Book is Due

Entitled to
Nothing

NATION OF NEWCOMERS
Immigrant History as American History

General Editors: Matthew Jacobson and Werner Sollors

LISA SUN-HEE PARK

Entitled to Nothing

The Struggle for
Immigrant Health Care in
the Age of Welfare Reform

NEW YORK UNIVERSITY PRESS
New York and London

NEW YORK UNIVERSITY PRESS
New York and London
www.nyupress.org

References to Internet websites (URLs) were accurate at the time of writing.
Neither the author nor New York University Press is responsible for URLs
that may have expired or changed since the manuscript was prepared.

Library of Congress Cataloging-in-Publication Data
Park, Lisa Sun-Hee.
Entitled to nothing : the struggle for immigrant health care in
the age of welfare reform / Lisa Park.
p. cm. — (Nation of newcomers: Immigrant history as American history)
Includes bibliographical references and index.
ISBN 978-0-8147-6801-3 (hardback) — ISBN 978-0-8147-6802-0 (pb) —
ISBN 978-0-8147-6833-4 (e-book)
1. Immigrants—Medical care—United States.
2. Health services accessibility—United States. I. Title.
RA448.5.I44P66   2011
362.1086'912—dc23   2011021036

New York University Press books are printed on acid-free paper,
and their binding materials are chosen for strength and durability.
We strive to use environmentally responsible suppliers and materials
to the greatest extent possible in publishing our books.

Manufactured in the United States of America

c   10 9 8 7 6 5 4 3 2 1
p   10 9 8 7 6 5 4 3 2 1

CONTENTS

ACKNOWLEDGMENTS

The writing of this book ebbed and flowed for some time. The project began in San Francisco and, after a number of crucial stops in between, has somehow ended in Minneapolis. Throughout the process, I benefited from the encouragement, kindness, and welcome distractions of some remarkable people.

At the Institute for Health Policy Studies at the University of California, San Francisco, Hal Luft was generous in his leadership and mentoring, and introduced me to Carol Korenbrot. There, I learned a great deal as a postdoctoral fellow at the Institute and as Carol's Project Director for the qualitative component of a larger study funded by the California Endowment. This experience became the seed from which this book took root.

The project continued during my time at the University of Colorado, Boulder, where I tested my ideas with friends and colleagues in the Women's Studies Program and the Department of Ethnic Studies. At that time, the research advanced further as I began my collaboration with Grace Yoo, a long-time friend at San Francisco State University. Working as co-PIs, we secured a grant from the California Policy Research Center's California Program on Access to Care to conduct fieldwork for the second phase of the research. I am grateful to both Carol and Grace for allowing me to use the data we gathered to formulate my own interpretation of its meanings and significance.

I then moved the project to the University of California, San Diego, where it began to mature into a book manuscript within the intellectually invigorating environment of the Ethnic Studies Department and the Urban Studies Program. I thank my friends, colleagues, and students there for pushing my ideas in seemingly never-ending directions. Finally, I arrived at the University of Minnesota, Twin Cities, in the Asian American Studies Program and the Department of Sociology to find a "warm" place with generous people. It was the perfect combination to guide me during the final writing of this book.

I would like to acknowledge a number of other individuals who provided crucial support for this project, in various ways: Cawo Abdi, Maggie Andersen, Martha Escobar, Yen Espiritu, Lynn Fujiwara, Brian Gran,

Michael Goldman, Teresa Gowan, Michiko Hase, Lynn Hudson, Adria Imada, Regina Kunzel, Jennifer Pierce, Jane Rhodes, Rhonda Sarnoff, Rachel Schurman, Rachel Silvey, Jaime Smith, Rickie Solinger, Dara Strolovitch, Stephen Suh, David Takeuchi, Alex Urquhart, Traci Voyles, Linda White, and Kim Yeager. I am also grateful for the opportunity to work with Ilene Kalish, Executive Editor, and the terrific staff at NYU Press. I would like to extend special thanks to the thoughtful anonymous reviewers who provided much-needed criticism.

On the home front, I also owe much to DN Pellow and JP Pellow for their patience and good cheer as I moved from place to place, room to room, trying to find the "perfect" space to get some words on paper. Thank you.

Finally, I saved my gratitude for the immigrant women and their advocates who participated in this research project till the end because I cannot thank them enough. I hope this book is received as a small token of my deep appreciation and respect. I dedicate this book to immigrant mothers everywhere, including my own.

CHAPTER 1

The Politics of Immigrant Reproduction

In 1998, twelve months after the birth of her twin girls, Sophia Chen[1] traveled to China to introduce the girls to their grandparents. When she and the twins returned to the Los Angeles International Airport a few weeks later, anxious to go home, they were detained unexpectedly by the Immigration and Naturalization Service (INS, now ICE, Immigration Customs and Enforcement). Ms. Chen, who legally resides in the United States, was asked how she had paid for the delivery of her babies. When Ms. Chen stated that she had received Medicaid, she was sent to another office to speak with a state Department of Health Services (DHS) agent. After hours of shuttling from one room to another, Ms. Chen was notified that she was suspected of Medicaid fraud and was a "public charge"—meaning, a public burden—for using a public health insurance program to which she is legally entitled. She was given two options: either she could immediately repay $4,000 for the medical expenses she had incurred during her prenatal care and delivery; or she could take the next flight back to China and come back when she had sufficient funds to cover the medical bill. Startled, Ms. Chen protested that she had filled out all the proper application forms and was legally eligible for those benefits. The INS official responded that that did not matter and that there were no avenues for appeal.

In the end, after speaking with her husband, Ms. Chen chose the second option. They could not raise enough money right away. Devastated, Ms. Chen left the twins alone at the airport and boarded the next plane back to China. Her mother-in-law drove down from Oakland to pick up the twins, while her husband rushed to the restaurant where he works nights after his day courses at the local university. Overwhelmed by their circumstances, the Chens contacted a local immigrant advocacy organization. The community-based organization investigated the situation and found that the Chens were not alone. They found that Latina and Asian immigrant women of childbearing age were targeted for a new health insurance fraud detection program run by the federal INS and state DHS agencies at ports of entry, including the border of California and Mexico, the San Francisco International Airport, and the Los Angeles International Airport.

This program was in existence for five years until it was terminated on the basis of a state audit that found the DHS-initiated programs poorly administered, inadequately planned, and legally liable for overstepping the scope of their authority by attempting to influence federal INS decisions on whether to admit or deport immigrants as well as improperly sharing confidential medical information in the process.[2] Despite its termination, I argue that this program is indicative of a significant historic moment in which notions of public charge were reinvigorated within the neoliberal ethos of the 1990s.

While these programs were initiated as an innovative approach to addressing health care fraud, the larger implications of the programs themselves and the way in which they were enacted require diligent investigation in light of the fact that these were not isolated events, but rather a concerted effort by various governmental and private entities that build upon the lessons of the past. This effort to control and discipline immigrants by targeting immigrant women's reproduction as they attempt to pass through national boundaries is part of a larger social phenomenon that has long historical roots in our national ideology. Debates regarding who should have access to public services such as health care (and how much, if at all) are important avenues for understanding the shifting boundaries of social belonging, legal entitlement, and the political implications of the welfare state today.

This book looks at the politics of access to prenatal care by low-income Latina and Asian immigrant women during a recent moment of dramatic federal and state policy changes regarding welfare, immigration, and health care. In 1996, President Clinton signed into law the "Personal Responsibility and Work Opportunity Reconciliation Act" (i.e., PRWORA or Welfare

Reform), which fundamentally altered the nation's welfare state by ending public benefits as an entitlement.[3] One month later, the immigration re-form bill, "Illegal Immigration Reform and Immigrant Responsibility Act" (i.e., IIRIRA or Immigration Reform) was also enacted, further restricting immigrant access to public services. These major federal legislations, in ad-dition to the Anti-Terrorism and Effective Death Penalty Act—all passed in 1996—which significantly increased surveillance of both documented and undocumented immigrants, marked the reconfiguration of immigration policy under neoliberal governance. The discourse surrounding these poli-cies isolated low-income immigrants as burdensome outsiders by reduc-ing their presence to the sole result of U.S. charitable generosity and there-fore contributing nothing to the everyday workings of the nation-state.

This framing, which placed immigrants clearly outside the national boundaries of social membership, was crucial to allowing for a neoliberal calculation of the value of immigrants as exclusively market-driven—the cheaper the better. The constant public fixation on their purported costs reached a fever pitch by the 1990s. The state of California took advantage of this political environment to revive the concept of a public charge to il-legally force immigrant mothers to "repay" reproductive health care costs for which they were legally eligible. This state initiative was part of an in-tense, ongoing battle over the boundaries of citizenship, nation, and the substance of social rights.

These far-reaching federal laws, coupled with persistent state measures limiting health care access by people of low income, will indelibly touch the lives of immigrant families living in the United States for years to come. This book argues that this moment marks the formal return of the immigrant as a public charge—meaning, a burden upon the state.

Immigrant Women as Public Charge

Public charge is a political classification used to exclude or deport those im-migrants perceived to be or to have the possibility of becoming a burden on the state. The latest U.S. Citizenship and Immigration Services' (CIS) defini-tion, refined in 1999, is as follows: "'public charge' means an individual who is likely to become primarily dependent on the government for subsistence, as demonstrated by either the receipt of public cash assistance for income maintenance or institutionalization for long-term care at government expense."[4] Public charge has been a part of U.S. immigration law for over a hundred years, used inconsistently to render "[a]n alien who is likely at any time to become a public charge [as] inadmissible and ineligible to become a legal permanent resident of the United States."[5] During its long existence, public charge was largely undefined and left vague in its applicability. Arguably, it is this vagueness that made this administrative law so flexible and therefore so useful in excluding immigrants over the years. As this study will show, it was only after the 1996 immigration and welfare reforms that the federal government attempted an actual definition with guidelines to clarify which public benefits are applicable for public charge determinations. Unfortunately, as this study will also show, this bureaucratic "clarification" did little to lessen immigrants' confusion and fear of using social services. What has been fairly clear over the life of this law, however, is its special concern about pregnant low-income immigrant women.

Pregnancy has long been categorized as a public burden with respect to low-income immigrant women. Scholars consider this designation as part of a continuing tradition of "selective immigration" that began in 1875.[6] When the Immigration Law of 1891 solidified the institutional mechanism for federal officials to inspect and exclude immigrants on the basis of public charge, Public Health Service agents were required to inspect and issue a medical certificate to all incoming immigrants for "loathsome or a dangerous contagious disease," including pregnancy.[7] According to historian Martha Gardner, "Between 1880 and 1924, 'likely to become public charge' (LPC) provided a catch-all category of exclusion through which vast numbers of women found themselves deported as potential paupers for moral, marital, physical, and economic deficiencies."[8] Gardner points out that while laws against poverty were usually applied to both men and women immigrants, LPC singled women out because the social mores of the early twentieth century linked immorality to indigence and, subsequently, poverty alleviation policies increasingly focused on women's morality and their "proper" role within the family. She writes, "LPC stigmatized women's work outside the home by dismissing the ability of single women, divorced women, or widows to support themselves and their families. Poverty, in essence, was a gendered disease."[9] Between 1895 and 1915, LPC designations accounted for two-thirds of all exclusions.[10] After the massive wave of migration during the turn of the twentieth century, public charge designations largely disappeared from the federal immigration agency's exclusionary repertoire. Then, in the mid-1990s, it reappeared on account of new heath care fraud detection programs in California.[11] In particular, access to and utilization of prenatal care by low-income immigrant women were targeted.

Governor Pete Wilson repeatedly and explicitly targeted prenatal care access in his efforts to halt immigration. In 1996, when a federal judge ruled in favor of Wilson's petition, arguing that the new federal welfare reform law allowed the state to end prenatal care for seventy thousand pregnant undocumented women, the governor was apparently "jubilant."[12] Wilson saw this judgment as a victory towards surreptitiously implementing a key component of the earlier anti-immigrant state measure, Proposition 187, which was legally stricken as unconstitutional. Despite evidence to the contrary, the governor insisted that prenatal care was "an incentive for immigration" and created great numbers of public charges who disproportionately drained state funds.[13] Regardless of the fact that studies have repeatedly shown that just a small fraction of America's health care spending is used to provide care to undocumented immigrants, Wilson and other anti-immigrant proponents continued to attack health care for immigrants (both documented and undocumented).[14]

In fact, immigrants are generally healthier than native-born Americans and have lower rates of health care use. A 2006 study of immigrant health care use found that a large number of foreign-born residents of Los Angeles County had almost no contact with the formal health care system.[15] In particular, prenatal care is consistently cited as cost effective.[16] One study reported an annual cost savings of $230 per mother.[17] Another study, conducted by the National Commission to Prevent Infant Mortality, estimated the cost of lifetime custodial care of low-birthweight children to be as much as $500,000 per child. The authors argued that since approximately 80 percent of mothers at high risk for low-birthweight babies can be identified in the first prenatal visit, prenatal care could potentially prevent long-term health problems and its accompanying costs.[18]

More importantly, prenatal care serves as the entry point for access to public health insurance (Medicaid) and other social services that can address underlying social inequalities. Writing in *JAMA*, Dawn Misra and Bernard Guyer point out, "Social factors also have strong influences, and it may be that changes in the woman's environment and resources are more important than medical services provided through prenatal care."[19] They add, "The stressful and impoverished environment in which many minority and low-income women live may be a fundamental factor that influences pregnancy outcomes but cannot be overcome easily with narrowly targeted interventions."[20] For low-income immigrant women, prenatal care can serve an important role in connecting them to valuable social services and resources for which they are eligible, in addition to the actual medical services.[21] This policy implication is cause for much chagrin for those who, like Wilson, want to limit the social rights of immigrants.

There are three basic methods that underlie how the United States has attempted to control the number and behavior of immigrants in the United States: first, by controlling initial immigration numbers through specific immigration and refugee policies, based largely upon U.S. domestic labor demands; second, by controlling the reproduction of those immigrants already in the United States; and third, by deterring future emigrants through punitive policies that limit access to social safety nets (such as health care access, public education, and welfare benefits) that are understood as basic rights of membership of U.S. society—making clear their second-class, temporary status.[22] Pregnant immigrant women, then, embody a walking target for the expression of a number of national anxieties regarding the quantity and quality of our citizenry. Consequently, services geared toward these women are deeply political and require careful critical analysis. As such, dissecting the social and historical implications of access to prenatal care goes beyond understanding the importance of health care per se, to the larger *social meaning* of this form of health care.

The recent (re)application of the public charge law upon immigrant mothers who utilize prenatal care encompasses all three methods of immigration control noted above. Legal scholar Dorothy Roberts argues that restrictions on who may give birth to citizens highlight the schism between the theory and practice of our civic nationalism. She argues that while we would like to believe that social citizenship is based upon shared political institutions and values, it is, in reality, defined by race. Here, Roberts joins the work of other critical legal scholars who demonstrate that, since the founding of the nation, definitions of who belongs within the boundaries of American citizenship have been based on the simultaneous denial of citizenship of others living within its borders.[23] One's inclusion is relational to another's exclusion.

Medicaid access is central to this issue of social inclusion and exclusion. A landmark achievement of the Kennedy-Johnson administrations, Medicaid is one of the largest and most established entitlement programs today.[24] This publicly funded health insurance for low-income families is a vital component of ensuring early and continuous use of prenatal care by women who would otherwise be uninsured for this care. Regardless of individual health risks, the U.S. Public Health Service recommends a minimum standard of eight visits starting no later than the second month of pregnancy for all pregnant women,[25] and the American College of Obstetricians and Gynecologists recommends fourteen visits starting no later than the third month.[26] During these visits women are screened for potential complications arising from their pregnancy, which can require additional visits, especially in the latter months of pregnancy. Low-income women, including immigrant women, have relied on Medicaid for these services. Both the federal and state governments fund California's Medicaid program, Medi-Cal.[27]

Studies show that uninsured women are less likely to make the recommended number of prenatal care visits, and they experience poorer birth outcomes than women with Medicaid.[28] Furthermore, foreign-born women are generally more likely than U.S.-born women to be uninsured for prenatal care, and are less likely to follow the recommended schedule of prenatal care visits.[29] When, in 1996, federal welfare and immigration reform legislation was passed, another barrier to access arose for low-income immigrant women by instituting greater restrictions on Medicaid for legal immigrants. Welfare reform restricted immigrants' access to health care by more narrowly defining the immigrant populations eligible for federal Medicaid funding, and immigration reform made it harder for more recent immigrants to establish income eligibility for Medicaid.[30]

In California, legal challenges to the implementation of welfare and immigration reforms and the use of state general funds ensured the eligibility of low-income immigrants for Medi-Cal coverage of prenatal care and other pregnancy-related services. The problem, however, is that the implementation of the federal welfare and immigration reforms, in addition to state health care fraud detection programs, produces a chilling effect that discourages the use of Medicaid by immigrants who are legally eligible in California.[31] There is concern that this decline in Medi-Cal enrollment will lead to lower prenatal care utilization among low-income pregnant immigrant women. This raises significant questions regarding the way in which federal and state policies collaborate to destabilize social safety net programs that were once viewed as fundamental to our national membership and identity. With the continued disintegration of the welfare state, a new relationship is apparent between the state and its members that goes beyond any distinction of citizenship status. Safety net protections are now more narrowly defined for all vulnerable people. What this study shows is that immigrants, particularly those who are low-income and women, function as easy markers to test the boundaries of this changing relationship, given their vulnerable gender, race, and class status. And the political economy of California in the 1990s provided a convenient opportunity for this test.

Reconfiguring the Burden in Neoliberalism

As immigrant women's labor became more central to everyday life, their presence was increasingly destabilized and marginalized as burdensome. While the notion of immigrants as public burdens is not new, a reassertion of formal, state determinations of public charge signals a critical political moment that highlights the role of immigrants. In this latest iteration in the 1990s, public charge reappears to test the rights of migrants within transnational free market governance.[32]

In the context of the current global economy, the surge in demand for service sector labor has by and large replaced the manufacturing industry in the United States. Unlike traditional manufacturing industries in the United States, the service sector employs large numbers of women, thereby increasing the global demand for women's labor. At the same time, economic globalization has increasingly feminized the workforce as multinational firms enter global South nations to establish assembly plants and take advantage of their low-wage labor.[33] Douglas Massey describes the creation of a socially and economically uprooted population in this way:

> The insertion of foreign factories into peripheral regions undermines traditional economies in other ways: by producing goods that compete with those made locally; by feminizing the workforce without providing

sufficient factory-based employment for men; and by socializing women for industrial work and modern consumption without providing a lifetime career capable of meeting these needs.[34]

The end result is a "migration prone" workforce composed of both men and women, with an accompanying demand for their low-wage labor. In addition, immigrant women are essential to providing care work (child care, domestic service, home health care, and so on) and continue to labor in the agricultural industry. The dilemma of the role of low-income immigrant women is highlighted as they become pregnant. What makes women's labor attractive in the global economy is its devalue (i.e., low cost) on the basis of their gender. However, when an immigrant woman uses her body for her own reproductive purposes, she is viewed as an irrational worker and punished for doing so. The bodily control that is necessary for the rationality and self-discipline of modern liberal subjects is denied to pregnant immigrant women workers. Global capitalist logic, which designates having babies and other forms of familial care-taking as inefficient for low-income migrant workers, becomes the basis for determining the rationality, and subsequently the deservingness of particular individuals. In this way, having babies is indicative of a lack of self-control.

In many respects, the timing appeared perfect. As Sanford Schram observed, even before the passage of major welfare and immigration reforms in 1996, there was "an ongoing 'privatization of public assistance'—a retrenchment of public welfare programs and the corresponding elaboration of a network of substitute services, often in the form of private aid."[35] Rather than entitlements or rights, publicly funded programs including welfare and health care were increasingly privatized and refashioned into a humiliating form of individual charity. The consequences are considerable. As Schram[36] predicted, we are seeing greater fragmentation and less accessibility, visibility, and effectiveness in the provision of social services, diminishing what little protection existed from structural issues that cause poverty including declining wages and eroding worker protections, racism and the dismantling of civil rights, unaffordable and inadequate childcare, underfunded public schools, and greater barriers to higher education.[37] Instead, poverty is individualized as personal moral failings so that the solution centers on disciplining non-normative bodies to perform in "responsible" and "entrepreneurial" ways.

This logic allows for the justification of discipline of women in poverty by defining dependency as a pathological disease indicative of those with weak moral constitutions who are unable to self-regulate and make the "right" choices. In their analysis, Alejandra Marchevsky and Jeanne Theoharis assess, "To confess one's dependencies is to forfeit one's individuality and rights in the American state."[38] As an example, they write,

> If we looked into most homes in America, we might find this same tangled mess of socks, jeans, and sweaters on the sofa, and perhaps a pile of dirty dishes in the sink. But, in Myrna's case, a messy home or an empty refrigerator could cost her her children because Myrna is on welfare. Twice, in fact, the government has inspected her home, checking for food in the refrigerator and men's clothing in the closet. There are only three populations in the United States whose privacy is not protected under "probable cause" rules: prisoners, undocumented immigrants, and welfare recipients.[39]

Dependency, then, is understood as indicative of whether or not one is deserving of rights necessary for social citizenship and almost entirely separated from actual need. Nancy Fraser and Linda Gordon note how this designation of deservingness is marked by specific economic, gender, and racial discriminations:

> What in preindustrial society had been a normal and unstigmatized condition became deviant and stigmatized. More precisely, certain dependencies became shameful while others were deemed natural and proper. In particular, as eighteenth and nineteenth century political culture intensified gender difference, new, specifically gendered senses of dependency appeared—states considered proper for women but degrading for men. Likewise, emergent racial constructions made some forms of dependency appropriate for the "dark races" but intolerable for "whites."[40]

By the 1980s, a decade after key western states enacted neoliberal policies, Ricky Solinger argues that the "core, essential attribute of a person in the state of dependency" was solidified as "the absence of the capacity to make sensible choices."[41] She writes that dependency and choice become fixed in an antithetical relationship with each other, creating the necessary justification for greater restrictions on women's behavior.[42] By this time, neoliberal interests had successfully usurped and redefined the discourse of "choice"—long championed by the women's reproductive rights movement.[43] By the 1990s, low-income immigrant women were firmly circumscribed as dependent public burdens. For Asian and Latino immigrants, their purported dependency as a public charge was used to criminalize particular legal behavior as "illegal," regardless of their actual citizenship status. This was the case for Sophia Chen, whose story began this book, and many other immigrant women who received publicly funded prenatal care.

Reproductive Control versus Reproductive Freedom

The contradiction between choice and dependency is thoroughly embedded in feminist discourse regarding women's reproduction. The linchpin issue in the struggle for women's rights remains reproductive freedom, and the composition and delineation of this issue continues to spark serious debate. Dorothy Roberts argues that the Supreme Court's *Roe v. Wade* decision is restrictive in its narrow understanding of reproductive rights as "the freedom to decide, without active government interference, whether to use contraceptives and whether to terminate a pregnancy."[44] Roberts argues for a broader definition:

> A woman's reproductive life is clearly implicated in more than just the decision to use contraceptives and to have an abortion. Reproduction encompasses a range of events and conditions from the ability to bear children, to conception, to carrying a fetus, to abortion, to delivering a baby, to caring for a child. Each stage in turn involves myriad decisions that the woman must make; her decisions at each stage may be affected by numerous factors—economic, environmental, legal, political, emotional, ethical.[45]

Reproductive freedom, then, would include access to health care, particularly prenatal care. This expansive idea of reproductive freedom also takes into consideration the experiences of low-income and other women deemed "undeserving" who were never allowed the opportunity to make "choices" regarding their reproduction. Solinger writes, "when choice was associated with poor women, it became a symbol of illegitimacy. Poor women had not earned the right to choose. . . . As dependents they were categorically excluded from good choice making."[46] Implicit in this assumption is a particular morality-based understanding of poverty in which people cause their own poverty as a result of bad decision making and consequently should not be allowed to make greater mistakes (i.e., to have children) that will produce yet another generation of burden upon the state. There appears to be a fundamental contradiction in this concept of "choice" in which there is only one correct decision and only those who "choose" that particular "choice" are allowed to do so. "Choice," then, is derived from self-control, which is, in turn, indicative of personal freedom.

Political theorist Lealle Ruhl addresses this philosophical dilemma of "choice" in the concept of "control," which is central to understanding the current politics surrounding women's reproduction.[47] She locates contemporary debates regarding birth control and fertility, which emphasize *self*-control, as a by-product of modern liberalism.[48] Seminal feminist theorists such as Simone de Beauvoir defined rationality and self-discipline as the central elements of liberal subjectivity.[49] However, Ruhl points out that "Modern liberalism relies implicitly on the capacity and willingness of its citizens to self-regulate."[50] Citing Mariana Valverde's[51] work on liberal governance, Ruhl argues that liberal citizens are "granted" the freedom to make choices only when they can be trusted to make the "right" decision. Meaning, "To act responsibly means to conform to an essentially middle-class, educated, and scientifically oriented worldview."[52] This definition of freedom appears oxymoronic given that an individual's decision is represented as one derived of freedom only if the "choice" represents a particular worldview. Any decision that is counter to that endorsed by the normative worldview, then, is understood as being against one's will and is dealt with accordingly. Under these circumstances, modern rationality is equated with conformity and the potentially exploitative powers of this logic appear great. Ruhl cites Margaret Sanger's use of eugenic arguments to promote birth control as one such example of punitive consequences for women who fail to prove their status as responsible citizens by controlling their fertility.

The subjectivity of low-income immigrant women in a modern liberal state deepens the complexity of this dilemma. Contemporary arguments for women's reproductive rights remain prone to such discursive practices in their use of the concept of control, which in the end does not truly encompass reproductive freedom but, quite possibly, the opposite. Ruhl asserts that "a fundamental challenge for feminists is to maintain a commitment to complexity of reproductive freedom while remaining alert to the possible misuses of a rhetoric of control."[53]

At a fundamental level, capitalist logic cannot form the basis for a feminist approach to women's reproductive rights. This is certainly made clear in the case of low-income immigrant women in which a "choice" to become a good mother marks her as a bad immigrant (i.e., a bad worker). True reproductive freedom must encompass the "choice" of low-income immigrant women workers to have children and not be punished with barriers to prenatal care for doing so. Only after such a broad understanding of reproductive freedom has been incorporated does it seem plausible to argue for reproductive control. A case in point is Rosalind Petchesky's fascinating contention for a "feminist revision of the body as property."[54] Petchesky argues for an alternative perspective to "rethink the meanings of ownership and thereby reclaim both a feminist idea of bodily integrity and a radical conception of property at large."[55] Citing African slave women's experiences as property and the consequent significance of "self propriety" as a powerful form of resistance, she writes that "we are better off thinking about property as a right—or . . . a relationship—than a thing, and about private, exclusive property as a historically and culturally circumscribed form of owning."[56] While the idea of self propriety is powerful, I am wary of this call for a revision of ownership as a form of feminist resistance, given the potential pitfalls in the use of this capitalist rhetoric and its accompanying logic with respect to racial minorities. First, the racialization of people of color as having no will, or antiwill, miscalculates their role in the marketplace. Patricia Williams writes,

> [O]ne of the things passed on from slavery, which continues in the oppression of people of color, is a belief structure rooted in a concept of black (or brown or red) antiwill, the antithetical embodiment of pure will. We live in a society where the closest equivalent of nobility is the display of unremittingly controlled willfulness. To be perceived as unremittingly without will is to be imbued with an almost lethal trait.[57]

"Thus," she explains, "while blacks had an indisputable generative force in the marketplace, their presence could not be called activity; they had no active role in the market."[58] Racialized initially as having no will, people of color are already irrational, making them illegible as economic actors. Consequently, their "contribution" or participation in the market is discounted, since they never made the "choice" to do so. Instead they are viewed as charity cases, without equal recognition of mutual humanity. This helps explain why low-income immigrants are not accorded social citizenship rights despite their strong labor market participation. The notion of self-propriety requires acknowledgment of will, which remains elusive for racialized immigrants.

Second, conveying bodies as property, whether it is a self-owned right or a privately owned thing, is a slippery slope. As a historically and culturally constructed concept, self-propriety may shift from one owner to another but, more important, it remains an entity in need of control/ownership. Instead, I see a more fruitful direction in expanding notions of freedom rather than control. It is a move away from privatization, which I believe is in line with black feminist theories regarding communal mothering. For instance, the works of Patricia Hill Collins, Linda Burton, and Carol Stack describe alternative family structures, including a network of fictive kin, that diffuses the responsibilities for familial care among "blood-mothers" and "othermothers."[59]

Here, Collins makes an important point in stressing that within these woman-centered kin units, the centrality of mothers is not predicated on male powerlessness. These diffused networks do not adhere to mutually exclusive and hierarchical gendering. In fact, they function in direct contradiction to privatized notions of responsibility in which a single person or household "owns" the child and the responsibility to support them. By documenting the existence of communal care networks in the face of structural adversity, these studies provide significant theoretical and practical insights to better understanding the potential paradox of choice/control and freedom. Without romanticizing the harsh realities of poverty, these approaches are worth revisiting for what it can tell us about the neoliberal conditions under which women must mother today.

The Deportability of Immigrant Women's Labor

The formal resurfacing of public charge was achieved by simultaneously capitalizing on the modes of racialization and gendering that already existed within state institutions while at the same time utilizing new forms of fear and anxiety associated with immigrants in the "War on Terror."[60] The purpose of this manufactured and enforced dependency is to preserve the political and economic vulnerability of immigrants during a time of unimpeded demand for their labor. Public charge policy is a technology[61] of what Nicholas De Genova calls "deportability." Writing about Mexican immigrants specifically, De Genova states, "It is deportability, and not deportation as such, that has historically rendered Mexican labor to be a distinctly disposable commodity."[62] He argues that U.S. immigration authorities do not actually intend to deport all undocumented migrants. On the contrary, it is deportability—a liminal state of perpetual insecurity—that ensures that some are deported in order that most may remain in the United States as vulnerable workers to ensure that U.S. citizens enjoy low food costs and home care. Similarly, the possibility of deportation through public charge maintains the vulnerable social location of immigrants (regardless of their legal citizenship status) and strictly disciplines their behavior.

In the end, neoliberalism promises that less government and more privatization will lead to greater individual freedom. This assertion raises a crucial question: "For whom?" In the case of many immigrants who are part of the growing population of the working poor, less government in the form of fewer state services has led instead to greater state surveillance (a different but continued government presence) and a diminution of individual rights and freedoms.[63] In his astute analysis, Matthew Sparke points out that although neoliberalism trumpets *de*regulation, in practice it is a form of *re*regulation. He writes that whether it is at the macro level of government policy (in the form of free trade, financial deregulation, welfare reform, and the like) or at the micro level of governmentality (audits, performance assessments, cultural cultivation of self-policing entrepreneurial individualism), "all these innovations in governmental policy and practice represent transformed patterns of state-making and rule."[64] This reconfigured governance produces a multitiered state in which the freedoms and rights of some are maintained by the reciprocal restriction of the same freedoms and rights of others.

Rather than greater rights in return for greater "personal responsibility," low-income immigrants must allow increased government surveillance of their movements as proof that they are in fact making the right "choices" and taking "personal responsibility." The assumption here is that immigrants are not doing these things and instead are "naturally" inclined to be burdensome. A fundamental contradiction underlying this assertion is the fact that most immigrants work. In fact, their rates of employment are higher than those native-born and yet, their social contributions are repeatedly questioned. This conflicts with the near obsessive focus of welfare reform on work as the sole route to self-control and making the "right" choices.[65] As Iris Marion Young notes,

> When welfare rhetoric invokes self-sufficiency today, it doesn't mean being literally independent from engagement with others to meet one's needs. It means only having a job and therefore, according to the terms of the welfare state, no longer being dependent on public funds. Even though many jobs do not pay enough to meet one's needs, are only part time, are very insecure, and make a person highly dependent on employers and co-workers, these facts are obscured by the language of self-sufficiency.[66]

Young is skeptical of paid employment as the primary means of achieving social citizenship.[67] The case of low-income immigrant workers supports Young's skepticism, given their diminished level of rights regardless of how many hours they labor. Instead, dependency of a different sort—to private employers—is expected. Relatedly, Marchevsky and Theoharis point to another contradiction in the construction of immigrants as public burdens. They note that immigrant women's domestic labor in their own homes is characterized as oppressive, while this same labor is viewed as an act of independence when performed in other people's homes. They call attention to the convenient timing: "Calls for immigrant women to liberate themselves from their culturally defined gender roles . . . conveniently corresponded to the nation's growing demand for immigrant domestic labor."[68] Evidently, the value and meaning of labor changes depending on where you perform it and for whom. What is considered pathological dependency in one context is viewed as libratory independence in another.

In tracing the genealogy of dependency, Fraser and Gordon point out that women historically have had to negotiate how to be "just dependent enough."[69] This has always been a difficult balance given how easy it is to "tip over into excess in either direction."[70] Patricia Hill Collins provides a powerful example in the case of controlling images of black women as "mammy" (too dependent) and "matriarch" (too independent).[71] Both stereotypes depict the black female body as ever-deficient and in need of discipline. Black women are placed in a racist dilemma, in which those "who must work are labeled mammies, then are stigmatized again as matriarchs for being strong figures in their own homes."[72] Collins writes, "While the mammy typifies the Black mother figure in white homes, the matriarch symbolizes the mother figure in Black homes."[73] Similarly, low-income immigrant women and the labor they produce are valuable only in specific circumstances (i.e., cheap labor for other homes/businesses) within neoliberalism and disciplinary images of public burdens function to maintain this market value. And, as this book will show, this maintenance requires continuous, deliberate care in presenting low-income immigrant women as either too much or not enough—excessive either way and in need of discipline in order to make the right choices. This paternalism supplants rights with charity, which in turn produces greater inequality among members of society as the giver receives moral credit while the taker is increasingly stigmatized. Charity, as a unilateral "gift" provided by a donor (who has no obligation) to a recipient (who has no claim), is a profound expression of power inequality.[74] Charity extracts significant costs for the recipient. However, the neoliberal framing of this exchange facilitates an altruistic, sentimental image of individual generosity while obscuring the fact that social entitlements are actually being taken away.

David Harvey observes that neoliberalism is "a failed utopian rhetoric masking a successful project for the restoration of ruling-class power."[75] This "masking" appears to play a key function in that the restoration of ruling class power requires the erasure of racism and sexism upon which it is based. Its discourse of individual choice and rational market actors absolves it from such "irrationalities" as racism and sexism. It seems imperative, then, for critics of neoliberalism to unmask this relationship and clearly articulate neoliberalism as a racist and sexist ideology, which is enforced by the state with such laws as public charge. Without an explicit challenge, market logic will continue to conceal the vast inequalities created for capital accumulation and our understanding of the complexities of migration will never advance beyond a mere debate about financial costs and benefits.

Racial Politics of Immigrant Births, 1990s Style

As it stands, one of the central arguments for the restriction of prenatal care for immigrants is the accusation that poor immigrants have a propensity for fraud and will abuse the generosity of the U.S. health care system. The core rationale of this position is that *any* use of the health care system by low-income immigrants is fraudulent and abusive. And more specifically, access to prenatal care, which may imply the encouragement of greater numbers of immigrants or their children of color, is understood as a special privilege which they do not deserve.

Respondents I interviewed across the state of California highlighted how recent federal and state immigration and welfare policies have contributed to a sense of fear among immigrants using Medi-Cal (California's Medicaid program), a legal entitlement. Beginning in 1998, my research team and I interviewed almost two hundred safety net health care providers, immigrant health advocates, government officials, and low-income immigrant women in specific regions of California, including San Diego County, the San Francisco Bay Area, Los Angeles, and the Central Valley. My objective was to assess the impact of federal welfare and immigration policy changes on access to prenatal care.

The consistency of the responses was striking. The social workers and health care providers repeatedly described their patients' dual fear of the consequences of negative immigration status for applying for Medi-Cal coverage, on the one hand, and the cost of obtaining prenatal care without Medi-Cal, on the other. At the heart of this fear are changes in health, welfare, and immigration legislation that have altered the implications of using Medi-Cal–funded health care benefits for the future immigration status of women and their families. They were afraid that using health care would harm their chances of attaining legal citizenship or permanent residency status. On the other hand, the women are faced with the increasingly high cost of health care if they are to pay for it out-of-pocket.

There is fear on both sides of this heated exchange. The fear expressed by those advocating greater restrictions upon immigrants focuses on the growing population of immigrants and interprets that flow as an "invasion."[76] The only solution to such threats is control, in its various forms. Consequently, pregnant immigrant women find themselves in the midst of an intense political debate over not only state control of women's reproduction but also immigration control. Within this predicament, the deeply racialized nature of immigrant women's reproduction is evident. For low-income immigrant women of color, having children is considered a selfish act, given their national role as temporary workers. This is in stark contrast to understanding the infertility of middle-class white women as a "tragedy," as expressed by many middle-class policy makers and politicians.[77]

Arguments that immigrant women abuse health care and have babies in order to obtain U.S. citizenship question the motive of low-income women in having children.[78]

These arguments are distinctly similar to the public obsession with the black "welfare queen."[79] Like the "welfare queen," low-income immigrant mothers are viewed as "working" the system by having children and therefore undeserving of social services for themselves or their children. Within this framework, new policies are introduced in order to deter such selfish behavior. These racist and classist assumptions preclude low-income immigrant births from any sense of protection derived from an understanding of mothering as "sacred" (as flawed as this understanding is).[80] From this perspective, immigrant women giving birth to any children at all is too much and therefore indicative of an out-of-control fertility. Consequently, any low-income immigrant woman of childbearing age is a potential public burden—in other words, a public charge.

For those who believe that the United States is threatened—economically, culturally, or racially—by immigration, control and discipline are the primary mechanisms to detect and deter the movement of immigrants. Technologies of control and discipline require that individuals have constant contact with the state. The Port of Entry Fraud Detection (PED) Program and the Medi-Cal eligibility process are just two examples of such a technology. Women who are "dependent" on state institutions are more closely monitored and controlled than those who are not. It appears that the dependency of immigrants on the state is enforced in policy, at the same time as it is decried in the public rhetoric.

The Politics of Immigrant Health Care Access in California

California is home to one-third of all immigrants living in the United States. One-fourth of the state's population was born outside the United States, making California the state with the highest concentration of immigrants. Asians and Latinos comprise the vast majority of immigrants to the United States. These two diverse ethnic/racial groups account for 80 percent of all incoming immigrants in the 1990s. Their individual and collective impact on the political, economic, and social landscape of

California is profound. In this regard, how California responds to these significant demographic changes is understood as the bellwether for the future of the entire nation.[81] Further, an investigation of the politics of immigrant health care access shows that immigration is indeed a pressing civil rights and racial justice issue in the United States.[82]

As part of this investigation, I found that despite the stark differences among the various immigrant communities, there are salient and strategic moments of interconnection that highlight some of the long-term consequences of federal policies and programs. In assessing the impact of the 1996 welfare reform on immigrant women, stereotypes of uncontrolled fertility—particularly Latina—played strongly into overall anti-immigrant sentiments.[83] In his study of the politics surrounding Latina reproduction, Leo Chavez states, "'Latinas' exist and 'reproduction' exists, but "Latina reproduction" as an object of a discourse produces a limited range of meanings, with an emphasis on 'over'-reproduction and on fertility and sexuality depicted as 'out of control' in relation to the supposed social norm."[84] Negative perceptions of motherhood and mothering by ethnic immigrant minorities played a considerable role in swaying California residents to restrict immigrant care in the 1990s. The growing presence of ethnic minorities was used to justify claims that immigrants in general overuse public health services and education, and take jobs from American citizens. The overwhelming passage of California's Proposition 187 in 1994, which restricted access to all publicly funded programs—including health care and education—for undocumented immigrants, clearly articulated this message. Lynn Fujiwara writes,

> Proposition 187 reflects fears that undocumented immigrants were over utilizing public resources such as health care, education, and economic assistance at the expense of poor working-class "Americans." Racial-gendered images of migrant women crossing the border to have their children and receive medical care through state-funded health care services played on working- and middle-class voters' resentments against "non-Americans" who allegedly received benefits from their tax dollars.[85]

Such sentiments are not uncommon. For instance, the *San Diego Union-Tribune* devoted significant resources to highlighting immigrants' use of health benefits in 1993 (a year before the passage of Prop. 187). The newspaper ran a five-part series entitled "Medi-Cal: The New Gold Rush," which focused on Mexican immigrants' use of health care in the United States. The first installment began with this subheading: "California's health program to treat the state's poor—Medi-Cal—has created a new gold rush as people from around the globe flood the Golden State to grab a share of the unsurpassed medical care available here. Who pays for all this? You do." The series reiterates many U.S. residents' misconception that immigrants migrate to the United States for welfare and health benefits and that immigrants do not contribute to this society (in taxes or otherwise). The imagery of California's gold rush of the 1800s that brought so many Chinese workers, as well as other immigrants, is also noteworthy. As the gold rush came to a close in the Sierra Nevada Foothills, Chinese immigrants experienced extreme hostility that resulted in the Chinese Exclusion Act of 1882. In fact, during this historical era, Chinese (along with Syrians and Greeks) were explicitly targeted in the medicalization and militarization of the U.S. border, as they tried to enter the United States as Mexicans. [86]

Also, a few months prior to this newspaper series in 1993, State Senator William Craven, chairman of the Senate Special Committee on Border Issues, was quoted as saying, "It seems rather strange that we go out of our way to take care of the rights of these individuals who are perhaps on the lower scale of our humanity, for one reason or another."[87] The separation of Latinos into an "undesirable" or "undeserving" category is clear; and so are the racist undertones that helped garner support for subsequent anti-immigrant legislation.

Finally, in February 1994, the *San Diego Union-Tribune* ran an "exposé" entitled "Born in the USA," which targeted Latina immigrants' fertility using what is by now familiar anti-immigrant rhetoric. The headlines read: "Births to Illegal Immigrants on the Rise," "California Taxpayers Finance Soaring Number of Foreigners' Babies," and "Border Baby with Medical Problem Costs $2.7 million." Such claims are in direct contradiction with numerous studies that have shown that individuals do not migrate to the United States for health or other social services.[88] Immigrants' overall use of welfare services and benefits is roughly the same rate as those of native-born persons. However, in 1994, immigrant women accounted for 60 percent of all publicly funded births (via Medi-Cal). This high rate is attributed to a number of issues, including the disproportionately large number of immigrants who live in poverty,[89] improvements in access to health care for immigrant women during the 1980s and early 1990s in California, amnesty granted through the Immigration Reform and Control Act of 1986, and liberalization of the family reunification policy.[90]

Historically, nativist concerns have a tendency to expand to encompass other vulnerable minorities under certain political and economic conditions. The Port of Entry Detection (PED) program, for instance, highlights the links among immigrants from Latin America and Asia. In this case, Latinas (particularly Mexicans) were the initial test, and once deemed successful, the program expanded from the U.S.-Mexico border to international airports to target Asian immigrants. The intersection of various policies exposes the ways in which different racial/ethnic populations are intertwined. At certain historical moments, particular ethnic groups rotate as convenient test cases to push the boundaries of citizenship rights.[91] For instance, legal scholar Bill Ong Hing writes that the legislative attacks on Asians in the late 1800s served as a model for the exclusion of eastern and southern Europeans.[92] Today, immigrants from Latin America are the most visibly attacked, both verbally and physically, for their use of public benefits. However, as the Port of Entry fraud detection program attests, the target can easily shift to others deemed foreign—including those presumed to be model minorities.

Another pressing concern in this investigation into the politics of access to immigrant health care is the unprecedented sharing of what was once considered private individual information across both state and federal agencies. While immigrant access to health services such as prenatal care was increasingly hindered, governmental access to individual information greatly expanded during this time. Five years prior to the September 11, 2001 attacks and the subsequent passage of the federal USA Patriot Act, immigrants in California experienced firsthand the effects of a new, intensified level of state surveillance of private information.

California's Proposition 187

Preparation for the collaboration and sharing of information between the state DHS and the federal INS departments in California was evident in 1994 with the passage of Proposition 187 and the creation of the PED programs. It was a sign of things to come for immigrants in the United States.

The passage of Proposition 187 conveyed the message to immigrants that they were not welcome in the state's publicly funded schools, clinics, and hospitals. This initiative, created by a coalition of nativist Californians and spearheaded by then-governor Pete Wilson (formerly the mayor of San Diego), was particularly punitive, given that undocumented immigrants were already denied health and welfare benefits.[93] In Ono and Sloop's study of the political rhetoric during this time, they note:

> For many, the policy conjured up memories of the racialized "alien" land law restrictions against Japanese Americans; legislation severely limiting Asian immigration; the incarceration of Japanese Americans during World War II; the 1930s repatriation campaigns to force Mexicans in the United States and their children to move back to Mexico; and the 1954 "Operation Wetback," in which more than a million Mexican migrant workers were forcibly deported from the United States to Mexico.[94]

Immediately after the passage of Proposition 187, a number of legal advocates filed legal injunctions questioning its constitutionality and successfully prevented it from being implemented. Despite the fact that this initiative was never enacted, the initial passage of this state legislation with overwhelming voter support sent a clear message to immigrants—both undocumented and documented—that they are viewed as a burden on the state and therefore unwanted. One of our respondents, a community clinic administrator, described the situation at that time as follows:

> After [Proposition] 187 passed, there was a lot of fear. Then we went back and forth as people were trying to get legalized. They did not want to apply for any kind of services that might jeopardize their applications. So some people wouldn't apply for Medi-Cal and we had to encourage and push them to apply for Medi-Cal because, let's face it, if you don't apply for Medi-Cal and you do not have the money, you're facing a $5,000 bill, at least—between prenatal care and the hospital. We basically sat down with them and said, "If you don't apply for Medi-Cal this is what your bill is going to be." And you know, when you look at what the bill is going to be, most of them ... a few of them wouldn't, but most of them would apply. If not for their prenatal care, at least for their delivery.

These initiatives, along with the subsequent passage of federal legislation on welfare and immigration reform in 1996, reinforced the message of a severely restricted entitlement to publicly funded programs. In a study of Latina immigrant women's perspectives on Proposition 187, researchers found that Latinas perceived this initiative as discriminatory and directed primarily at their community. The study also found that Latinas were reluctant to seek medical care as a result of this initiative.[95] This finding was supported by another study conducted by the Urban Institute that showed a significant decline in applications for Medi-Cal and welfare benefits by immigrants in Los Angeles County.[96] Apparently, immigrant access and utilization of key public benefits declined immediately after the passage of this anti-immigrant proposition, reflecting a pervasive fear in these communities.

Federal Welfare Reform and Immigration Reform of 1996

Such hostile perceptions and treatment of immigrant women were further solidified in 1996 with the passage of the federal welfare reform bill (PRWORA—Personal Responsibility and Opportunity for Work Reform Act—PL 104-193) and the federal immigration legislation (IIRIRA—Illegal Immigration Reform and Immigrant Responsibility Act—PL 104-208). The welfare reform restricted immigrants' access to health care by more narrowly defining which immigrant populations were eligible for federal Medicaid funding. Federal Immigration and Welfare legislation explicitly linked immigration status to eligibility for public benefits by creating new categories of exclusion: "pre-enactment" and "postenactment."[97] For those immigrants who arrived (legally) after August 22, 1996, this legislation ended their eligibility for federal means-tested entitlements, including federal cash assistance, food stamps, and Medicaid. Along with a five-year lifetime limit on cash benefits and new work requirements imposed on all welfare beneficiaries, the PRWORA implemented additional restrictions on legal immigrants.[98] Remarkably, restrictions on immigrant benefits alone accounted for almost half of the total federal savings.[99] Ostensibly a budgetary measure, the savings from eliminating almost the entire safety net for immigrants came from denying benefits to *legal*—not "illegal"—immigrants. Undocumented immigrants are already ineligible for most major means-tested entitlement benefits.

A year later, some food stamps and Supplemental Security Income benefits were restored to a narrowly defined group of immigrants through the Balanced Budget Act. States were also given the option to determine immigrants' eligibility for Medicaid and state cash assistance programs. California opted to continue Medi-Cal coverage to legal immigrants irrespective of their date of entry to the United States. However, state and local government agencies continued to require documentation of immigration status from applicants for means-tested programs.

At the same time, the federal immigration reform made it more difficult for more recent immigrants to establish income eligibility for Medicaid by requiring sponsors of new immigrants to sign legal affidavits that they had incomes greater than 125 percent of the federal poverty level. This legislation also required that the income and assets of sponsors be considered when determining Medicaid eligibility for a new immigrant (i.e., "deeming"). This deeming provision created another barrier to health care access because the addition of the sponsor's income and assets significantly decreased the number of new immigrants eligible for Medi-Cal. This was in addition to the other major provisions in this legislation that affected both documented and undocumented immigrants, including new legal affidavits by family unification sponsors, nearly doubling the number of Border Patrol agents, increased civil and criminal penalties for illegal entry, greater restriction on asylum admittance, and limitations on possible challenges to deportation rulings.[100]

The passage of these two laws also facilitated the exchange of information regarding immigration status and the receipt of Medicaid-funded services between states and the federal INS (now Immigration and Customs Enforcement—ICE).[101] For instance, PRWORA explicitly prohibits the use of federal funds for Medicaid benefits other than emergency care for specific groups of immigrants. Therefore, unless they have a specific, verifiable immigration status, immigrants are only allowed coverage for emergency care. States must now verify the immigration status of a foreign-born Medicaid applicant with the INS if the person applies for a Medicaid benefit that includes federal financial participation.[102] This is a departure from previous policies in California wherein verification of immigration status was only required for those seeking full-scale benefits and, when required, a social security card or birth certificate was sufficient to establish legal immigration status. Consequently, an immigrant was eligible for emergency and pregnancy-related services without any documentation of immigration status.[103] Chapter 3 will illustrate this issue further, using as a case study a class action suit against the California Department of Health Services.

Moreover, these federal policies have prohibited state and local governments from restricting communication between state and local agencies and the INS regarding the immigration status of benefits applicants. This information link between the INS and DHS can occur through local Medi-Cal eligibility offices. When immigrants apply for Medi-Cal, the information they provide about their income, assets, and the information in documents they used to establish their California residency can now be turned over legally to the INS. This institutionalized sharing of what was once private information is a public health issue, given that the increased level of fear may deter immigrants from using preventive health care such as prenatal care. The disciplinary, governmental reach of INS/ICE continues to expand into other entities, often to the detriment of these organizations. Thus, the mission of safety net health care hospitals and clinics to care for their underserved and vulnerable populations is jeopardized as they become increasingly intertwined with immigration enforcement. For instance, public hospitals seeking federal reimbursement for emergency services provided to nonqualified aliens are required to follow federal procedures regarding verification of immigration status.[104] In this way, public hospitals are forced to verify their patients' immigration status in order to be compensated for their care. Verification of immigration status is central to federal Medicaid eligibility requirements.

Currently in California, legal challenges to the implementation of welfare and immigration reforms and the use of state general funds have ensured the eligibility of low-income immigrants for Medi-Cal coverage of prenatal care and other pregnancy-related services. The problem, however, is that the policy implementations of the welfare and immigration reforms have created a chilling effect that has discouraged use of Medicaid by immigrants who are *legally* eligible in California. There is concern that this fear may have long-term health consequences for low-income pregnant immigrant women.

Since the passage of the 1996 laws, information concerning people who apply for and receive Medi-Cal has been provided on an ongoing basis to the state DHS office by local Medi-Cal eligibility agencies. Prior to the INS clarification, the issue at stake was whether Medicaid, a non-cash public benefit, fell within the domain of public charge since the benefit is not cash assistance, but health care coverage.

Surprisingly, the official clarification of public charge in 1999—stating that Medi-Cal use alone cannot be used to determine public charge—did little to diminish the initial fears created by the federal and state policies. The trust required to deliver quality preventive health care such as pre-natal care to immigrant communities was badly damaged as a result of a history of anti-immigrant sentiment.[105] The 1996 policies helped to solidify this distrust of government programs. The power of the INS to arbitrarily prevent an immigrant they judge to be a potential public charge from ob-taining legal permanent residency helped to create this antagonistic rela-tionship. In addition, the INS can refuse readmission to immigrants who leave the United States for more than 180 days, and are judged likely to become a public charge upon their return. And the ever-present threat of deportation as a public charge (while rarely done) has created an intensely hostile environment for low-income immigrant women in need of pre-natal care. Again, the message is that low-income immigrant women do not have the same freedom as middle-class native-born women, to have healthy children. The threat of deportation is severe.

It appears that what California began with Proposition 187 in 1994 was en-acted de facto across the nation with the Immigration and Welfare Reform Acts of 1996. The restrictions to public services enforced by the state Prop. 187, which were deemed unconstitutional and never legally enacted, were in effect reinstated by federal policies two years later. The chilling effects ini-tiated by Prop. 187 were further solidified nationally through these federal legislations that reinforced the stereotype of immigrants as public burdens.

Methods

For this project, 196 participants were interviewed in two stages from Sep-tember 1998 to December 2001. Using qualitative methods, key respon-dents were interviewed to document the impact of recent immigration and welfare reforms on health care access for low-income pregnant immi-grant women in California. Initially, we focused on four areas of the state that together comprise more than 75 percent of California's foreign-born population: San Diego, Los Angeles, the San Francisco Bay Area, and the Central Valley. In this first stage, we selected a purposive sample of 101 respondents from 76 different organizations knowledgeable about immigrant health care in California since 1994. These respondents were from three different types of organizations, thus revealing the multiple dimensions of immigrant women's experiences with health services: safety net health care providers, immigrant organizations, and government agencies.

A little over a year later, I returned to my respondents and interviewed them once again to document any changes in access to health care since our first interview. This time, I limited my sample size to three geographical areas to provide greater depth: the San Francisco Bay Area, Fresno County, and San Diego County. The San Francisco Bay Area remained the northern California sample, Fresno the rural, Central Valley sample, and San Diego the southern California sample. However, during our return visit, we found a high turnover rate in these positions, making it difficult to locate the same individual we had interviewed earlier. Consequently, whenever possible we spoke with the newly hired replacements of those we had interviewed earlier, holding the same positions. In some instances, the positions had been eliminated altogether. We interviewed a total of 95 key informants in this second stage.

My objective, in this second phase of data collection, was to document whether the women and their health care providers had experienced less confusion after a number of key attempts were initiated to clarify federal and state policies regarding health care for immigrants. I paid particular attention to federal policy clarifications regarding public charge, which was intended to alleviate the fear of the consequences of accessing health care. A more detailed description of my data collection methods is provided in Appendix A.

Outline of the Book

This book begins by framing the social context of immigrant women's reproduction within major welfare and immigration reforms in the 1990s. I first outline the history of "public charge" and its strategic political use to portray low-income immigrant women as burdens on the state. I discuss the contemporary neoliberal twist to this idea and how immigrant access to prenatal care pertains to and contributes to debates about immigration in California. In extending these arguments, I analyze the role of immigrants in what is left of today's welfare state in chapter 2. Here, I focus on pregnant immigrant women's experiences with the Medicaid eligibility process in California.

In chapter 3, I investigate the impact of public charge fears on low-income pregnant immigrant women's access to Medi-Cal, a publicly funded health insurance program for low-income Californians. Here, I begin with a more detailed discussion of the Medicaid fraud detection programs established at the Mexico-U.S. border, and later at the Los Angeles and San Francisco International airports to illustrate the extensive and complex influence of policy on an everyday level. Of particular significance is the impact—or lack thereof—of government efforts to backtrack or "clarify" their mistakes (i.e., unintended consequences). As data, I provide two key case studies. First, I use documents and interviews relating to a lawsuit brought against the State Department of Health Services regarding its handling of fraud detections programs at the border. This lawsuit brought to light largely secretive initiatives to deter low-income immigrants from accessing health care and to illegally collect funds from immigrants who had already done so. Second, I analyze a remarkable state audit of a specific fraud detection program aimed at documented, low-income immigrants re-entering the United States through border crossings in San Diego County and the international airports in Los Angeles and San Francisco. These cases show that federal policies have little room for error, given these policies' actual consequences on people's everyday lives.

Chapter 4 focuses on the role of social workers in ensuring the necessary level of community trust in sustaining medical safety nets. I show how these social workers play a pivotal role in holding up the fraying health care safety net. To do this, I analyze the clarification of public charge policy in 1999 and its impact on community-based safety net organizations. In chapter 5, I pay attention to San Diego as a constructed "illegal" space where local and national anxieties about immigration come together to push (seemingly) new initiatives to dismantle health care for low-income immigrant workers. The U.S./Mexico border allows for an extranational space of experimentation to see how far rules and regulations can be bent in keeping with the ebb and flow of global financial investment, national security fears, and political capital. I look particularly at two health care clinics in San Diego County who care for indigent residents. These clinics are indicative of the last frontier of immigrant health care.

I conclude, in chapter 6, with a summary of how the notion of public charge promotes a neoliberal ideology of personal responsibility and criminal dependency. The criminalization of low-income Asian and Latino immigrants in the 1990s as public burdens recast their legal behavior as "illegal," regardless of their actual citizenship status. In response, various health care clinics, hospitals, and organizations developed innovative strategies to alleviate some of the chilling effects of public charge allegations on low-income immigrant families. These innovations are essential, given the grave consequences of these federal and state policies. By simultaneously capitalizing on the modes of racialization and gendering that already existed within these government institutions, understandings of burden and citizenship are reframed by neoliberal logic to the detriment of all people—both immigrant and native-born.

CHAPTER 2

The Health of the Welfare State

Especially since the 1970s, the norms of good citizenship in advanced liberal democracies have shifted from an emphasis on duties and obligations to the nation to a stress on becoming autonomous, responsible choice-making subjects who can serve the nation best by becoming "entrepreneurs of the self."

—Aihwa Ong[1]

Creating "Entrepreneurs of the Self"[2]

The massive economic restructuring of the 1970s was pivotal to the development of global capitalism. This economic transformation, driven by a ferocious faith in a global market free of barriers to facilitate the flow of capital, fueled a parallel demand for transnational labor migration.[3] In fact, Saskia Sassen argues that immigration is largely a result of the economic, political, and social conditions of the *receiving* country. She states, "Immigration flows may take a while to adjust to changes in levels of labor demand or to saturation of opportunities, but eventually they always have tended to adjust to the conditions in receiving counties, even if these adjustments are imperfect."[4] At the same time, the Hart-Celler Act of 1965 not only rearranged which and how many persons could enter the United States but also the entire process by which these decisions were made.[5] The new category of "family unification" helped to alter the composition of the immigrant population to comprise approximately 40 percent from Latin America and another 40 percent from Asia. In a stunning turn-around, European admissions fell to less than 20 percent during the 1970s. Thus, the 1970s brought in a new wave of large-scale immigration from what were, at the time, nontraditional sending nations. Subsequently, the number of Latino/as surpassed the African American population to become the largest racial minority group in the United States today. In addition, Asian immigrant communities also experienced significant population increases—so much so that Asian Americans became the fastest growing minority group.

The decade of the 1970s was also an historic era of civil rights legislation. Consequently, particular forms of discrimination, including racism, were legally prohibited. Here, we see the impact of the civil rights movement in opening access to welfare benefits to African Americans. In 1939, when AFDC was created (Aid to Families with Dependent Children), the major welfare program for poor families, 89 percent of the recipients were white and 61 percent were widows.[6] These numbers began to change in the 1960s as black women and other welfare rights advocates collectively won greater access to AFDC by contesting the exclusion of certain industries from coverage under the programs and discriminatory practices of state agencies that administered the programs.[7] However, by the mid-1970s, retrenchment of the welfare state was institutionalized through a concerted political attack on the acceptability of entitlement. Teresa Amott describes this coordinated process as follows:

> Starting in California, a movement to limit state taxes was able to mobilize the concerns of moderate income citizens over their stagnating earnings. Fundamentalist Christians focused on the erosion of "family values" and the rise in divorce and out-of-wedlock births. Corporations facing falling profit rates sought to impose labor discipline through cutbacks in government programs, sophisticated anti-union campaigns, and demands for deregulation. At the state level, these movements combined to sharply limit the never-strong political support for AFDC.[8]

As the U.S. economy began to stagnate in the 1970s and neoliberal political and economic doctrines took root, the concept of entitlement underwent severe scrutiny as age-old moral fitness arguments were reinstated

to question the "deservingness" of Black mothers. Gwendolyn Mink observes that welfare, as a maternalist innovation, was once understood as
a "Mother's pension," but it became "discursively transformed into a 'way
of life' by the late 1960s, and the worth and rights of single mothers were
displaced by the icon of the Black 'welfare mother.'"[9] Mink describes today's postmaternalist welfare policy as pathologizing women's dependency
to justify punishing mothers who do not conform to legislated morality—
a "shape-up-in-the-home or ship-out-to-work" principle: "Today's welfare
reform . . . rejects the idea that the poverty of mothers and children is a
social concern and seeks to privatize economic uplift: hence the notion of
coercive work requirements."[10]

By 1990, Linda Gordon writes,

> In two generations the meaning of "welfare" has reversed itself. What
> once meant well-being now means ill-being. What once meant prosper-
> ity, good health, and good spirits now implies poverty, bad health, and
> fatalism. A word that once evoked images of pastoral contentment now
> connotes slums, depressed single mothers and neglected children, even
> crime. Today "welfare" means grudging aid to the poor, when once it re-
> ferred to a vision of a good life.[11]

As access to social services included more people of color, the service
itself became defined as morally questionable. The few publicly funded
programs of assistance to the very poor were so despised that even self-
defined liberal progressive organizations did not want to touch the matter. For instance, the National Organization for Women (NOW)'s Legal
Defense and Education Fund tried to appeal for financial support for an
economic justice litigator through direct mail but its request was met with
so much hate mail that it stopped mailing any literature mentioning welfare issues.[12] Gordon provides this bleak assessment of the state of welfare
in 1994:

> "Welfare" is hated by the prosperous and the poor, by the women who
> receive it and by those who feel they are paying for it. It stigmatizes its
> recipients, not least because they are so often suspected of cheating,
> claiming "welfare" when they could be working or paying their own way.
> It humiliates its recipients by subjecting them to demeaning supervision

and invasions of privacy. Yet it does nothing to move poor women and their children out of poverty and often places obstacles in the paths of women's own attempts to do so.[13]

By 1996, women who accessed welfare were openly treated as "reckless breeders who bear children to avoid work."[14]

While the drive for reform is not surprising, given such assessments, the extent and depth of the 1996 welfare legislation's long-term effects on low-income immigrant families and its implications for our national identity is profound. These policies describe a retrenchment or retraction of the welfare state itself. One of the most remarkable elements in this legislation is the disproportionate focus on immigrants. In the initial form passed, almost 50 percent of the overall welfare cuts were directed at the limited services for immigrants. Clearly, the focus of national anxiety over welfare use highlighted immigrants.

Given this vitriolic reaction to anything defined as "welfare," health care activists advocated for prenatal services for low-income immigrants by framing prenatal care as a form of preventive care that was relatively cheap compared to emergency care and by defining the patients as deserving, self-sufficient people who valued their children. Linking cost effectiveness and morality, good mothering was evoked to distance their patients from the negative imagery of "welfare mothers." However, this argument was to little avail as the political climate toward immigrants increasingly chilled to a point where even immunization for citizen infants of immigrant mothers was viewed as asking for too much.[15] Ironically, by focusing their arguments on costs, morality, and mothering, public health efforts may have functioned to further solidify the negative stereotype of welfare mothers as real. Rather than dispute the representations themselves as false, harmful, and racist, public health advocates may have missed an opportunity by presenting certain immigrant women as "model minorities," in opposition to others who fall into this stereotype.

There is another pitfall with this representation, in that strong, independent women are problematic in a welfare system in which recipients must show "neediness." The welfare state's role as disciplinarian is well established. From Mimi Abramovitz's historical analysis of welfare policy as a systemic way to regulate women's lives[16] to Michel Foucault's theory of governmentality,[17] studies have illustrated how the state utilizes a discourse of "needs" to justify institutional social control. What has changed is the degree to which discipline was meted out during the neoliberal era of the 1990s.[18]

Despite the rhetoric of low-income immigrant women as public burdens, real independence is troublesome for the nation-state in its current drive to control the border and the immigrants within it. Ironically, the nation-state requires a certain level of subservience or dependency from these women and the welfare system enforces this. The eligibility process to gain access to the system, for example, enforces a strict code of behavior, as do most forms of charity. The move toward privatization through personal responsibility has diminished what were once state entitlements to almost complete dependence on individual charity. This is particularly the case for low-income immigrant women who are seen as public burdens. For immigrants, the consequences are considerable. The following section of this chapter outlines in greater detail the ritual—that is, the procedures and performance— of enforced dependency that many low-income women encounter as they try to access prenatal care for which they are eligible. I will also discuss the impact of intergovernmental collaboration as a persistent barrier that contributes to this ritual. Then, I will conclude by examining the political quagmire of motherhood for low-income immigrant women who need prenatal care. Many of these women are trapped between being viewed as either too dependent or too independent of the state, both of which are deemed irresponsible subject positions.

With the "enforced and induced compliance"[19] of the individualistic logic of neoliberal capitalist discipline, the existence of the welfare state is treated as an eyesore. And the anxieties regarding immigrants and immigration have contributed to the latest, near-fatal blow to the welfare state. What images of the "welfare queen" crippled, the "immigrant public charge" has decimated, perhaps even nailing the coffin shut.

Rituals of Enforced Dependency

The Medi-Cal Eligibility Process

Medi-Cal—California's Medicaid program—provides health care coverage for over 5.1 million low-income families and individuals who lack health insurance. Both the federal and state governments fund Medi-Cal. It is administered by the Department of Health Services (DHS) at the state level, and by the Department of Social Services (DSS) at the county level. It is at the county level that "Medi-Cal eligibility workers" determine eligibility. These eligibility workers are based in welfare offices and in some health care hospitals and clinics. [20]

However, Medi-Cal does not cover everyone who is poor. One must meet a number of property, income, institutional status, residence, and citizenship requirements to qualify. In 1998, there were 107 categories or "aid codes" for eligibility. The welfare and immigration flegislative changes after 1996 made what was already a complicated Medi-Cal eligibility process even more intimidating for immigrants. The Medi-Cal eligibility process is commonly described as a "hassle." [21] The complicated income and residency requirements and intimidating investigators all contribute to the barriers that surround access to Medi-Cal. A community clinic director explained:

[I]t is very difficult for people to understand all the eligibility [categories]. My professional eligibility staff—it is a miracle that they understand all that. Understanding all these little rules. It is just such an incredible waste of wealth as well as a deterrent to care. I think that is the real impact of how this comes together. And it is with such concentration, particularly aimed at immigrant families. It is sort of academic whether or not you are eligible under these certain circumstances. Overall message is you are really not welcome, you are really not eligible.

Respondents in each region stated that even though immigrants may want health care, the lengthy paperwork involved in signing up for Medi-Cal deters them from enrolling. The time spent on completing the application and then getting approval for the services is a lengthy and time-consuming task that has discouraged some immigrants from enrolling in Medi-Cal. A health care provider in San Diego illustrates the level of frustration that characterizes this process by saying:

There's absolutely no assistance in completing an absolutely monstrous application. Most of the clients we are dealing with are really not in a position to complete application forms. . . . So if you've got a huge document this thick, what's the likelihood of having tremendous miscommunication? Massive.

The inability to fully complete an application may mean that it will be months before an individual is eligible for Medi-Cal, resulting in delay in seeking and receiving the needed health care. A San Diego health care provider describes the problems that can surface with the completion of these applications as follows:

> People have to apply two or three times because they don't get the paperwork done. They're not actually denying a person because it's actual ineligibility, they just don't have either what they want or what they need to determine that eligibility. So I think it's becoming more and more clear that all of our clients really need help in completing the actual applications so that when the eligibility technicians get the forms, they can actually determine eligibility and then go ahead and grant, or deny if in fact they are ineligible.

These difficulties involved in Medi-Cal access are also evident in the income and residency requirements of these applications.

Income Requirements

As part of the Medi-Cal application process, an applicant's household income must be assessed. For some immigrant applicants, this is no easy task. Many immigrants, particularly the undocumented, work in the "informal economy"[22] where there is no written record of their labor or the wages they receive. As a community clinic outreach worker explained:

> One of the major problems they have here is that a lot of them do work under the table—for instance gardening work—and they get paid in cash and when they go to apply for Medi-Cal; well, Medi-Cal says, "we need proof of income" and they go back to that person and they say, "you know, can you give me a receipt or a little ledger that says that I worked here and I made $40 today." People refuse to do that because they know that they are hiring an illegal and they don't want to be involved. And they deny that the person has worked there. So they go back to the Medi-Cal worker and say, "you know, I cannot provide this because this person doesn't want to give me this," and then this is the end of the story.

The outreach worker described a number of cases in which her patients experienced a series of disruptions in her prenatal care as they and/or their partners jumped from one "informal" job to another. Even those who are initially enrolled in Medi-Cal find themselves in difficult situations regarding their employment. The informality of this labor force creates problems for Medi-Cal recipients when they file mandatory quarterly reports declaring their income and assets. As they go from one job to the next, there is no guarantee that their current employer will provide the necessary documentation for the quarterly Medi-Cal form. Those patients who are unable to provide proof of income may be cut from the program. Due to the stricter eligibility requirements and immigrants' inability to provide sufficient documents, providers have reported growing numbers of denials for Pregnancy Only Medi-Cal[23] applicants.

In these situations, immigrant health care advocates are essential for minimizing or eliminating the disruptions in prenatal care. One outreach worker related the following experience of one of her patients who needed prenatal care:

She was five months pregnant, had a stack of [medical] bills, and the employer refused to sign the [form] because he did not want to be in trouble for hiring somebody knowing that they have a fake social security number. He did not want anything to come back to him. So, that is why I called the social worker and I just gave her the situation. I said, "What can she do, her employer doesn't want to sign this form. They have already closed her case, her Medi-Cal case."

In the meantime, this outreach worker ensured temporary access to prenatal care through presumptive eligibility so that her patient could have at least another sixty days to disentangle her enrollment problems. The outreach worker also made some phone calls and found that there was a supplemental form she could use to explain her employment situation. The eligibility worker did not inform the patient that this supplemental form could replace the original income eligibility requirement.

Immigrants working in the agricultural industry also find themselves in difficult situations as their employment is not year-round but seasonal. They follow the agricultural cycle and work nine months out of the year. While most immigrant agricultural workers' gross annual incomes fall well below the federal poverty guidelines, health care providers in these areas find that during the peak harvest season—when all the household members are working overtime—families make more than the designated income eligibility level (at or below 200 percent of the federal poverty level) for Medi-Cal. Some also earn more than the limit imposed by alternative payment programs that were established by individual safety net providers for immigrants unwilling to apply for Medi-Cal. A community clinic outreach worker explained:

> We offer a sliding fee scale—but sometimes they don't qualify because they were at that peak season where they made a lot of money, you know, overtime hours with her husband and herself well, then it would be too high for them to pay on a cash basis. Sometimes they'll hold off and not apply until the season's over.

Medi-Cal policies do not allow for the unique difficulties that seasonal workers face. This is one of many hurdles some immigrants confront when trying to access basic care for which they are eligible.

Residency Requirements

Residency requirements can also prove to be an obstacle for some immigrants. A director of women's services at a safety net hospital said that her immigrant patients experienced difficulties in providing a seemingly simple requirement, namely, proof of residency. This is particularly so for those who work in the informal agricultural sector. The director said:

> With Medi-Cal you have to have an address, you have to previously live here. We have a lot of migrant farm workers up here that work in the fields. They have no way of proving, of giving an address. So they are unable to sign up for Medi-Cal for that reason.

Residency requirements may be difficult to fulfill for low-income immigrants living in metropolitan areas as well. A coordinator of a home-visiting program for high-risk infants born to immigrant mothers explained that many of the families with whom she worked lived in small one-bedroom apartments with several other families. The high cost of living, particularly for rent, had forced many low-income immigrant families to share the cost of housing. However, this has led to problems in establishing who legally resides in a particular household. Not all occupants are listed in the lease or on an electricity bill, making the proof of residency requirement difficult to fulfill.

An immigrant advocate and social worker in the Bay Area discussed the recent barriers constructed for the undocumented to establish their residency as follows:

> They ask them for a utility bill in their name. And before, they could bring the brother or sister-in-law's utility bill with a letter from the person saying she lives here. But now they can't do that. There has to be something with their name. So, they go back and forth, back and forth, and they have this form from the state saying specific items that they need for them to bring to apply for Medi-Cal. And one is a California ID. And they cannot get California ID because in order for them to get California ID, they need to get a social security number, and they are undocumented so they cannot get social security. So there is no way around. And so they go and get fraudulent papers; and then they get caught. It is really difficult. A lot of women go through pregnancy with no Medi-Cal, and after the baby is born, then they try to figure out how they are going to pay, or Medi-Cal will send them papers to come and apply, but it is a hassle to just go back and forth, back and forth, to try to get the papers that they require for Medi-Cal to get prenatal care.

To make matters worse, in San Diego, an invasive investigation is conducted for those whose Medi-Cal applications are in "pending" status. In that county, if there are questions regarding an applicant's residency requirement, an investigation is launched wherein DHS peace officers, armed with guns and badges, appear at the applicant's door. In these circumstances, people have no option but to let the officers in and give them permission to search their home. A local community clinic coordinator explained that, if immigrants did not let the DHS officers into their house: "Then [DHS] will say there is not enough information and they will reject [the application]. So, it is very, very intimidating."

Another clinic outreach worker in San Diego reported:

Many times, if there is a question about someone's eligibility, an investigator is sent to their home to check to see if they really live there. They show up in uniform and armed with a gun. It's really intimidating. They go inside and look through everything, including their underwear drawers to see if they actually live there. They count the underwear. Lots of times, they'll go during the workday when no one's home. If no one answers the door, then, they're denied Medi-Cal. It's invasive and you feel like a criminal.

The Medi-Cal Eligibility Worker

Stricter income and residency requirements, combined with intimidating eligibility investigators, have created greater barriers to care. One of the most common complaints expressed during my research team's interviews concerned the disrespectful treatment of immigrant Medi-Cal applicants by eligibility workers. The problem arises from the fact that there is little or no trust between the applicant and the local Department of Social Services (DSS), whose job it is to determine their eligibility for Medi-Cal benefits. While trust is imperative in alleviating fear among low-income immigrant communities, it is difficult to achieve in an environment where there is high turnover and burnout rate among DSS workers.

Many outreach and social workers who work with low-income pregnant immigrant women described a hostile environment at the eligibility office, where there is no sense of comfort or safety. However, there are some women who enjoy a good relationship with their eligibility officer, and have developed a level of trust where the social worker and/or the immigrant applicant feels free to ask questions regarding eligibility requirements and, more importantly, is confident about the reliability of the response. Having DSS workers "outstationed" at the clinic site has helped to regenerate some trust. A clinic coordinator in San Diego said:

One thing we do is, we have DSS workers who come on site and do the eligibility determinations right here. So people can avoid going to the DSS offices entirely. And that is a benefit for our patients, because they are very intimidated by the DSS offices.

As one outreach worker in Santa Clara County told us, "They [immigrant women] just want to be treated like human beings." Respondents described many DSS investigators as frustrated, disrespectful, and poorly trained. According to outreach workers we interviewed, the job turnover rate is so great among Medi-Cal eligibility workers that there is very little consistency and the workers themselves are ill-informed about policy changes. Participants discussed how a single misinformed eligibility worker could damage trust in the system and prevent many immigrants from accessing the services they need and are entitled to. "Many are scared off," stated one administrator at a Fresno health clinic. "There are negative connotations, but also large [amounts of] paperwork and dealing with incidents with eligibility workers being rude or insensitive that turns them off from applying."

A health educator in Fresno described some of her interactions with Medi-Cal eligibility workers as follows:

> Sometimes [immigrant patients] are treated with very little respect. . . . [Eligibility workers] are overworked and you call the Department of Human Resources and you leave 20 messages and you won't ever get a response. So it's hard. I've tried to call myself from the office and leave messages, talk to supervisors and you usually come to a wall. You're banging yourself against this wall.

A Medi-Cal eligibility worker's lack of sensitivity or knowledge can seriously affect an immigrant's trust and heighten the fear of government programs. One statewide advocate said:

> Medi-Cal is a great program. . . . Unfortunately, it doesn't take many eligibility workers to wreck it for everybody. If you don't have the advocacy component to get in there and fix those problems, you don't get the trust back.

In San Diego, focus group participants repeatedly stated that the health care eligibility workers consistently and purposely tried to prevent immigrants from obtaining Medi-Cal. Medi-Cal fraud is an important focus in San Diego County due to a powerful conservative constituency (similar to that of many border towns) and media attention surrounding a relatively small number of immigrants who inappropriately obtained Medi-Cal and health services. As a result, eligibility workers have focused their efforts on detecting fraud at the expense of authorizing needed health care services. In other words, the job becomes one of fraud detection rather than public service provision. A program manager from San Diego stated:

> [I]t's fraud prevention that they are more concerned about. . . . [I]n this county, we don't have a county hospital, we don't have anyplace for these poor people to go except for the community clinics and other kinds of places along that line. . . . In a sense, they are saying that unless you are a citizen, you don't deserve it. And it's a subtlety; they won't say it to your face, but that's really what they mean.

Moreover, there is an attitude that permeates the work of eligibility workers. One San Diego health care provider said:

> [A]s long as the attitude at the top is that, "we don't want to increase our case load, we really aren't interested in helping these people, they really ought to go home," and all of those other kinds of things, the attitudes of the workers are not going to change and even when you get a bright, fresh, new employee that comes in and starts working and really wants to help, after a few years of being beaten down, you give up or you leave.

The Medi-Cal Eligibility Office

The sharing of DHS information between local health and human service departments and the INS is also evident in DSS offices in San Diego where women go to apply for Medi-Cal eligibility. The San Diego County Board of Supervisors directed its County Health Department staff to provide INS information regarding documentation status for any immigrants applying for TANF, Food Stamps, or General Relief. The county went so far as to place signs in the local social service offices where individuals apply for Medi-Cal. A San Diego legal advocate described the signs:

It said, "Please be aware that we can send any information you give us to INS" and went on to state that they may send information to the INS if you are applying for Cal Works or Food Stamps. Finally, the last paragraph stated: "We will not send information from people who are applying for Medi-Cal only."

The advocate noted that many people did not read past the intimidating introductory sentence down to the last paragraph that exempted Medi-Cal only applicants. These signs have had a reverberating impact in San Diego's immigrant community. A health care provider explained:

There was a lot of concern about the public charge issue and particularly in San Diego County, which is a very conservative county in which the board of supervisors interjected its policies . . . with the Department of Social Services. So, what we were seeing was that people were very much aware that information was being shared between the DSS and the INS. There were posters for a period of time in the Department of Social Services offices saying information will be shared with the INS and that just made people crazy. We had about 70 percent of our patients who were interviewed by the eligibility technician going on pending status. They would be investigated and many of them received visits by peace officers who—carrying weapons—would actually go into their homes and look at their underwear, look at their letters, look at their wallet, and use that to determine whether they were eligible. It was extremely, extremely intimidating for people.

A midwife at a safety net clinic in San Diego spoke about her patients' reactions to the signs:

[W]hat the women told me is that they feel threatened when they go in and they say that whatever you say here can be reported to immigration [INS] or something, so a lot of them, even if I tell them that they all have the right to go and apply because the law still provides for them to have Medi-Cal, they feel threatened. They say, no I don't think so. They say, they've heard stories that somebody got deported or something. And unfortunately, even though we gave out a pamphlet that says you have the right, even if you don't have papers, to apply for Medi-Cal, a lot of them when they go to the office and when they see that poster they turn around and they don't do it.

The perinatal manager of this clinic, which relies on Medi-Cal patients, reported a dramatic decline in the number of pregnant immigrant Latinas coming into their clinic. She has had to lay off one of her two providers and views the hostile Medi-Cal eligibility process as the culprit.

Intergovernmental Collaboration: Sharing of Personal Information

Before 1996, state government agencies did not formally share information with the federal Immigration and Naturalization Service (INS) about individuals' immigration status or use of public benefits. Provisions of the Social Security Act expressly prohibit the sharing of information in regard to individuals' receipt of public benefits with other government agencies.[24] However, both the 1996 welfare and immigration reforms included new provisions that allow for the sharing of information between the state Department of Health Services (DHS), which is responsible for the state Medi-Cal program, and the federal INS (now called Immigration and Customs Enforcement or ICE, housed within the Department of Homeland Security).[25]

Under the welfare reform legislation, states are now required to verify the immigration status of a foreign-born Medicaid applicant with ICE if the person applies for a Medicaid benefit that includes financial participation by the federal government.[26] In the past, a social security card or birth certificate was sufficient to establish legal immigration status. Moreover, state and local governments are prohibited from restricting communication between state and local agencies and the Department of Homeland Security regarding the immigration status of benefits applicants. This information link between Homeland Security and DHS can occur through local county Medi-Cal eligibility offices. When immigrants apply for Medi-Cal, the information they provide about their income and assets, as well as the information in documents they used to establish their California residency, now can be turned over legally to the federal immigration authority.

In addition, public hospitals seeking federal reimbursement for emergency services provided to certain noncitizens designated "nonqualified" are now required to follow federal procedures regarding verification of immigration status.[27] Public hospitals are now forced to verify their patients'

immigration status in order to be compensated for their care and verification of immigration status is now central to federal Medicaid eligibility
requirements. This institutionalized sharing of information across state
and federal government agencies created an unnerving precedent for
many ethnic minorities regardless of their legal citizenship status. State
surveillance powers increased dramatically with these new policies and
many immigrants expressed fear in accessing even those social and health
services for which they were eligible. The governmental interconnection
institutionalized through these new policies delivered a blow to the hard-
earned trust gained by community advocates who had successfully promoted preventive health care, such as prenatal care, in immigrant communities throughout California.

Unfortunately, these hostile welfare and immigration policies make
health care access an excruciating choice for those with limited financial
resources and legal protections. A Bay Area community clinic director described an incident involving a low-income mother of two young children,
a three-year-old girl and a three-month-old baby, respectively. A month
earlier, the older sibling had developed an alarming fever. The mother took
her child to the emergency room and incurred a hospital bill in excess of
$1,000. The clinic director continued:

> So, the bill was sitting on the kitchen table and then the three-month-
> old baby starts choking. The mother is holding the baby and the mother
> is thinking, "OK, what do I do?" She is looking at this $1,000 bill and
> thinking, maybe I panicked that time; maybe I didn't need to take her to
> the ER. So she is second-guessing herself, and ends up calling five differ-
> ent relatives and friends. On the 6th call, she calls the clinic, and the doc-
> tor goes, "What?! She's choking? Get off the phone right now and call
> 911." And she did but the baby died. The irony was the baby was three
> months old so technically was still covered under Medicaid for another
> three months after delivery.

For many immigrants, health insurance continues to be a luxury and
even the prospect of utilizing emergency health care is a difficult decision
that requires careful balancing of costs and benefits.[28] Even in such life-
or-death situations (or perhaps particularly in these situations), the decision to go to a hospital is not a simple one. The confusing and frequently

humiliating health insurance eligibility process, hostile health care workers, possible negative ramifications for the individual and his or her family's immigration status, in addition to the costs of the care are just some
of the barriers that contribute to a situation in which health care is frequently out of reach. The confusion and hostility is, at times, so great that
community rumors of prison time for not paying back Medi-Cal benefits
are received as truth. Health care providers conclude that many immigrants simply do not get care until it is too late.

The Specter of Bad Mothers

Since overtly racist rationales for exclusion might be accompanied by the
discomforting specter of eugenics, ideologically charged labels of "good"
and "bad" mothers become a convenient cover for media and policy dis-
courses on immigrant access to health care. As a legacy from the Victo-
rian ideal of motherhood, the "good" mother is self-sacrificing, domestic,
and instinctively attuned to her children's needs, while the "bad" mother is
deemed to fail on one or more of these measures.[29] As part of this legacy,
women's place in the new nation was explicitly tied to "good" mothering.
A self-sacrificing mother was the ideal citizen. Ladd-Taylor and Umansky
write, "Women were formally excluded from most rights of citizens (such
as voting), but they were assigned informal responsibility for the moral education of their citizen-sons."[30] This education was considered the foundation of a successful American democracy. Ladd-Taylor and Umansky note
that in practice, the label of "bad" mother has fallen upon three general
categories of people: "those who do not live in a 'traditional' nuclear family; those who would not or could not protect their children from harm;
and those whose children went wrong."[31] Consequently, "bad" mothering
does not actually denote particular practices, but rather implicates entire
categories of people. During the late nineteenth century, the idea of a "scientific motherhood" provided a modernist twist for creating a hierarchy
of "good" mothers. Proponents argued that evolutionary theory deemed
Anglo-Saxon or northern European women as the true "good" mothers.
Women of other races further down the evolutionary ladder inevitably
produced inferior offspring.[32]

In addition to the persistence of race in discussions of immigration and the use of motherhood as a strategic state ideology, a third characteristic is common in these eugenic arguments: the link between motherhood and childhood. On this last point, sociologist Evelyn Nakano Glenn points out that new notions of motherhood arose as industrialization propelled a new understanding of childhood as priceless.[33] She writes, "Childhood came to be seen as a special and valued period of life, and children were depicted as innocent beings in need of prolonged protection and care."[34] This new conception of childhood required a complementary conception of motherhood as a serious responsibility, one that required total and exclusive devotion. Here, we see the beginnings of the extraordinary mother as normative social convention. This new concept of childhood and accompanying motherhood placed many working-class immigrant women and women of color in a difficult position. The new "science" of eugenics defined them as bad mothers on the basis of their "inferior" racial stock, but at the same time the demand for their labor in the domestic sphere—as nannies and housekeepers—increased sharply.

Ladd-Taylor and Umansky note, "Although proslavery ideologues declared black women to be lacking in maternal feelings for their own children, they sentimentalized the mammy, always there to protect and care for her young white charges." Working-class immigrant women today find themselves in a similar dilemma. Glenn argues that these women are not expected or allowed to be "good" mothers. She states, "Because [women of color] were incorporated into the United States largely to take advantage of their labor, there was little interest in preserving family life or encouraging the cultural and economic development of people of color."[35] Anti-immigrant policies that restrict access to prenatal care services construct low-income immigrants as social burdens and an uncontrollable internal threat to the nation's economic, cultural, and political stability.[36]

As a social institution, motherhood is so taken-for-granted and pervasive in its idealized form that real women with children negotiating everyday life with its endless details are viewed as bizarre—so much so that *extraordinary* mothers are now the social norm. The cultural romanticization of motherhood has shifted the definition of a "good" mother to that of an extraordinary one. An extraordinary mother, then, is a miraculous woman who can provide for her family—emotionally and materially—beyond the resources available to her. As Ladd-Taylor and Umansky write,

"To most Americans, 'bad' mothering is like obscenity: you know it when you see it."[37]

In practical terms, extraordinary mothers are those who can achieve particular outcomes without adequate resources to do so. This includes women who work outside the home who can accomplish as a parent what she would have accomplished had she stayed at home full-time.[38] Consequently, the normative good mother is now an extraordinary one who can make the impossible happen, and at great cost to herself. In fact, it is this impossibility that makes motherhood "sacred." In her discussion of the cultural contradictions of motherhood, Sharon Hays writes, "Giving of oneself and one's resources freely is the appropriate code of maternal behavior, and any concern for maximizing personal profit is condemned."[39] The sacred nature of mothering is the diametrical opposite of a rationalized market economy that encourages personal profit. A good mother must somehow participate in a capitalist system as a consumer and, for most women in the United States, as a worker, but she must eschew any personal benefit that may result from the system while at the same time meeting the many needs of her growing children. A bad mother, on the other hand, is one who cannot extract sufficient capital from the market economy and must depend, at least in part, upon public benefits to care for her family. Extracting the necessary services or cash assistance from the state to care for one's family is viewed with severe disdain and understood as a sign of selfishness. [40]

Clearly, this idealized notion of motherhood has a class and racial bias. A good mother must exhibit adequate self-sacrifice and forgo personal profit but at the same time provide a comfortable, stable, and safe home for her children. This ideal is far more difficult to achieve for women with limited financial and social means than it is for middle- and upper-class women. Self-sacrifice entails an entirely different regimen for families whose basic needs are met and taken for granted. On the other hand, low-income immigrant women of color experience an essentially impossible proposition. They must provide all the trappings of a middle-class childhood for their children, but with far fewer resources and greater barriers to success. Access to basic, preventive health care is a prime example of this impossible situation. A basic level of healthfulness is essential, given that a sick child is symbolic of "bad" mothering. However, preventive prenatal care for immigrant women is a constant target for elimination among those in favor of anti-immigrant legislation, not to mention social conservatives pushing for traditional family values. Consequently, immigrant mothers are blamed for any negative health outcomes of their children while at the same time being restricted from accessing services that can prevent or minimize potential health problems.

Legal theorist Dorothy Roberts points out that mothers are primarily responsible for childrearing but many poor women of color are denied the compensation, power, and support they deserve and require to achieve that goal. Roberts contends that this scenario conveniently absolves the state of liability. She writes, "It pretends that poor minority children's deprivation is caused by maternal negligence and not by joblessness, deplorable housing, inadequate health care, and dilapidated schools."[41] Evidently, it is far easier and politically more salient to police the behavior of low-income mothers than it is to address such complex structural inequalities as health care access.

The Good Mother versus the Good Immigrant

If motherhood, as a historical and social construct, is the link between the family and the nation, what then of immigrant mothers? Certainly within nativist narratives, low-income immigrant mothers of color are a threat to a "healthy," unified national identity. Beyond this eugenic notion of nation building, low-income immigrant mothers pose further ideological difficulties in upholding the nation as a family. This difficulty in inclusion stems from the fact that immigrant mothers are expected to silently exist outside the national family but at the same time uphold the ahistorical and fictive national narrative of "the American Family." This is evident in the construction of the ideology of the "good immigrant,"[42] which functions in contrast to the "good mother." A good immigrant is one who provides particular kinds of necessary but generally denigrated labor at below market value and does not expect the same access, protections, or privileges as a full national member. Therefore, a good immigrant cannot be a mother—good or otherwise. Within this system, the children of today's largely Asian and Latin American immigrants are viewed as costs, given their contentious position within the national family. Studies of the second generation portray an ambiguous scenario in which their inclusion or adaptation as full citizens is far from certain. Even those misinterpreted as "model minorities" feel compelled to refute the persistent assumption of their "foreigner" status.[43]

And yet, the demand for immigrant women's labor remains unfettered. In defining a new "commodity frontier," Arlie Russell Hochschild writes that public and private resources for intimate or domestic care are declining at the same time that demands for longer work hours are increasing.[44] In response, immigrant labor becomes an increasingly necessary component in meeting the average family's daily expectations. Immigrants are essential to ensuring that their employers adhere to the national ideology of family; and in particular, that the "mother" be a good one. Immigrant women's labor as domestic and service workers becomes increasingly necessary for many families in the current 24/7 global economy. In fact, their labor is evidence that meeting the impossible goal of being a "good" mother in today's economy actually requires a second, silent mother. However, this silence is disturbed when immigrant women have their own children. It is discomforting, to say the least, to know that one family is maintained at the expense of another. On the surface, transnational mothers who leave behind their own children and thereby externalize the cost of reproduction appear to embody a tidy solution. But even here, there are difficulties. In their study of Latina transnational motherhood, Hondagneu-Sotelo and Avila found that raising other people's children and taking care of other people's homes is a "radical break with deeply gendered spatial and temporal boundaries of family and work."[45] These transnational mothers from Mexico and Central America redefine the good mother in ways that are at odds with the U.S. national narrative. They write,

> The daily indignities of paid domestic work—low pay, subtle humiliations, not enough food to eat, invisibility—means that transnational mothers are not only stretching their U.S.-earned dollars further by sending the money back home but also, by leaving the children behind, they are providing special protection from the discrimination the children might receive in the United States.[46]

Counter to nativist assumptions of the "American Dream," these immigrant women feel the need to protect their children *from* the United States in an effort to be good mothers. In addition, long-term separations for employment are understood to be a part of being a good mother. These definitions fall outside the established narrative of motherhood that acts as a normalizing tool to link familial hierarchies to national inequalities. At their core, strong and independent immigrant mothers are a problematic necessity in upholding the ideal American family.

While the rhetoric of public charge positions poor immigrant women as problematic on account of their "dependency" on the state, it seems that *independent* poor immigrant women pose an even greater problem. As the nation becomes increasingly dependent upon immigrant women, independent immigrant women who define their identity as mothers apart from the U.S. national ideology are viewed as a growing threat. Consequently, such women are forced to be dependent on the state. This is evident in the technology of the state bureaucracy, which actually enforces dependency among low-income immigrants as a mechanism for detecting and limiting their movement within the United States. This enforced dependency also reinforces the "natural" national narrative wherein women are appropriately dependent upon the (male) head of state, mirroring their rightful subordination to the male head of the family. This paradox is evident in prenatal care policy and rhetoric. The growing restrictions on access to prenatal care for which immigrant women are eligible come largely in the form of greater bureaucratic hurdles that allow increased state surveillance, despite the state's repeated emphasis on "individual responsibility."

Historically, the national anxiety regarding the number of immigrants and their economic and social influence has reached hysterical proportions every few decades. Common within these anxious moments are arguments regarding one's "deservingness" to not only participate in social programs open to the "public" but also their "deservingness" to labor in the United States. The nativist core of these arguments views immigrants from global South countries—especially women with limited financial means—first and foremost as public burdens, regardless of any economic and social contributions they may make. The fact that low-income immigrant women may give birth to racial minorities with rights of legal citizenship threatens the nation's sense of control of our national identity.[47]

A good immigrant is an invisible laborer who upholds the fictive imagery of the American family and gladly accepts his or her exclusion from that unit. A good mother, on the other hand, is an extraordinary, self-sacrificing woman who magically provides for the well-being of her children without adequate resources to do so. It appears that a good immigrant cannot be a good mother—since having children, particularly citizen children, interrupts her invisibility as a worker. Immigrant mothers are, by definition, a public burden, and are consequently bad mothers. Like the Eugenicists of the late nineteenth century, this construction of the immigrant mother as threatening and burdensome solidifies her secondary citizenship status. Roberts writes, "One of the tests of privileges of inclusion in a community is the ability to contribute one's children to the next generation of citizens."[48] Immigrant mothers find themselves in difficult circumstances in which they are necessarily included as laborers but are excluded from the most basic privilege of community membership—the right to have children.

CHAPTER 3

The Politics of
Public Charge

> The Department of Health Services (department) inadequately
> planned its port of entry fraud detection programs—Port of Entry
> Detection (PED) and California Airport Residency Review (CARR)—
> before launching them. It did not fully research essential legal aspects
> of the programs before it adopted guidelines and protocols. As a
> result, the department opened itself up to lawsuits charging that the
> department's operation of the port of entry programs led to abuses.
>   —California State Auditor[1]

The Eugenic Beginnings of Public Charge

It is no coincidence that the notion of a "public charge" was formalized
during the height of mass migration and the subsequent popularity of eugenics in the early twentieth century. The prominence of the American
eugenics movement occurred in part as a response to social anxieties
about immigrant female sexuality and reproduction. In his seminal text,
Backdoor to Eugenics, Troy Duster notes the importance of immigration
to the development of scientific racism in the United States.[2] During the
early 1900s, the mass migration of poor European immigrants put into
motion a number of efforts to distinguish this group as different and inferior to those Europeans who had immigrated earlier. Duster writes that
scientific racism via eugenics was a central element in making this differentiation: "[T]he growth of a body of research showing that genetic disorders were distributed differently through different racial and ethnic groups
[provided] empirical evidence that one group was more likely to have genetic disorders than another."[3] The fact that these genetic differences were
produced *socially* through enforced patterns of mating did little to diminish the far-reaching usefulness of eugenics as a palatable (i.e., "scientific")

evidence of racial superiority and inferiority.[4] The popularity of eugenics reached both sides of the political spectrum, including social radical Margaret Sanger and staunch conservative Madison Grant.[5]

Sanger and other Progressive Era reformers embraced eugenics as a civilizing force that would further increase women's rights. She and her contemporaries viewed eugenics as the advancement of an "objective" scientific tool to control reproduction rather than the moral rationale employed in the nineteenth century. On the other hand, Madison Grant, author of the bestseller *The Passing of the Great Race*, embraced eugenics as a way to limit immigrant rights by deterring births by immigrant women deemed sexually promiscuous. Historian Wendy Kline writes,

> White middle-class authority and middle-class manhood both were in jeopardy because of social and economic changes that undermined established race and gender hierarchies. By regulating the sexuality of working-class and immigrant women, eugenics would reform the sexual behavior of "women adrift" and limit the procreation of the "less civilized"—that is, nonwhite and working-class—races. And by encouraging middle-class white women to return to full-time motherhood, eugenics would both prevent the new woman from succeeding in her "vain attempts to fill men's places" and ensure that the white race once again would be healthy and prolific.[6]

During this historical period, Kline argues that a nationalistic goal of "building a better race" brought strange bedfellows together to focus on immigrant reproductive decisions. The logic of eugenic ideology assumed that restricting the reproduction of "feebleminded" mothers would eliminate feeblemindedness in future generations.[7] This logic solidified the notion of feeblemindedness or being a "moron" as the result of illicit sexual behavior by women. Across the political spectrum there was broad agreement that immigrant women and their innate propensity for reproduction posed a significant social problem.

Almost a century later, immigrant women's reproduction remains central to national anxieties over race and class. However, this time the majority of immigrants are from Asia and Latin America. And while eugenics has fallen out of favor as the explicit operating logic governing immigration or reproductive policies, "it remains just beneath the surface."[8] Duster outlines the general ebb and flow of this racist logic in U.S. history, citing 1900 to 1935 as the height of its popularity, followed by an abrupt disenchantment from 1940 to 1965, and a gradual resurgence beginning in 1970 and continuing into the 1990s.[9] Not surprisingly, this latest resurgence coincided with the newest wave of mass migration.

However, the use of the term eugenics was considered socially distasteful. Instead, other forms of discourse were used, with differing levels of success. In the late 1960s and early 1970s, the rhetoric of overpopulation and welfare dependency gained greater currency in discussions of "the immigrant problem." This was evident in the massive sterilization campaigns directed at poor women of color during that time. In her study of coerced sterilization in Los Angeles County, Elena Gutierrez argues that the rhetoric of overpopulation, rising welfare rolls, increasing Mexican immigration, and the perception that the costs of delivering immigrant children were excessive made Mexican immigrant women a prime target for forced sterilization in the 1960s and 1970s.[10] Here again, there was collaboration across the political spectrum. This time, environmentalists (generally understood as politically left-leaning) encouraged sterilization as a way to reduce the ecological strain of population growth on the earth's resources.[11] And conservative nativists remained consistent in their belief that childbearing was part of a plot to recolonize the United States.[12] These concerns by both the political left and right converged to define low-income immigrant women's reproduction as a significant public threat.

The constant surveillance of immigrant mothers, whether from below or above the surface, is a result of their delicate position in the broader Western idea of the nation as "family." Anne McClintock argues that since the mid-nineteenth century the trope of family has functioned as the organizing rationale for the social hierarchies within Western nations. She writes, "Because the subordination of woman to man and child to adult was deemed a natural fact, hierarchies within the nation could be depicted in familial terms to guarantee social difference as a category of nature."[13] She goes on to note the fallacy of this rationale, in that the family—a metaphor for a unified national narrative—is actually an institution devoid of history and excluded from national power.[14] In other words, notions of the family, as an ahistorical and largely politically powerless entity, strictly limit the role of women. The mother, then, functions as a central metaphorical figure in national narratives as a "naturally" dependent and subordinate member.

While all wage-earning mothers have the potential to disrupt this national narrative of dependence, low-income immigrant women, like most working-class racial/ethnic minorities, are not "protected" or bound by traditional notions of the family. Rather, many of these women were employed as maids and nannies to uphold the ideal family for white, middle- and upper-class women.[15] This is not to say that the national trope of the family did not affect these immigrant and working-class women. Rather, the powerful ideology of the family functioned to enforce dependency in order to control their movements without even the possibility of subordinate membership of the national family. The family trope facilitated the "disappearance" of their necessary roles in maintaining the larger social hierarchy. Their continued invisibility is perpetuated through intense governmental surveillance and negative public scrutiny of their illegitimate (i.e., "illegal") presence, which enforces their silence. At the same time, they must endure the controlling, disciplinary tactics of the state. In the end, low-income immigrant women are forced into a dependent relationship with the state, largely for the benefit of the state, and are simultaneously punished for this dependency.

Public Charge, 1990s

Legal policy scholar Kitty Calavita convincingly argues that public charge provisions are one of the most important ways in which the United States tries to resolve the contradiction whereby immigrants are desirable as a source of cheap labor for the growth of capitalist markets while being disavowed as public burdens for allegedly causing overall wages to stagnate and incurring high social welfare costs.[16] While I would agree that these provisions are important venues to interrogate the oppositional positioning of immigrants, I would add that rather than resolving this contradiction, public charge provisions actually maintain it by preserving a counterbalance between the two approaches. Public charge provisions function to heighten the supposed social costs of immigrants to offset their labor benefit/value. In reality, the desirability and disavowal of immigrants are two sides of the same coin. What makes immigrant labor desirable is their cut-rate wages, which follow from their disparaged social position as a noncitizen racial minority. Both approaches work together to reinforce capital growth through racial subordination.

Public charge—in policy and sentiment—has existed just beneath the surface of U.S. immigration policy since its inception in the late 1800s, and has reared its head at key historical moments. Apparently, moments of high demand for immigrant labor allow for public charge determinations to become a feasible, formal state response. Public charge tempers the desirability of immigrant labor by clearly positioning immigrants as dependent and undeserving/irresponsible burdens upon citizens and the state. In this way, "desirability" can be more broadly construed to include an increasing sense that their presence is "normal," which consequently leads them to have a greater potential for political influence. The mid-1990s, which saw the passage of major welfare, immigration, and health legislative reforms at the state and federal level, were one of these "corrective" moments in which the labor and political desirability of immigrants was counterbalanced by heightened public policy disavowal.

In California, the formal return of the immigrant as public charge is evidenced through the state's Port of Entry Fraud Detection (PED) programs. In this chapter, I discuss in greater detail the process and significance of this health care fraud program, run by the California Department of Health Services at transnational border sites. I then highlight the intricate strategies of state-level immigrant health policy advocates, each of whom was identified as instrumental in responding to the resurfacing of public charge policy, and analyze their generally pragmatic assessments of their own efforts. The advocates' experiences provide a parallel narrative alongside the state's documents in articulating not only the purpose of these particular health care access programs but also the (ir)responsibility and (il)legality of the state in their relationship with immigrants. These data support my argument that immigration policies produce a double reinforcement of the desire for cheap immigrant labor and the social subordination of these populations in that the PED is an instrument that serves to mark immigrants as populations in need of surveillance and control.

Port of Entry Detection Programs

The Port of Entry Detection (PED) programs were part of the effort by the California Department of Health Services (DHS) to discourage the fraudulent use of health care. The first Port of Entry Detection program officially began in 1994, in the midst of and strategically under the radar of the intense battle over Proposition 187.[17] The pilot PED program in 1994 combined two specific tactics to root out Medicaid fraud: first, prevent fraud before it happens,[18] and second, target documented immigrants/noncitizens trying to return to the United States through ports of entry.[19] The PED programs were part of a larger state effort to cut Medicaid costs by targeting individual access to health care.[20] By increasing the number of investigations of people suspected of inaccurate or fraudulent reporting of income, property, residence, or household composition, DHS was able to proudly tout a 55 percent denial rate on applications for public health insurance for low-income, disabled, and elderly residents, resulting in "substantial cost savings."[21] The program's success was particularly noted in San Diego County. In addition, these suspicions were given top priority from the DHS Investigations Branch and processed within seven days, and the findings were reported back within ten days of receipt of the referral[22]—a significant feat of lightening speed relative to most state bureaucratic procedures.

The PED programs assumed that immigrant health care use was suspicious from the start and required the greatest level of surveillance to prove otherwise. In effect, this program institutionalized greater restrictions on health care access for immigrants, without initiating the far more cumbersome (and democratic) process of legislative reform. In addition, the state specifically targeted immigrant women's use of prenatal care. With the strong support of then Governor Pete Wilson and the tidal wave of anti-immigrant sentiment that passed the landmark state Proposition 187, DHS and INS viewed the PED program as an exciting collaborative effort that would lead to greater sharing of information across government agencies. Watched with growing interest by neighboring states, PED increasingly pushed the boundaries of immigrant rights, health care access, and constitutional due process.

There were two PED programs. The first was located at the three U.S./Mexico ports of entry: San Ysidro, Tecate, and Calexico. As these three sites brought in more and more revenue, the program quickly expanded to include the Los Angeles International Airport a few months later, and then the San Francisco International Airport in 1996. The later program located at the Los Angeles and San Francisco airports was called the California Airport Residency Review (CARR). In these programs, immigrants and noncitizens returning to the United States through these border checkpoints were asked about their use of Medi-Cal.[23] Women who had *legally* received health insurance coverage for prenatal care and delivery in the past five years were told to repay the benefits before reentering the country. This was the dilemma that Sophia Chen confronted upon her return to the United States from a family visit to China (see chapter 1). The assumption was that immigrants without permanent residency status (i.e., green cards) are nonresidents and therefore do not meet state residency eligibility requirements for Medi-Cal.[24] However, it is also the case that nonimmigrant and qualified aliens are indeed eligible for state-only funded Medi-Cal emergency and nonemergency pregnancy-related services.[25] This logistical conundrum led to disparate accounts about the mission and administration of these programs. The different narratives illustrate differing understandings of the states' responsibility to immigrants, and vice versa.

For instance, according to an official of the DHS office of Audits and Investigations I interviewed, the mission of these programs is to stop the illegal use of health care. The administration of this goal was reportedly fairly straightforward.[26] The DHS official explained that INS officials first identified potential fraudulent beneficiaries and referred them to DHS for further investigation. The referral decision was reportedly made solely by the Immigration and/or Customs official and was separate from DHS's jurisdiction. In a separate office, DHS officials asked for proof of California residency and determined if the individuals had or were receiving AFDC (Aid to Families with Dependent Children) or Medi-Cal, using the Medi-Cal Eligibility Data System (MEDS). This was estimated to take twenty to thirty minutes. If they suspected residency fraud, DHS then referred them back to the INS, with information about the results of their initial review, and wrote a "notice of action" to the DHS field office to determine residency status and money owed for medical care or AFDC.[27] The DHS official I interviewed stated that while they received many referrals from the INS, they only followed up and collected money on a few cases. He noted

that this procedure was relatively new—they used to determine fraud at
the initial meeting at the airport or port of entry rather than refer the case
to field offices (e.g., county welfare offices) for an independent review. A
process for appeal and a hotline to report inappropriate treatment during
the investigation were also new features of the program.[28]

One of our respondents, a Bay Area community health clinic director, had an opportunity to visit the California Airport Residency Review
(CARR) site in San Francisco in November 1997. During an interview, she
provided a detailed account of the program's administration. She became
concerned about the program after half a dozen of her clients, who were
documented immigrants, reported having problems trying to reenter the
country. The health clinic director was able to set up a meeting with DHS
and INS officials to find out how the program operated.[29] One of her first
questions was how they chose particular people to interview. She learned
that flights from Asia and Latin America, principally Mexico, and women
of childbearing age were targeted. She described the extra screening conducted near the customs checkpoint in this way:

> They are looking at women of Asian and Latino origin, [particularly]
> if they had little children with them or they were somewhere between
> the ages of 20 and 45. Then, [they were] asked a series of light interview
> questions. And in those light interview questions, [if] either determined
> that they had children within a certain period, then they would ask, who
> paid for it? What kind of insurance did you have? Who was your health
> care provider? . . . [A]nd if someone ended up showing their Medi-Cal
> card, then they were totally in the next realm of interview.

Interviewees were then sent to a second level of screening. The director
went on to explain:

> There were three levels of interview, and if you got to the third level, you
> were basically brought into a small cubicle, way inside, and at this point
> you have been detained several hours. And then, by the end of that, they
> had determined that you . . . were either a potential public charge or
> that you should not have gotten services. It was purely arbitrary as far
> as we could see.

Here, she describes a complex administrative process where an individual is physically moved from one space to another, deeper into a bureaucratic maze, and is made to wait for hours as a judgment is passed as to whether she will be able to leave the airport and join her family. From the clinic director's point of view, these judgments appeared to be made randomly, given that the women in question had received their medical care legally. She described the process further:

> [T]hey are basically convincing you that you should consider paying back the money that Medicaid had paid for your health services. They would have someone from DHS stationed there with a computer. . . . [A]nd they say, "Well, when it got down to it, you could have been eligible under DHS criteria, but the INS could be taking a different interpretation . . . of public charge."

The clinic director portrays a complicated interplay between the federal INS official and the state DHS representative. Rather than a clear determination of Medi-Cal fraud, the state health care representative used innuendos of public charge to persuade the individual to "voluntarily" repay the state for health services delivered. The exchange played on the fear clearly associated with public charge. The clinic director explained that the DHS and INS officials coordinated a "good cop/bad cop" script. While the INS agent questioned the woman, the DHS official sat quietly, letting the INS play "bad cop." The INS agent would raise questions as to whether she was truly eligible for Medi-Cal and advise her to consider paying back the benefits to avoid being sent to court for an eligibility determination, or the more severe penalty of possible deportation and permanent denial of future entry. After creating these doubts and fears, the woman was advised of the costs of the services she had received and "provided the opportunity" to repay DHS. The clinic director said:

> [T]he DHS person knows that it is against the law for them to demand money back, repayment of services that under their guidelines the person was eligible for. So they will sit there and say, sign this letter that you are voluntarily asking how much it cost. And if they sign the letter, it supposedly cleared DHS [of] any culpability of going out of their bounds. They look up in the computer, and go, it was $4,000, you had

a cesarean section. . . . And this was by admission of the DHS and INS people: that they were so grateful to be able to have the opportunity to pay this thing back rather than face the potential jeopardy of going to a court and then being deported and permanently banned from ever coming back into the United States.

[A]t a certain point, they were doing this so much that there were lines, sort of like going to your check cashing, there were lines at the airport of people who were making payments for services that they had gotten under Medicaid.

Contrary to the account from the DHS official from the Office of Audits and Investigations, the clinic director's narrative had little to do with actual health care or Medi-Cal fraud. Instead, the state officials functioned illegally in demanding repayment of legally utilized health care services. And the PED programs racially profiled and gender profiled specific immigrants of color from Latin America and Asia. While the DHS account emphasized a clear separation of the state Department of Health Services from the federal Immigration and Nationalization Service, the clinic director witnessed a far closer interaction between the two government entities. In fact, the state and federal agencies strategically preyed upon the dual vulnerabilities of health care access and immigration status experienced by low-income immigrants who want to ensure a healthy baby as well as permanent residency. Public charge appears to be the crux of the interaction between these two powerful government agencies. INS needs DHS and vice versa to make real the fear of consequences from a public charge determination.

Unfortunately for the DHS and INS, their actions in operating the PED programs were found to be outside the bounds of legality. A lawsuit and an audit led to this conclusion, which precipitated the program's demise.

Rocio versus Belshé: Linking Health Care and Migration

Rocio v. Belshé was a pivotal lawsuit that fundamentally altered the administration of the PED program and forced the DHS to deal directly with public charge, which it had been avoiding by claiming that this was strictly within the purview of the INS. The DHS had feigned innocence regarding the INS's use of health care information to make public charge

determinations. At the same time, the INS distanced itself from any culpa-
bility by defining the program as solely a DHS venture in which it was only
peripherally involved because the programs happened to be located at the
ports of entry.

The lawsuit, which was filed in March 1997 with the U.S. District Court
of Southern California, serves as an informative case study of how public
charge links together health care and immigration concerns. This class action suit alleged that the DHS went beyond its legal mandate and "routinely, knowingly, and deliberately" collected benefits lawfully paid to immigrants. The lawsuit went on to state,

> This practice violates federal statutory and constitutional protections,
> including Federal Medicaid law which provides that states may not re-
> cover Medicaid benefits which are correctly paid, and regulatory, statu-
> tory, and constitutional due process provisions governing the procedure
> for collecting Medi-Cal overpayment.[30]

The central plaintiff of this lawsuit was Rocio R. She and her husband
were documented residents living in San Diego County with their citizen
children. Mrs. R had legally received Medi-Cal benefits for the births of her
children and completed all the appropriate DHS paperwork. The family's
troubles began when Mrs. R applied to the INS to change her temporary
immigration status to legal permanent resident (i.e., a green card holder).
In response to her application, INS asked her to obtain a letter from Medi-
Cal disclosing any debt owed by her to Medi-Cal. When she did this, Mrs. R
received a letter from the DHS stating that she owed a debt of over $6,000
for "illegal receipt of Medi-Cal benefits." This was the first time she had
ever heard from the DHS that she owed any money or that she was ineligible for the health care that she received. When she contacted the DHS's
Audits and Investigations office for an explanation, she was told that she
"had to pay all of the money 'owed' or Mrs. R would not receive her legal
permanent resident status from the INS."[31] Given that Mrs. R was approved
for the health care benefits by the same state government agency that
later deemed it an "illegal" "debt," the question arises as to how and when
the benefit became "illegal." It seems that legal access and use of health
care can become illegal when they coincide with another request upon

the state—in this case, legal permanent residence. Here, a clear connection is made between the use of health care and one's ability to become a permanent resident of the United States. For low-income immigrants, health care of any kind—legal or otherwise—is punishable as irresponsible and burdensome.

When Mrs. and Mr. R received the DHS letter, they contacted Sofia Immigration Services,[32] a nonprofit immigrant advocacy organization, for legal representation. Sofia then contacted Mrs. R's Medi-Cal eligibility worker at the County Department of Social Services and the department worker confirmed that Medi-Cal benefits were appropriately accessed and the costs were correctly reimbursed to the clinic that cared for Mrs. R. However, the DHS continued to refuse to provide a letter clearing Mrs. R of any debt. This stalemate not only delayed Mrs. R's application for change in immigration status, but also led to Mrs. and Mr. R's decision to withdraw their citizen children's Medi-Cal benefits, for which they were eligible, for fear that their use would further hinder Mrs. R's immigration status and potentially lead to her deportation and the rest of the family's as well. These fears were not unreasonable or illogical, given Mrs. R's extralegal treatment. Mrs. R was not afforded the legal protections guaranteed to others by the state. What basis did she have to expect that the state would act within the boundaries of its own rules and regulations?

This uncertainty is institutionalized in the vagueness of policy and the secrecy with which the policy is administered. Rocio R's predicament was part of the DHS's larger "Border Project" (which includes the PED program) and the lawsuit points to the lack of information about DHS health care fraud detection initiatives: "Most of the rules governing the procedures are secret, are not made available to Medi-Cal recipients or the public, have not been published for notice and comment as required by the State Administrative Procedure Act."[33] This, coupled with the overall vagueness of the definition of public charge (e.g., "immigrants who have or *will become* dependent on public benefits"),[34] have allowed for wide variations in its interpretation of fraudulent behavior, health care access, and public burden. The fact that the DHS issued form letters notifying Medi-Cal recipients that they owed a debt to the state for benefits received without any determination as to whether or not the benefits were correctly paid assumes that all use of health care is fraudulent for immigrants. And this initiative clearly targeted low-income immigrants by tying a "release" letter from the DHS as a condition of having their immigration application approved by the INS.

The *Rocio v. Belshé* lawsuit based its complaint on four main statutory infringements: first, restricting access to state Medicaid programs;[35] second, lack of protection of personal information, including health and immigration status;[36] third, recovery of medical costs correctly paid to beneficiaries;[37] and fourth, absence of due process.[38] On May 4, 1998, a settlement was reached between the plaintiffs and Kimberly Belshé, Director of the California Department of Health Services, and the DHS. And while the final settlement agreement was sealed, the subsequent actions by the DHS in response to this lawsuit make clear that the plaintiffs "won" the argument. An All County Welfare Directors Letter dated March 14, 2000[39] directly addressed the settlement and advised all DHS county workers to:

1. Stop seeking repayment of Medi-Cal benefits that were legitimately received;
2. Stop "advising Medi-Cal applicants or beneficiaries on the interpretation or application of immigration and Naturalization Service (INS) rules or regulations, or the effect that receipt of Medi-Cal may have on a person's immigration status;"[40]
3. Review new clarification of public charge determination rules;
4. Send notification to all affected that DHS had incorrectly acted in claiming Medi-Cal benefits as a debt that required repayment; and
5. Refund any money paid to DHS since March 19, 1996.

In fact, these five directives met almost all the demands of the lawsuit. The class action had insisted that DHS stop:

1. Collecting Medi-Cal benefits correctly paid;
2. Issuing overpayment notices which do not advise recipients of due process and statutory rights to a fair hearing;
3. Coercing Medi-Cal recipients into cancelling or repaying their Medi-Cal benefits, by reporting or threatening to report them to the INS;
4. The "Border Project" unless and until procedures are formally adopted as regulations and made available to the public; and

5. Providing Medi-Cal recipients and applicants with incorrect or misleading information regarding the effect of Medi-Cal receipt on their immigration status.

As part of the settlement, it seems defendants were asked to not only notify all class members of the DHS's wrongdoing but also to refund the amount paid. In accordance with this demand, the DHS issued a refund notice with instructions, a two-page flyer from INS on the most recent clarification of public charge policy, and a claim form on two separate occasions.[41] The second notice was part of a modified settlement agreement[42] made in light of the fact that the first notice was written only in English and so few had filed a claim requesting a refund. This second notice also included a Spanish, Vietnamese, Cantonese, Tagalog, Korean, Hmong, and Cambodian translation. Class members were given until March 15, 2003 to postmark their claim form.

In both notices, all questions by potential claimants were directed to the plaintiff's counsel. In these "All County" letters, welfare offices were strictly forbidden from assisting anyone with questions regarding the refund or broader public charge questions. Claimants were instead directed to the counsel and/or they were simply told to read the two-page INS Fact Sheet on public charge (written only in English and Spanish) that was enclosed with the refund notice. While the official number of refund requests is unclear, health care advocates I interviewed reported that the numbers were low on account of the continued lack of trust of government agencies and the clear directive made to welfare offices to not discuss public charge issues with their clients, which limited efforts to disseminate the significant public policy changes in health care access for immigrants. The burden of notifying immigrants regarding the public charge clarifications that arose due to this lawsuit and the PED programs was entirely privatized to individual hospitals, clinics, and nonprofit organizations that clearly lacked the resources to do so.

This lawsuit greatly affected the administration of PED programs and was a crucial factor in dismantling the programs. *Rocio v. Belshé* altered the repayment collection procedure by forcing the DHS to actually take into consideration whether the health care was legitimately received through Medi-Cal, and if it was, to stop "asking" the Medi-Cal recipients to repay these benefits. These administrative changes resulted in most of the cases being referred back to the INS with the understanding that no fraud was suspected. Ultimately, the cost of running these programs became greater than the recovery of funds.

PED Audit: "Unjustified," "Poorly Administered," and "Abusive"

In April 1999, the DHS terminated all the Port of Entry Fraud Detection programs. A few days later, both the state assembly and senate budget subcommittees formally defunded the programs. These actions followed a particularly negative review of the programs by the Bureau of State Audits, declaring both Port of Entry Medi-Cal Fraud Detection programs "unjustified."[43] The audit cited operational and administrative deficiencies and found that the department was no longer recovering sufficient fraudulent Medi-Cal payments to justify its investment in these programs. The settlement required the state DHS to return at least $3 million to immigrants who were "improperly ordered to return Medi-Cal benefits" to the PED programs. State auditors documented intimidation by way of threatened imprisonment or reduced chances for citizenship, and demands for repayments higher than the actual cost of the Medi-Cal benefits received. Approximately fifteen hundred families were eligible for refunds under this settlement. As of April 1999, only one-third of these families had filed for a refund.[44]

In their assessment, the auditors reviewed DHS policies regarding the two fraud detection programs, written communications between the state DHS, federal Department of Health and Human Services, and the federal Health Care Financing Administration, as well as a memoranda of agreement between the DHS and INS and another MOA between the DHS and San Diego and Imperial counties. They also researched state laws that governed Medi-Cal, and federal laws that governed the relevant immigration issues. They also reviewed lawsuits filed against the PED programs and interviewed opponents of the programs. This was in addition to reviewing 440 case files of individuals investigated by the programs. Their conclusions overwhelmingly supported the administrative process described by the community health clinic director and other immigrant health advocates I interviewed.

According to the auditor's report, using Medi-Cal was especially onerous for women. Of the 440 case files, the audit team found that *97 percent*

TABLE 3.1
Profile of Individuals Investigated at PED and CARR (N = 440 case files)

Gender:	97%	Women (430 cases)
Age*:	86%	21–40 years old
Documentation status:	80%	nonimmigrant aliens living in CA and eligible only for pregnancy and emergency services
Families with children:	89%	
Nationalities/PED:	98%	Mexico
Nationalities/CARR@LAX:	40%	Mexico, El Salvador, Guatemala, Honduras
	17%	Philippines, Korea, China
	43%	unknown
Nationalities/CARR@SFO:	19%	Mexico
	51%	Philippines, Korea, China
	30%	unknown

*Average age ranged from 29 to 35 yrs old
Source: California State Auditor 1999.

of all the individuals investigated by the Port of Entry programs were *women* and the type of health care coverage most frequently identified was pregnancy-related. This was despite the fact that women accounted for only 50 percent of people eligible for Medi-Cal benefits.

The profiles of people investigated by the PED and CARR programs contrasted sharply with the general profile of people eligible for Medi-Cal benefits. For example, just under 20 percent of people eligible for Medi-Cal in July 1998 were between the ages of 21 and 40, yet this age group represented over 80 percent of the individuals investigated by both programs. And in 1997, nonimmigrants and undocumented aliens living in California represented just 7 percent of the eligible Medi-Cal population. However, they accounted for at least 80 percent of the investigations for the programs.[45] These individuals were not "illegal" immigrants; they held some form of documentation—including a temporary border pass, U.S. tourist visa, student visa, or a temporary visa. And as noted in my earlier interview with the community health clinic director, there appears to be a targeting of particular nationalities at specific ports of entry. Most of the people detained at the U.S./Mexico border were Latinas and more than half of those detained in San Francisco were Asian.

The audit's central criticism was that there was poor planning, which led to poor administration and, consequently, to lawsuits against the abuses. The report describes a rush by the DHS to discontinue or deny Medi-Cal benefits by changing eligibility procedures without requesting appropriate changes in state regulations.[46] And, as the *Rocio* lawsuit contended, the auditor found that the DHS routinely demanded repayment of Medi-Cal benefits without actually determining whether recipients were indeed ineligible. Also, the report documented evidence that the DHS went "beyond the scope of their employment by trying to influence the federal Immigration and Naturalization Service's (INS) decisions on whether to admit immigrants and visitors at ports of entry."[47] Here, the fear of public charge—an administrative law within the purview of INS—was used by DHS for its own purposes. The report states, "Upon reviewing the minutes of 1996 meetings of the PED program, we found repeated discussion of the link between repayment and improvement in immigration status."[48] They found similar problems at the international airport sites (CARR):

> According to a discussion we had with a CARR program investigator, investigators sometimes led subjects to believe that repayment, or an expressed willingness to repay, might improve their chances of admission to the United States. In addition, according to the minutes of meetings and correspondence we reviewed, investigators solicited repayment of Medi-Cal benefits in exchange for the release of passports INS held. Nevertheless, the department characterized repayments made under these circumstances as voluntary.[49]

This mischaracterization of repayments as "voluntary" was used as cover for the state to circumvent legal protections including due process: "[T]he department believed that the subjects voluntarily repaid benefits; therefore, it was not necessary to notify them of their rights to a hearing."[50] The audit's report took pains to explicitly lay out the laws and legal procedures that pertained to these programs. The administrators appeared to have strayed so far from legal bounds that a reminder was necessary. For instance, the report clarifies what the DHS already knew but had conveniently overlooked:

> The department was aware prior to 1997 that individuals may possess nonimmigrant documentation and still be eligible for public assistance,

if sufficient additional evidence indicated they were also residents of California. Federal statues in 1986 extended Medicaid benefits for emergency medical assistance, including labor and delivery, to undocumented and nonimmigrant alien residents. These individuals often possess nonimmigrant documentation but reside in California. Thus, the department's change in the eligibility regulations made such individuals automatically ineligible for Medi-Cal benefits in California, in spite of federal law.[51]

By automatically denying eligibility for emergency health care to nonimmigrants, the DHS had essentially instituted a new policy without complying with state requirements to do so. To properly adopt a new regulation, government agencies were required to seek public comment and forward the proposed regulation to the State's Office of Administrative Law for review. The report makes clear that the contention that repayment was the low-income immigrants' "choice" and technically not required did not absolve the DHS of responsibility for its actions.

In addition, the auditor documented an increasing level of harassment and threats in the letters suggesting "voluntary" repayment. By the time the last port of entry site—CARR at San Francisco International Airport—was established in November 1998, DHS investigators were sending letters making unsubstantiated accusations of criminal violation and threatening imprisonment. The report takes particular issue with a letter that inaccurately stated that the person's use of health care through Medi-Cal constituted three felonies and that a conviction would lead to state prison. This letter was sent prior to the department's investigation of whether the person was actually ineligible. There were also numerous accounts of CARR investigators making demands for random amounts of funds. The auditor wrote:

> We reviewed one such letter, which demanded a repayment of over $33,000 even though actual Medi-Cal payments totaled just $3,200. Another letter requested a $12,000 repayment for Medi-Cal services. It was followed two days later by a second letter requesting repayment of $8,700 for the same services.

These letters indicate an increasing level of desperation on the DHS's part. By the end of 1998, the return on the state's investment in these programs

TABLE 3.2
Port of Entry Costs, Benefits, and Return on Investment

Fiscal Years	1995–96	1996–97	1997–98	1998–99
PED Program				
Costs*	$1,093,096	$1,234,067	$990,289	$430,468
Benefits**	$7,055,130	$5,399,127	$4,775,488	$995,082
Return (for every $1 of cost)	$6.45	$4.38	$4.82	$2.31
CARR Program				
Costs*	$164,659	$242,066	$216,406	$97,834
Benefits**	$1,243,721	$1,297,710	$1,744,508	$43,224
Return (for every $1 of cost)	$7.55	$5.36	$8.06	$0.44

* Costs include department investigators, county eligibility staff, and contract private investigators.
** Benefits include repayments to DHS and cost avoidance from termination of each active case.
Source: California State Auditor 1999.

began to truly plummet, especially at the airports. Table 3.2 shows a significant drop in return from $8.06 to $0.44 for every $1 in cost, in just one year at the CARR sites.

The effect of modifying the operations of these programs in 1998, as a result of lawsuits and concerns from the federal Health Care Financing Administration (HCFA), was dramatic. When they no longer demanded repayment from detained Medi-Cal beneficiaries until a thorough investigation was completed, their return on their investment was significantly lower than before.[52] In fact, after these modifications, the programs were no longer financially viable. In other words, the only reason these fraud programs were "successful" was due to illegal procedures that exploited low-income immigrant women with children.

In the end, the audit highlighted three major conclusions: first, due to significant operational and administrative deficiencies,[53] continuation of the programs was no longer justified; second, the cost-effectiveness of the programs diminished after the department modified its operational procedures; and third, the state and the Medi-Cal program would be better served if the department redirected its funds to other fraud detection programs.

The report also added that despite the improvements to the PED and CARR operations since the lawsuits, the programs continued to share confidential information about beneficiaries of Medi-Cal and other public assistance programs with the INS even though the DHS has not met the legal requirements allowing this. The PED investigators provided three kinds of information: first, recipients' names, birth dates, social security numbers, and addresses; second, names and birth dates of family members receiving benefits on the same case; and third, the type of benefits received. This was done with the understanding that the INS would, in turn, supply the DHS with useful information about the person's residency, income, work history, and immigration status to help in the investigation. According to the auditor's report, the INS had never reciprocated and the DHS had never followed up and asked why. The auditor concluded: "[I]t does not appear that the department's disclosure of confidential information has contributed to its investigation of Medi-Cal fraud."[54] However, the DHS continued to contend that these PED programs were a separate issue from public charge since they were primarily concerned with benefit fraud and not whether an immigrant was or would become dependent on public benefits. But, in reality, it appears that public charge was a concern for the INS and when the DHS collaborated with the INS, immigrants were screened for both benefit fraud and public charge within a single program. For most immigrants, the differences between the two were academic, if not insignificant. For them, the message was clear: using Medi-Cal can be detrimental to your immigration status.

Overall, the PED Programs have had a profound effect on immigrants throughout the state of California. The fact that *documented* immigrants who legitimately used health services could be asked to repay their Medicaid expenses, be denied reentry, or even be deported by an arbitrary process of public charge determinations is a frightening proposition for *all* immigrants. One health care provider I interviewed in San Francisco put it this way: "People don't trust the government. They will see what the government gives them and wonder what the government will take away from them. They will always have that fear." The women and children (many of whom were citizens) were forced through an invasive and humiliating system that reinforced their perception that they were unwanted and that the U.S. government was a hostile authority.

Clarifying Policy: Key Role of Policy Advocates

In the midst of all this policy confusion on the part not only of Medi-Cal recipients but also those administering state programs, there are important policy advocates who monitor the slippery slope of policy enforcement to ensure at least minimal health care access for immigrants. The following section analyzes the role of five key players, who work in nonprofit organizations on behalf of low-income immigrants in California. These advocates, whom I interviewed on multiple occasions, were women who functioned as mediators between the state and the on-the-ground legal practitioners and health care providers who cared for immigrant communities. As the California State Auditor's report illustrates, convenient interpretations or misreadings of legal provisions, particularly in times of significant policy change, can lead to questionable practices that have serious ramifications for vulnerable populations. These interviews with state-level policy advocates provided another level of understanding of how intricate the policies governing immigration and welfare are and how this intersection impacts access to health care for low-income immigrants. The advocates' intense behind-the-scenes efforts to combat the formal reintroduction of public charge determinations outline these intersections and their implications.

Calling the Port of Entry Fraud Detection program a "witch hunt" that was a "scandalous misuse of state power," a strong network of key immigration advocates successfully worked to undermine the PED programs. They approached these programs as a "very challenging, high-stakes issue" because they understood that the underlying concerns of public charge and its implications within PED went far beyond the specific programs at hand. The detrimental effects of a wide-reaching public charge policy could have grave consequences for not only low-income immigrants but for the general constitutional protections of due process and equal rights for all U.S. residents.

As the confusion regarding public charge reached their doorstep, California state-level legal advocates worked with agencies and advocates at the federal level to clarify the legal boundaries of public charge determinations. They were able to convince the Department of Justice and the INS to issue new field guidance regarding the regulation of public charge in response to the growing confusion surrounding its definition and the standards by which this measure was applied. In May 1999, it was clarified that noncash benefits, such as Medicaid, and special-purpose benefits that were not intended for income maintenance were not subject to public charge consideration.[55] In other words, the use of Medi-Cal or other health services alone would not affect immigration status unless these and other government funds were used to pay for long-term care (i.e., nursing home or other institutionalized care). In addition, the use of food stamps, WIC, public housing, or other noncash programs was protected from public charge consideration. However, receipt of cash welfare, including SSI, TANF, or general assistance could affect one's immigration status.

An advocate described their efforts to clarify public charge as "a classic textbook example of policy change." A grassroots mobilization of policy makers, a media campaign, and the assistance of strategic community (i.e., minority) members in positions of power within the federal government pushed the INS to more clearly define public charge and the ways in which state agencies could apply this rule. This effort was initiated as reports about the PED program spread to immigrant communities, their health care providers, and to legal advocates for immigrants. A staff attorney at an immigrant advocacy center who worked closely with federal officials to develop the clarification of public charge applications said, "People across the country were reporting to us about the abuses, in particular in the health care arena and in California, where people were inappropriately being asked to repay benefits as a condition [for] coming back to the country." She described the effort in this way:

> We helped, along with many, many other organizations, to document the abuses. When it got to a critical point and health care providers were saying that this was just making it impossible for them to deliver health care to their communities, our D.C. office compiled the stories and submitted them to federal agencies. At the same time, county and state officials who noticed the impact of the public charge simultaneously wrote to public officials asking for clarification. At some point the federal agencies got together and decided to do it.

According to this attorney, the severe misapplication of this law occurred with the passage of welfare reform in 1996. She explained: "The main thing that happened was that across the country there were a lot of abuses of existing law. The clarification was merely a clarification of existing law. But after the welfare law passed there was a lot of misinformation about whether the law had changed." Given the intense nativist sentiments in the 1990s that helped bring about Prop. 187 in California, and the federal welfare and immigration laws, the clarification—which stated that

Medi-Cal use alone could not be used to determine public charge—was viewed as a significant win.

Crucial to this win was a broad-based mobilization that convincingly appropriated a social justice frame. An advocate explained, "It was relentless, high quality, and well-informed." She said,

> The facts were well-documented. It got to the heart of health access and social justice. There were people unquestionably eligible for benefits who were playing by all the rules. It was just the INS and state Medicaid agencies and food stamp agencies that were misapplying the law, either due to confusion or ignorance or whatever. Clearly the communities were right on this. It was a powerful moment.

However, in assessing their overall efforts, the advocates were pragmatic about their short-term gains and more than a little ambivalent about the long-term impact. One advocate said, "I don't think any of us wants to minimize the impact of that [clarification] victory, but at the same time the difficulty is, when we look at the 1996 welfare reform, the impact of the law was so devastating that I don't think we'll ever be able to get back to the point where we can finally say things are safe."

In their successful challenge of public charge determinations, immigrant advocates effectively combined two crucial strategies. First, advocates at various levels worked to intervene and insert an alternative understanding of the effects of public charge applications and essentially flipped the standard script of the legislations' intent. Second, it took a broad network of advocates—of various racial/ethnic backgrounds and citizenship status—to create a systemic approach to disseminate this alternative narrative.

Flipping the Script

The first strategy required that the issue be understood in broad-based terms to bring together the stakeholders or participants who were affected and that the response be specific. Advocates and community constituents developed a system of gathering solid, accurate information in response to state discourse, which was largely silent if not misleading on the issue of public charge. As one advocate explained, we have to figure out "what it takes to educate everyone in the system at the appropriate junctures." An up-to-date networking structure was imperative in this systemic approach that linked together a wide spectrum of knowledge and could flow from one end to the other. The formal two-page clarification of public charge from the INS only came after years of concentrated pressure that was strategically organized by these advocates.

During this time, thousands of Californians were detained and threatened with severe immigration sanctions that would forever alter their family's futures. And a far greater number of people altered their health and social services utilization as news spread through word-of-mouth—some of which was accurate and much of it not—that the Migra[56] had yet another plan to round up community members. The length of time it took to clarify confusing policies varied greatly but all the advocates agreed on the necessity to get and disseminate good, solid information as soon as possible.

By doing so, community health workers were able to document the effects of this misapplication by governmental agencies and "flip" the "personal responsibility" trope on its head and place the responsibility for clearing up the confusion on the state. The power of these stories, in addition to the shaky legal grounds on which this program stood, pushed the federal government to more clearly limit the reach of public charge.

The second strategy required the meticulous reading of policies (particularly when new laws were introduced) in order to ascertain the most effective way to insert the alternative narratives of policy impact. These personal stories relayed by community clinics and organizations were used as powerful correctives to government narratives. An advocate based in San Francisco explained, "[W]e always have to be monitoring and vigilant. Bureaucracies make mistakes, either unintentionally or willfully, so we have to pay attention. . . . Getting people networked and hooked up to the same kind of educational and information-sharing systems is a huge challenge." It was a tedious but necessary foundation for their advocacy. These immigrant rights advocates were part of a loosely-structured coalition of nonprofit organizations, who, in effect, functioned as a regulatory body keeping government actions in check. Their jobs required that they know not only the language of the state and regulation but their intersection with other policies and how it was actually experienced by people.

Continuing Consequences of Public Charge

As important as clarification was from a policy standpoint, it did not resolve all public charge issues, nor did it increase immigrant families' overall sense of freedom or security. One advocate recalled her disappointment
from "[j]ust peeling off one layer of issues [to find] that there were other
issues that remained." Perhaps the biggest source of continued confusion
for immigrant families was that public charge still existed, though in more
prescribed terms. The advocate explained, "[T]he public charge test is still
in operation, so somebody who is low-income who is sick, who is elderly,
or who has other factors that make them likely to become a public charge
will have to worry about public charge. We can't guarantee the person
they're going to get their green card."[57] For example, the clarification did
not quell concerns regarding sponsor liability. Sponsor liability became a
new, pressing concern with the passage of welfare reform and immigration
reform in 1996.[58] A San Francisco-based advocate said,

> The next day [after public charge clarification] we started getting tons
> of calls on sponsor liability. . . . We don't know what to tell folks. You
> will find that a lot of folks who are on the new affidavits of support are
> eligible for Medi-Cal but not accessing it because they or their sponsors
> are worried that their sponsors are going to be sued to pay back those
> benefits. It's a legitimate fear.

These new federal laws created a new requirement that all family-spon-
sored immigrants[59] who applied for an immigrant visa or adjustment of
status on or after December 19, 1997 must have an affidavit of support (INS
Form I-864) from a qualifying sponsor. Without this form, he or she would
be found inadmissible as a *public charge*. The main statutory requirement
to be a sponsor was an annual income of more than 125 percent of the federal poverty level.[60] This affidavit of support was a legally binding promise
that the sponsor would provide support and assistance to the immigrant
if necessary. The sponsor also agreed to repay the government if the immigrant used certain benefits and the government requested repayment. The
sponsor's obligation under the legal affidavit lasted until the immigrant
became naturalized, had logged in 40 fiscal quarters of work (this usually
took ten consecutive years), left the United States permanently, or died.

Interestingly, if the sponsor died, the sponsor's estate was still required to repay any obligations accrued before the sponsor's death.

Pressing questions remained regarding what kinds of benefits sponsors were obligated to repay and what, if any, avenues of appeal or legal waivers were possible. There remained considerable opportunity for greater clarity on public charge determinations resulting from sponsor liability issues. However, a policy analyst cautioned against rushing into a situation that would make things worse for those for whom they are advocating. Peeling back all layers of a policy at once may not be the best strategy. The analyst explained, "[T]he policy that was passed in 1996 is so horrible that quite frankly we don't know what a clarification would look like and whether or not the government would come out with something that again would scare people away from accessing things they're entitled to." The analyst's caution demonstrated the fickle nature of policy making. This was also present in this person's approach to the audit: "Quite frankly, until we all knew what the situation really was out there and what the state was doing and what the community's involvement was, we weren't sure we wanted an audit." The audit was a final step in a two-year strategy that required a close study of immigrant rights and the public benefits for the community.

Interpretations of law are open to the influence of the larger social, political, and economic mores of that historical moment. Consequently, a systemic understanding of policy change and the constant vigilance of bureaucratic maneuverings sharpened the focus of policy advocates as they carefully peeled one layer of issues away to expose another. An interviewee put it this way:

> Did we learn a lot? Yes . . . [but] it's not like you can pull any of this stuff off the shelf. It's important background, and it saves you a lot of time on some of the basics, but what government does is invent a new strategy. I may sound a little too cynical. I don't mean to be a conspiracy theorist but how it plays out is that the next political spin on this will be some kind of variation on the theme. I can't predict what that will be.

Perhaps one of the most profound lessons learned from this effort was how difficult it is to regain the trust of immigrant communities once it is broken. Many public health workers, community clinics, and safety net hospitals in California have worked diligently for years to ensure that they achieve their mandate of serving the health care needs of their community. Given the high concentration of foreign-born populations in California, immigrants comprise a significant portion of potential constituents for many health care providers. In addition, many safety net health care providers depend upon Medi-Cal reimbursements from caring for low-income residents. This has meant that many health care facilities have worked very hard to reach out to these communities and develop bonds of trust. The public charge test deeply debilitated this trust between immigrants and their health care provider. Since immigrants were initially told that it was safe to use publicly funded health care, the public charge scare questioned the reliability of the doctor's reassurance and raised the possibility that prenatal care was another "trap" for immigrants. One advocate said, "The main lesson is that once you destroy the community's trust, people are not going to give it back to you easily. You have to work to get it back. You misinformed them in the past. People aren't stupid."

Trust is a hard-earned sentiment, given the level of reticence and the fear of accessing public benefits experienced by immigrants. Given the political climate of growing nativism, many immigrants reported enduring a sense of siege and preferring to avoid undue scrutiny. Those areas that reported a strong sense of trust despite these fears were ones where people felt the clinic staff had deep knowledge and expertise relating to their community. However, even these clinics found themselves in a very difficult situation trying to retain a meaningful level of trust with their immigrant patients following the 1996 welfare and immigration reforms. A policy analyst working with a strong immigrant collaborative on issues of welfare and health care noted the following reaction from immigrant communities they worked with:

> As soon as we got the clarification, we were all very excited. We thought, "This is great. This will address a lot of the fear and confusion that's been in our communities for very legitimate reasons." We immediately started to do outreach, presentations, work with other providers. What we noticed was, when we would tell the providers or advocates or attorneys, they would think, "Oh, that's great news." But there was a total disconnect between folks who work with the community and with people who are directly affected.

This stark disconnect was perfectly illustrated at a community event to disseminate news regarding the clarification of public charge:

> The day after the clarification, some of our L.A. partners pulled together a press conference to announce the public charge clarification as a way to get a word in the community that it's no longer a problem. People should feel safe to access benefits. They invited a woman community member who herself had been in the position of not enrolling her kids or herself in any health care programs because she thought it would be an issue. They talked to her several times beforehand and invited her to speak. She was great. She really spoke to the impact the policy had had prior to the clarification. The funny thing is, afterwards, some of our folks said, "Thanks for speaking at the press conference. Are you going to enroll in health programs now?" She said, "No, no way."

While the community member intellectually understood the importance of health insurance and encouraged others to access Medi-Cal, the fear of future punitive government action kept her away. Dissemination of public policy change in this political environment posed a formidable challenge. Compounding the problems posed by this challenge, Governor Gray Davis took office in January 1999 in the midst of the public charge clarification and the PED audit investigation, and took what advocates viewed as a very unfortunate reading of the government's responsibility in clarifying public charge.

An advocate explained, "They've interpreted the settlement agreement in *Rocio v. Belshé* much more broadly than attorneys on the case interpret it, telling counties not to conduct public charge outreach unless they were specifically approved. They sent out INS letters that actually conflicted with some of the local entities' work with counties." This advocate saw the Davis Administration's move as a passive-aggressive act against immigrants: "The Davis administration tried to prevent money [from being] allocated specifically to public charge outreach and in general has thwarted any efforts to do outreach on public charge." Immigrant advocates interpreted the administration's inaction as deliberately sitting on the political fence on immigration, which did not strengthen its political stature in their perspective.

A state-level advocate took particular care to separate the successful public charge policy change from any actions by Gray Davis: "In the technical analysis, at the end of the day, technically it was this governor who agreed to a budget agreement that defunded the Port of Entry. But really I think that was just technical and administerial." Advocates argued that the appropriate response should have been more forceful and proactive. He should have said, "This is abhorrent to me, I'm going to eliminate it from my budget," according to this advocate. Instead, "He let the process play itself out. He made some members of the legislature prove that it was not cost-effective to the state and the system had run really amok before he acted. And then he didn't even publicize his action. He hoped it would go unnoticed." Following this line of analysis, the governor not only played little to no role in the policy change, but made a difficult situation worse by sitting on his hands for personal political reasons. In the end, the advocates viewed Davis, a Democrat, as hostile to immigrants—a deep disappointment for those who had struggled against the vicious anti-immigrant policies of former Republican governor Pete Wilson. A federal-level immigrant rights advocate based in California provided one reason for their disappointment:

> When the audit came out the program was disbanded. A couple of weeks later, Governor Davis somehow put in another request for funding to do some kind of fraud detection, but we were able to clarify that the focus was to be on health care providers rather than beneficiaries. There was some kind of attempt to refund it, even after that audit.

This statement reinforces the second lesson learned from this effort to clarify public charge policy—the need for constant vigilance of state practices, particularly with respect to immigrant populations, regardless of which political party held state office. This statement also reminds us of the persistent nature of public charge, which remains just beneath the surface. As another advocate retorted, "I would never underestimate the potential for that kind of thing to happen again if the politicians think it's in their interests, for whatever reason."

TABLE 3.3
Immigrants Excluded From the U.S. via Public Charge, 1892–1990

Period	Total	L.P.C.*	% of Total Exclusions
1892–1900	22,515	15,070	67
1901–1910	108,211	63,311	59
1911–1920	178,109	90,045	51
1921–1930	189,307	37,175	20
1931–1940	68,217	12,519	18
1941–1950	30,263	1,072	4
1951–1960	20,553	149	<1
1961–1970	4,833	27	<1
1971–1980	8,455	31	<1
1981–1990**	19,759	NA	NA

* L.P.C.: "Likely to Become a Public Charge"
** The INS Statistical Yearbook discontinued listing the number of L.P.C. exclusions in the mid-1980s.
Source: "Aliens Excluded by Administrative Reason for Exclusion, Fiscal Years 1892–1990," Table 67, p. 226,
U.S. Department of Justice, Immigration and Naturalization Service, 1998 Statistical Yearbook of the Immi-
gration and Naturalization Service (Washington, D.C.: U.S. Government Printing Office, 2000).

Public Charge, Redux

This latest surfacing of public charge tests will likely not be the last. This legal provision is a powerful tool in its strategic ambiguity and quiet location on the outskirts of public notice. As an administrative law, public charge is a statutory provision under the jurisdiction of nonjudicial staff within government and not subject to oversight by legislatures or courts. Since its inception in the late 1880s,[61] this administrative law has undergone very little change. In her careful study of public charge, Patricia Evans argues that while other administrative laws evolved during the twentieth century, public charge determinations reached a stage of "arrested development" as they moved out of public view, limited largely to the confines of American consulates abroad.[62] Writing in 1987, Evans states that public charge reached its "zenith" with a presidential directive in the 1930s to exclude as many immigrants as possible from Depression-stricken America.[63] INS records illustrate a steep drop in its use after the Depression.

However, the ability to exclude or deport on the basis of someone potentially becoming a public burden was established as a powerful tool for social engineering purposes. And despite its disreputable history as a frequently used mechanism within the eugenics movement, it continues to exist. This is due in part because public charge provisions allow for the contradictory social location of low-income immigrants in order to preserve their political and economic vulnerability. This arbitrarily administered immigration law not only lies in wait just underneath the surface of public notice, to arise at the appropriate moment, but it also serves as a constant threat of deportation and a reminder to immigrants that they are allowed to live in the United States only for the purposes of laboring for capital growth.

Debates about immigrants as public burdens also confines our understanding of immigration to calculations of costs and benefits. Regardless of which side of the argument one falls on, immigration and immigrant labor are misunderstood as purely market-driven phenomena. While immigrant labor is fundamental to the U.S. and global market economy, immigration law is a product of broad social and political factors during a particular historical moment. While the tightening labor market of the Depression helped to explain the utilization of public charge determinations in the 1930s, the more recent turn of events is the culmination of an historic anti-immigrant political climate in combination with dramatically changing racial demographics and the ever increasing speed and reach of global capitalism. Demographically, California officially became a majority minority state in the 1990s. The "browning" of America is evident in the numbers provided by the U.S. Census Bureau. From July 1, 1990 to July 1, 1999, the nation's Asian and Pacific Islander population grew 43 percent, and the Latino (or Hispanic, as defined by the Census Bureau) population grew 38.8 percent.[64] California had the greatest numeric increase in both racial/ethnic groups. At the same time, the white population declined from 17.9 million in 1990 to 16.5 million in 1999, bringing down the percentage of whites to 49.8 percent of the total state population.[65]

And while the contemporary number of exclusions based on public charge may not rival that of the early twentieth century, it is still a pressing concern. For many immigrants, public charge is yet another avenue for expulsion. If public charge is unavailable as a tool for nativism, there are always other options. For example, Operation Gatekeeper, a federal "control through deterrence" program initiated in 1994 (the same year as the passage of Prop. 187) funded the construction of fences and militarization of the U.S.-Mexico border and set the stage for the Anti-Terrorism and Effective Death Penalty Act of 1996.[66] However, as the policy advocates learned in their fight against public charge threats targeting immigrant women's use of Medi-Cal, each method of expulsion requires constant, careful vigilance and monitoring. There needs to be a systemic analytical approach to these policies to understand the various layers and interconnections between one regulation and another; with the goal of devising an effective challenge that will bring together the appropriate people with the necessary information.[67] This is essential if we are to repair the trust required to ensure health care access. And, in the midst of all the many methods of deportation, public charge remains, quietly waiting in the wings, with the potential to resurface in various incarnations—some more egregious than others.

However, across the variations on a nativist theme, there has been consistency in the particular scrutiny paid to women in public charge investigations. Their propensity for pregnancy placed them just below those with "loathsome and dangerous" contagious diseases in the hierarchy of excludable offenses.[68] This was certainly evident in the profile of individuals targeted for Medi-Cal fraud investigations at the Port of Entry Detection program. The federal INS and state DHS agencies collaborated in targeting immigrant women with children in an attempt to interrupt both the flow of immigration and the likelihood of more childbirths by low-income immigrant women. According to INS records, "alien removals" of women steadily increased in the 1990s. "Removal" of an "alien" from the United States is considered appropriate "when the presence of that alien is deemed inconsistent with the public welfare."[69] The INS has several possible removal procedures, including deportation, voluntary departure, and exclusion; however, the Illegal Immigration Reform and Immigrant Responsibility Act of 1996 (IIRIRA) significantly changed these procedures. Deportation and exclusion proceedings were consolidated and relabeled "removal" proceedings (with voluntary departure continuing as an option at the government's convenience). But perhaps the most significant change was the new authority for expedited removals, in which an arriving immigrant is judged to be inadmissible due to improper documentation, fraud, or misrepresentation, and is removed without any further hearing or review unless a plea is made for asylum. In addition, there are significant penalties associated with a formal removal that include not only the removal but possible fines, imprisonment for up to ten years, and a bar to future legal entry (the bar is permanent for aggravated felons and up to twenty years for other immigrants).

Between 1992 and 1995, women comprised approximately 6 percent of "alien removals." The proportion of women in this category rose to 12 percent in 1996, 16 percent in 1997, and 21 percent in 1998. Much of this increase is attributable to women from Mexico who attempted to cross the ports of entry into San Diego and Imperial counties. By the end of the 1990s, women constituted 39 percent of all expedited removals—an increase attributable to the PED program and the passage of IIRIRA.[70]

However, recent immigration numbers show that these policies, including the welfare and immigration reforms of 1996, have not worked entirely as intended.[71] Sassen explains that these reforms and others that have increasingly militarized the U.S.-Mexico border have not only failed to slow migration but have also increased other social problems. She writes, "The combination of such sanctions and a regularization program that excludes a large number of undocumented workers will contribute to the formation of an immigrant underclass that is legally as well as economically disadvantaged."[72]

These barriers to health care access increase the reluctance of immigrant women to receive prenatal care that may prevent potentially costly future health problems. Low-income immigrant families' already tenuous financial situation becomes more stressed as they try to find other means to cover a public benefit for which they are eligible. The recent 1996 welfare reform measure sends a clear message against the use of public benefits in the United States. Those who argue for stricter immigration laws view the use of public benefits as an indication of declining "quality" of immigrants admitted.[73] This notion reinforces the idea that use of public benefits implies dependence and that dependence is a sign of weakness or moral deficiency.[74]

Ironically, many immigrants share the general "American dream" in which one should "pull themselves up by their bootstraps." In addition to the structural barriers to accessing Medi-Cal, health care providers who work with immigrants report that many immigrants are reluctant to access public benefits in the first place. One advocate said:

Many of our immigrant women, because of their cultural values, would prefer not to be on public benefits because they feel that it is not a good thing to do. They feel they should be on their own, depend on themselves. So, sometimes we need to work with them more; need to work with them for a longer time to tell them that, "[L]ook, this is what you need to do because it is OK. If you work in the future you will be paying into the government, therefore you are not getting a free ride."

Health care providers and advocates find that they must persuade their patients and clients to access Medi-Cal not only by addressing their fears of public charge, but also by enhancing their sense of themselves as productive members of society. This is despite the fact that low-income immigrants remain substantially less likely to use welfare than working-age U.S.-born people who are poor.[75] A state policy analyst highlighted the particular vulnerability of pregnancy:

> The point at which parents are willing to risk their concerns over public benefits or just their general reluctance to take something from the government is the point at which their children are most at risk, and there isn't a more important time than pregnancy for that kind of balancing. The state data bears that out. Most immigrant Latino women use the Medi-Cal program for the pregnancy-related programs and services.

Here, the analyst explains that the state strategically focuses on prenatal care and delivery, knowing that these are the kinds of health care for which immigrant women would be most willing to risk governmental surveillance and discipline.

It is apparent that within the contemporary social welfare discourse, welfare dependence, not poverty or unemployment, is viewed as the social ill that the state should target for remedial action.[76] The focus on welfare dependency erroneously simplifies the source of the problem as the individual rather than the structural, institutional mechanisms that constrain the individual.[77] It is always easier to blame the victim than to clean up the problem. The threat of public charge, or the potential dependence on welfare benefits, has made it clear that immigrant women and their children are undeserving and unwanted.

The following chapter focuses in more detail on the work of safety net health care providers and community outreach workers as they try to build a relationship with their patients in the midst of a broken sense of trust.

Living with Uncertainty under Ever-Shifting State Policy

It just seems like every week it's a different story and in the past year it has been incredibly terrible. I mean like we've had a week-by-week thing. "Okay, starting July 1st, we're cutting off prenatal care. Oh just kidding, starting August 1st. Okay, now if you're already on, you're going to be taken off and we're not accepting new people. Okay, starting September 1st." . . . [Y]ou know, sometimes, a little bit of news is worse than no news at all because it caused a lot of apprehension among staff members and among the patients.
—Community Clinic Coordinator, Bay Area

Social Workers and the Medical Safety Net

This chapter focuses on the role of social workers in safety net hospitals and clinics who work with low-income immigrant communities in California. In particular, I discuss how the federal and state policies outlined in earlier chapters have affected social workers in health care settings as they find themselves in a delicate dilemma trying to uphold their obligation to

"First, do no harm . . . " while fighting for their own existence. Social workers who work in these safety net health clinics and hospitals find themselves in a difficult position as they try to allay their patients' fears while battling their own financial uncertainties in a highly competitive health care market for prenatal care patients eligible for Medi-Cal. Their experiences provide important insights into the everyday, messy realities of policy implementation.

The role of social workers in medical settings is generally invisible despite the fact that they are invaluable as the central link between safety net hospitals and clinics and low-income and/or uninsured immigrant communities. Various job titles—Maternal and Child Health Social Worker, Case Manager, Social Worker, Community Outreach Worker, CPSP Outreach Educator, Perinatal Health Educator—fall under a general umbrella term of social worker. While the job descriptions vary, there is a common central goal across these positions: to act as a liaison between the patient and the health care provider in ensuring access to quality prenatal care. Given the welfare and immigration legislation's construction of low-income immigrant women as "undeserving," the task is formidable. These major legislative changes foster an environment of confusion and frustration not only for immigrant women but also for the social workers and other health care providers. However, their job requires that they interpret the policy changes for patients, put them at ease, and at the same time assist the safety net clinics and hospitals to implement the changes.

In this study, health care social workers across the state of California report a sense of fear among low-income pregnant immigrant women about using Medi-Cal to cover their prenatal care. This was evident within the Medi-Cal eligibility process, a humiliating and frightening experience for many low-income women. This process questioned the legitimacy of such women's presence in the United States, their choice to have a child, as well as their attempts to provide health care for themselves and their babies. The increasing barriers raised to limit low-income pregnant immigrant women's access to prenatal care—services for which they are eligible—reveal an important dimension of today's anti-immigrant political climate: having children is an entitlement not afforded to low-income immigrant women. Within this climate, social workers in safety net health care settings find themselves in a difficult, yet crucial position.

The social welfare system endured severe cuts in the 1990s. As part of this system, California's public hospitals and community clinics experienced a growing crisis as the number of uninsured and vulnerable patients increased while the availability of funds to pay for their care decreased.[1] As a result, a number of public safety net hospitals, which are required to treat everyone regardless of the patient's ability to pay, closed or came under private ownership. Since 1990, seventy hospital emergency rooms and trauma centers have closed in California.[2] Consequently, the challenge of social workers in this setting is daunting. To make matters worse, changes in immigration policies at this time have added greater complexity to their jobs within the diminishing welfare state apparatus.

Outreach workers and advocates play an enormous role in allaying the fears that arise from the sharing of information between the DHS and the INS, and the confusing and intimidating bureaucracies associated with Medi-Cal and the use of prenatal care. Their roles may include a wide range of services including home visits, translation of documents and policies, transportation, addressing eligibility questions, and, most importantly, "hand-holding" through the entire Medi-Cal process. As one clinic coordinator put it, "At the end they decide to go for Medi-Cal. In between, a lot of them have questions." It is in this "in-between" stage that social service workers play a crucial role. Another health advocate discussed how she assists her patients with the Medi-Cal process:

> We can help them fill out the Medi-Cal application. There is a fine line between assisting and coaching, so we are very conscious of that, so we won't coach them as to where they can get documents, but we can say, "Why don't you talk to your neighbors and see where they get a photo ID?" And so, that is another barrier. Most of these women, for example, do not have a photo ID. And they have no idea where to get one. We can't tell them where to get one, but we can say, "Why don't you talk to your neighbors, maybe they can tell you where to go?" A lot of this is just hand-holding through the process.

The growing reluctance of pregnant immigrant women to enroll in Medi-Cal has created a serious conflict for safety net providers. They feel an increased need to promote the use of Medi-Cal, both to ensure continuing reimbursement for the pregnancy-related services they provide, and to ensure that their low-income clients avoid paying unmanageable out-of-pocket costs. At the same time, however, social workers and health care providers worry that there may be future immigration repercussions for the women or their family members when they apply for a change of immigration status or try to sponsor additional family members.

This confusion regarding the ramifications of Medi-Cal enrollment creates a particularly burdensome dilemma for the social workers whose job it is to build a level of trust between the health care provider and the immigrant community. Many times, social workers are immigrants and mothers themselves, and so they find themselves "riding a fence" between the two communities. However, it is clear that these recent policies have significantly taxed the tenuous relationship between immigrants and their safety net health care providers.

In the pages that follow, I show how these social policies impact the work of social workers during a historic moment of fear over public charge. The social workers help to decrease the barriers to health care for low-income immigrants and their children, and they demonstrate that low-income immigrant women and children are "deserving" of public benefits. They are, in fact, "normalizing" immigrant motherhood in opposition to the popular anti-immigrant rhetoric, as solidified by recent federal and state legislative measures. They are encouraging access to and utilization of prenatal care as a normal part of an immigrant woman's life—a benefit that they deserve and should expect, as do other (i.e., middle-class and native-born) pregnant women. Medical social workers help alleviate the confusion and hostility surrounding the new federal and state policies by advocating for immigrant women through the difficult Medi-Cal eligibility process, rebuilding trust by "treating" the whole person and the needs of their families, and providing consistent and reliable information. These influences help redefine immigrant mothers and their families as contributing members of our society who deserve access to quality prenatal care.

The Public Charge Fiasco

The 1990s were a time of heightened fear and confusion over public charge. Not only were immigrant communities severely tested but so was the safety net health care system that cared for them. From 1994 to 1999, as epitomized by the Port of Entry Fraud Detection program, the INS and state DHS officials made public charge determinations based solely on the use of Medi-Cal.[3] It was later clarified that this practice was in conflict with INS policy that stated that public charge determinations should be made on the basis of the individual's total circumstances, including age, health, family status, assets, resources, financial status, education, and skills. This five-year period and the months immediately after the clarification about public charge policy are particularly informative in understanding the role of safety net health care centers in immigrant communities and how immigrants negotiate their health care needs during times of great strain. Here again, the importance of trust in overcoming fear is repeatedly evoked.

One community health care clinic director told us of an incident wherein she received a phone call from a family member of someone who was having a heart attack. They had called to ask how much an ambulance would cost for a full fee, cash paying patient. Despite the fact that they were documented immigrants, they did not want to use an ambulance for fear of a public charge determination for doing so. In another case, a Korean immigrant woman in the San Francisco Bay Area burned herself badly in the bathtub. The clinic director described the situation as follows:

> [H]er family were all documented citizens and working in one of the suburbs. And she was so afraid of not getting her family in trouble, or getting herself in jeopardy that she didn't show up in the emergency room for 30 days after having scalded herself, and by then she was so infected that she was not able to survive. She died.

These immigrant communities have little expectation or sense of entitlement to public goods—even for emergency care. Because the reach of public charge policy is uncertain, they assume the worst.

For many social workers who work directly with low-income immigrant women, the damage has already been done and the trust that is crucial in ensuring access to quality prenatal care has suffered dramatically. The authors of a study by the National Health Law Program and the National Immigration Law Center, state, "Throughout the country, advocacy groups and healthcare providers are reporting that immigrants are medically 'on the run,' too afraid to obtain health care, even when they legally are entitled to it."[4] As a result of this chilling effect, low-income pregnant immigrant women are left with few options. They can either opt not to seek care, choose to self-pay, or enroll in Medi-Cal and run the risk of public charge. Whichever option they choose, the threat of public charge sends a clear message: low-income immigrants are not welcome to use public benefits. The passage of these policies underscores the secondary status of immigrants and the popular assumption that immigrants have a "natural" tendency for public dependency.

Overall, approximately half of all providers interviewed felt there were health consequences as a result of public charge. While it is unclear whether the cases raised by the interviewees are part of a growing trend, the stories are provocative in that they are preventable. We asked if the key informants could identify any major health consequences as a result of public charge, and for those who could, the responses were immediate and detailed. These were stories that the providers could not forget. For instance, a clinic director in San Diego recalled:

> Quite a few women have had serious illnesses but wouldn't do anything about it because they were afraid that they'd be deported or that their family would be deported or somehow somebody in their family would get in trouble for this. No matter what we say or do, it does not change their opinion. The case that really stands out is the one that needed a hysterectomy. She had uterine cancer but she wouldn't go any further with the treatment.

Others recounted patients entering the emergency room for delivery without prenatal care. One health care provider in Fresno remembered a number of patients who had limbs amputated due to untreated gestational diabetes. The patients told her that they were too afraid to come to the hospital. Thinking about such cases, a midwife put it this way: "So much suffering, you know? Unnecessary."

Unfortunately, the fear and confusion regarding the potential immigration consequences of using Medicaid for health care services does not end with immigrant patients. Many doctors, nurses, medical outreach workers, and even legal advocates are also confused about the implications of the welfare and immigration reforms and the subsequent ramifications of these legal provisions in the everyday lives of their patients. They are frustrated by their inability to provide the direct assurances that the women need. A community clinic director said:

> There was this one woman who had come in asking can we assure that she is going to be able to access Medi-Cal during her pregnancy and also after her pregnancy. I am guessing that she was concerned about public charge issues. She was saying that we had to be able to assure her that she would be able to be eligible for Medi-Cal and it would not have any negative repercussions. Otherwise she was going to have an abortion. She was asking us to tell her what to do.

Clearly, the implications of federal and state policy can have a direct and intimate effect on people's lives and their reproductive health. In this case, the clinic director felt she could not unequivocally guarantee the patient's immunity from negative public charge repercussions. So the patient left the clinic and did not return. Safety net providers find themselves limited in what they can say or do for their patients. This was particularly so prior to the federal clarification of public charge. A San Diego county health advocate explained:

> There is a great deal of confusion about what being a public charge means. So, even for women who are here legally and who, either for themselves or family members may be going through the naturalization process, there is great reluctance to apply for any kind of benefits because it is not being clearly defined. We've had flyers and so on that have come from immigrant rights and welfare organizations saying this is a public charge and that isn't, but even with that . . . I began to distribute them and then found that our Legal Aid Society down here had some concerns about some of the information because it's such a case-specific area of the law. It's very hard to give out information [that] is generalizable because it may not be true for certain circumstances [and it] can't go into a brief flyer.

In this scenario, even legal policy advocates could not provide solid information. The health care outreach workers found their hands tied when trying to address even seemingly straightforward questions.

Some safety net clinics and hospitals feel inclined to "push" their patients into Medi-Cal. The cost of prenatal care alone is an incentive in some cases. As a number of immigrant health care advocates mentioned, pregnancy and delivery are particularly vulnerable times for immigrants.

The importance of safely delivering a healthy baby will in most cases trump the fears associated with the risk of a public charge determination. And while there is great uncertainty in the Medi-Cal system, safety net health providers also agree that the benefits of health care outweigh the potential risks. A director at another county clinic explained:

> We have to do it. We are all a little nervous about it because we don't want to be leading our people down the wrong path only to find out in another 3 to 4 years from now, when they really do go for citizenship, that more of them are being penalized. But we collectively feel that we can't afford [not to].

This director reported that some of the county health centers in her area had had to pay 30 to 40 percent of their costs out of their general funds rather than through Medi-Cal reimbursements. Understandably, this presents a significant hardship for safety net health care providers that depend on Medi-Cal funds for a large portion of their revenue.

The complexity of the public charge policy, in addition to the vagueness with which it is implemented, makes it difficult for health care providers and advocates to allay the fears associated with Medi-Cal. This is a central concern for safety net providers who depend on Medi-Cal funds for a large number of their patients. Also, the fear produced by public charge degrades their authority within the immigrant community. Their inability to reassure their patients weakens the sense of trust that is imperative in working with immigrant families, particularly those who are undocumented.

Clarification? What Clarification?

The Immigration and Naturalization Service provided new guidance regarding public charge only in response to the considerable public attention and political pressure brought to bear by immigrant health care advocates. This clarification, which took place on May 25, 1999, stated that use of Medicaid, CHIP (children's Medicaid), or other health services would not affect immigration status unless these and other government funds were used to pay for long-term care (i.e., nursing home or other institutionalized care). Nor would the use of food stamps, WIC, public housing, or other non-cash programs affect one's immigration status. In addition, the INS clarified that use of cash welfare by children or other family members would not affect one's immigration status unless these benefits were the family's sole source of income. However, one's own use of cash welfare (including SSI, TANF, or General Assistance) could affect one's immigration status.

In our interviews with health providers one year after this announcement, the majority of key informants reported that access to prenatal care and other health services had increased with clarification. However, there was little optimism, as they remained cautious. Clinics that were geographically isolated and subsisting at or above their capacity as a safety net health care provider had experienced little or no effect as a result of clarification. Their patients relayed their fears of accessing health care, as they always had. One immigrant health care advocate replied, "It's the same. There's so much fear and such a strong perception. It's going to take a long time to change the perceptions. There's probably some change but not nearly enough." For their patients, the onslaught of problems was constant and the clarification of public charge guidelines did little to alleviate all the other barriers to health care, much less all their other concerns related to poverty and discrimination.

For most, news of the clarification was welcomed with hesitation. Fifty-six percent of respondents reported greater prenatal care access and 53 percent reported an increase in access to other health services by their immigrant patients. An outreach worker based in San Diego summarized the general sentiment: "It's a little better, but they still have fear. Some [Medi-Cal] investigators and some people are still telling them that they can be deported, that they [should] not apply for legal residency, but it's a little bit better than like two or three years ago." Given the tumultuous experience of many who served low-income pregnant immigrant women, one health service provider replied, "Is anyone really going to believe them?" What makes matters worse is the almost complete lack of dissemination of information by the state regarding the clarification of public charge. This has led to the spread of *mis*information by various stakeholders: immigration attorneys, ethnic and mainstream media, and even some health care providers and advocates.

Others presented a more positive, but still cautious, outlook. A clinic director said:

It takes time. Community opinion is not something that changes overnight, and certainly the trust doesn't come overnight. I see it getting better all the time, but still we are always confronting patients who say, "I
don't want to apply for Medi-Cal because we're afraid it's going to hurt
my immigration status. I'm in the process of fixing my papers. I don't
want to get Medi-Cal." So the word is getting out, but slowly.

However, this clinic director also added:

There isn't the trust factor. It's very true that we have clients who say,
"OK, you're telling me this now, but how do I know it's always going to
be like this? How do I know that in the future they won't ask me to pay
back my benefits?" All we can say is, "This is the ruling now. This is our
understanding now. We'll give you written verification of the ruling and
you can always go back and say, 'This is the ruling I relied upon.'" But it
is true that people have had the rulings changed in the past. That's why
they don't have a lot of confidence that it's the final word on the subject.

In the day-to-day operation of clinics and in the work of providers, public
charge clarification had a direct impact on how providers and clinics op-
erate. The policy clarification led to positive changes in job descriptions,
organizational priorities, and the way health care providers interact with
their immigrant patients, particularly for those working in the border region of San Diego County. In San Francisco, 70 percent of respondents
stated that the clarification of public charge had affected how they worked
with their patients, 40 percent stated that it had altered their job duties, and 50 percent stated that it had resulted in organizational changes.
In San Diego, all the respondents replied that the clarification of public
charge had led to organizational changes in their clinics and the way they
worked with their patients. They also felt better prepared after the clarification of policy. In the Fresno region, 43 percent of the respondents sug-
gested that clarification had had an impact on the way they worked with
patients and 86 percent felt better prepared in their jobs.

However, this sense of better preparation is apparently derived less from
the official clarification document issued by the INS, than from the actual
process of bringing about the clarification. A San Francisco-based outreach worker who works with the Asian immigrant community explained,

"We have a taste of what we need to do when issues [like this] come up. We need solid information, set up strategies, collect data, and go back to policymakers. The system has been set up." A nurse working with medically fragile infants and their families in the Latino community of Oakland emphasized the importance of her role as an advocate in bringing about policy changes to benefit her patients: "I've learned that our system of service is not set up to meet the specific needs of specific communities and so it becomes incumbent upon conscientious, individual service providers to raise [these issues]. It causes more work. It changes how I work with families."

Health service providers repeatedly cited the need for an increase in the intensity of advocacy. One advocate stressed the importance of alliances between community-based agencies and health care providers in order to form a foundation for future activities. Social workers have intensified their advocacy by increasing their time with their clients as they accompany them to Medi-Cal offices and learn to argue aggressively with hospitals to admit them for care. All these actions have required health care providers and their support staff to take on additional roles—including that of immigration law interpreters. One community clinic director replied that her job has become more difficult as she must now decipher the constantly changing federal, state, and local policies that affect her clients.

Also, with the continuation of the public charge test, low-income immigrants continue to worry about the confidentiality of the information they provide to benefits agencies. And, sponsor liability is another area of concern and confusion. As stated earlier, affidavits of support are legally enforceable contracts that a U.S. resident must sign in order to sponsor an individual to live permanently in the United States. Prior to PRWORA, this affidavit was considered a moral rather than a legal obligation. Now, sponsors must accept this legally enforceable responsibility until their "charge" becomes a citizen or has worked forty fiscal quarters (usually ten years).[5]

A significant part of the confusion lies in the fact that although technically sponsor liability is considered a separate immigration issue from public charge, yet a sponsor may be liable for the costs of benefits incurred by an immigrant he or she sponsored. Consequently, for all practical purposes, a sponsor could be charged as a public charge and made to repay benefits legally accessed by someone whose immigration he or she helped facilitate. An immigration policy analyst explained:

[W]hen we say public charge isn't an issue [and] it's now safe, people say, "Oh, great, sponsors aren't going to be sued." Then we have to say that's a separate issue. Very confusing. People see them as anyone would, as all the same issue together.

Despite the limitations of clarification discussed so far, state advocates acknowledge that change is slow and that there remains hope for positive change for immigrant access to health care. In some ways, health service providers and advocates may have had unrealistic expectations of the impact of clarification.

It is apparent that barriers continue to exist for many low-income immigrants and that the damage inflicted by welfare and immigration reform has far-reaching implications. However, on a more positive note, some valuable lessons were learned. An advocate said, "That's probably the most positive thing, that people from all corners came together to push on this and were able to show the problem." If nothing else, another advocate replied, "We are better prepared to deal with the issue if it comes back."

The Everyday Impact of Ever-Changing Policies

The sharing of information between the California Department of Health Services and the Federal INS agency, together with recent welfare and immigration reforms, have created an increasingly confusing environment. The devolution of federal welfare policy is a slow process that undergoes constant revision and rearticulation, as policies filter down from the federal to the state and county governments.[6] It involves making both exclusive and shared decisions that take time and that are often revised repeatedly before they become stable. Policies generally filter down from the federal level to the state, and then to the county governments, and ultimately trigger decisions and actions at the lower levels of government. For safety net health care providers, the wait is frustrating. Many social workers described a sense of helplessness while they waited for clarification on policies that could have had detrimental effects on their patients' health. When a patient came to a county clinic administrator, worried about new federal deeming regulations, she found that she could do little:

It takes one or two years for all the bureaucracy at the federal level, the state level, the county level, to work out the regulations and interpretations and so forth. [During this process] we can't find a reliable source. I have called up the INS. I have called up Medi-Cal. I talked to supervisors—"Well, at this time, yes, they [the policies] are changing." "Can you send anything in writing?" "No, we can't do anything." We can ask our people in the central office, the Director's office, and they try to keep up with information and send information back to us. But we are told two conflicting things.

In this process of filtering information, each level struggles to keep up with the impending changes and their implications. Misunderstandings are common in situations where complex policies are being translated and tested at each bureaucratic level. The complexities and frequent changes in rules for the implementation of policies often result in a lack of adequate knowledgeable personnel who are able to decipher and explain the welfare and immigration reforms and their implications to individual immigrant clients. Social workers have mentioned that maintaining timely information in light of the constant changes is difficult for eligibility workers and clinic staff. Moreover, immigrants feel uncomfortable about relying on informational phone lines to determine their case-specific options and the implications of their using Medi-Cal. One provider explained:

They want somebody to say, "Yes, you have the right and nothing is going to happen to you." I cannot make that kind of statement because if something happens I am 100 percent responsible. And the recent number they gave us in Los Angeles said that if people had questions regarding immigration and their Medi-Cal status, they can call there, an 800 number, I think, but several of the people that called there said that they didn't get very far. Either they didn't get through or the information they got again was kind of hazy so they didn't feel comfortable applying anyhow.

This confusing process of policy devolution, coupled with ill-prepared eligibility workers, is detrimental to providing timely health care services such as prenatal care. Some immigrant women have had to endure almost nine months of delay in receiving approval for Medi-Cal for prenatal care. A safety net provider in San Diego County reported:

> One of my patients just delivered a couple days ago, and luckily we just got her on Medi-Cal two weeks ago. It took us her whole pregnancy to get her onto Medi-Cal because it is so much more difficult these days to qualify for Medi-Cal, that it took the whole three trimesters to get this woman on. It was the paperwork and she kept getting denied and denied. That's one of the things that . . . is happening now. It is much more difficult to get Medi-Cal and it is much more difficult to stay on Medi-Cal.

Given the complexity and lack of clarity with regard to the implementation of these recent reforms, constantly changing information may worsen, rather than alleviate, the situation. A county clinic administrator said, "[I]n this last year, more information and regulations are coming out. And as they do, it sends a lot of fear and concern throughout the community for access to health care." For her, the issue of deeming[7] is of particular concern. Questions concerning whether the sponsoring family will be held financially responsible for the Medi-Cal use of someone they sponsored (including prenatal care) and if their use of health care will affect the sponsoring family's application for citizenship, remain unanswered.[8]

The impact of these changing policies is evident in the fluctuating number of patients, which corresponds to the onset of particular legislative reforms or threat of reform. This was the case surrounding Presumptive Eligibility (PE) Medi-Cal, a method for certified prenatal care providers to serve pregnant women who are eligible for Medi-Cal while the application is being processed. Given the time-sensitive nature of pregnancies, PE Medi-Cal facilitates the early initiation of prenatal care because the costs incurred during the first sixty days are covered by Medi-Cal while the application is being processed. A nurse described what happened at the community clinic where she works:

> In the last six months we have actually had an increase [in patients]. There was a period of time where it seemed to be flat. That was back around six, seven months ago, there was a lot of talk that the PE Medi-Cal was going to be discontinued. When that was really active, then we saw a real decrease, and then there was a period of time when there were a lot or rumors going around that if you try to get on PE Medi-Cal or Medi-Cal to have the baby, then Immigration [the INS] was going to come to your house.

Irregular or discontinued care directly impacts not only the patients involved but also their health care providers. Early and continuous care is necessary for the health of mothers and the facilities that care for them. One clinic coordinator described the environment in which policies, particularly for the undocumented, are constantly threatened, as "death row." She explained:

> So many of our patients are fee-for-service Medi-Cal,[9] and that is what enables us to offer the CPSP[10] program. If we did not have Medi-Cal, we could not offer all those ancillary services that people need. So we know that if the Medi-Cal program for the undocumented were to disappear, we would have to lay off staff. *And so it is kind of like being on death row.* . . . [S]omething like twenty-five times in the past two years it has been announced that prenatal care for the undocumented will disappear. Not only does that unnerve the staff, but the community is really aware of that, too. They may not know exactly what is going on in terms of what is happening in the legislature or in the Governor's office. But they do hear that it is threatened, so it poses a barrier.

These policy changes have produced fear and confusion not only for the immigrant patients but also for the providers who care for them. In these circumstances, both the patient and the provider are on edge, bracing for the next blow. It is a stressful environment that makes providing quality care difficult. A Bay Area community clinic coordinator described her working conditions in these terms:

> I think there are misconceptions with the population and there are misconceptions with staff and Medi-Cal workers themselves. It just seems like every week it's a different story and in the past year it has been incredibly terrible. I mean like we've had a week by week thing. "Okay, starting July 1st, we're cutting off prenatal care. Oh just kidding, starting August 1st. Okay, now if you're already on, you're going to be taken off and we're not accepting new people. Okay, starting September 1st . . . ." It was just like that, just week after week and then there were court appeals and you know, sometimes, a little bit of news is worse than no news at all because it caused a lot of apprehension among staff members and among the patients.

In the meantime, prenatal care providers have had to find alternative ways to ensure that patients receive some form of prenatal care. This effort creates a significant strain on the already limited resources of a safety net clinic. For instance, these policy changes have altered many social workers' job descriptions to include greater legal advocacy. An executive director of a community clinic in San Francisco reported, "Now we have an additional role in terms of advising patients and interpreting these legal issues. . . . And we have to learn about it ourselves." A nurse at another clinic in the same region said:

> I'm almost having to serve as an immigration expert, trying to explain the situation when I really don't have that expertise. As far as I know, I still don't have a clear idea [of public charge] because what if I tell them, "No it's not going to affect you," and then somewhere along the line it does, I'd feel really bad.

Fears about public charge have increased the difficulty and workload for health service providers who serve low-income immigrants. Social workers are overextended as they personally struggle to full an informational void. They must wade through the built-in vagueness and bureaucratic jargon that create significant spaces of ambiguity in the interpretation of policy. These intermediaries find themselves in an on-going "natural" experiment that tests how far the boundaries of the welfare state will contract before it is collectively contested.

Rebuilding Trust

As the connecting link between the provider and the patient, social workers are privy to the everyday impact of these policies on immigrant women and their families. A social worker for a San Francisco Bay Area hospital said, "[T]he clients that we see [now] seem to be more stressed. They cry a lot more. They're so overwhelmed, they just burst into tears." It is in fact this increased level of stress that has spurred some clinics and hospitals to understand the greater need for social workers. A social worker at a neonatal follow-up center described how home visits to immigrant families with medically fragile (e.g., premature) infants created a new program in the Bay Area:

> Well, as the nurses started going out, they started finding that they were going out into families that were having an incredible amount of stress; lots of other stresses including the stress of raising a fragile baby. So, there was a decision made to expand the program and to bring on a different staff. At this point, we have a developmental pediatrician who is our Medical Director. We have a medical component that includes: nurses, physical therapists, nutritionists, and we have a mental health team. We have another social worker, myself, and a psychologist. So we each then work individually with families so that we can bring the expertise of all these other people on our team to work specifically with this specific unit.

This model of medical intervention is a unique one that places social workers in a central position. It is particularly well suited for working in low-income immigrant communities because it treats the whole person rather than simply the medical condition. Respondents in this study repeatedly asserted that trust could only be regained by treating patients in their entirety—including the needs of their families, an understanding of their history, and their reasons for migration. Because public charge fears are so embedded in the lives of low-income immigrants, social workers find that they must address this issue as a *systemic* concern that affects the patient and her family. In order to regain trust, the provider must attend to all the various barriers to accessing medical care—above and beyond attaining Medi-Cal for the pregnant mother. A Regional Perinatal Program coordinator in Fresno explained:

> [F]rom a care provider perspective, they become more or less social workers like they have to deal with all the other issues before they can actually effectively provide the medical care. [It's] not just providing health care to the individual person but providing resources or hooking them up with existing resources within the community.

A significant challenge is the "word-of-mouth" communication system in many immigrant communities. Many immigrants live in close-knit communities wherein they rely on information from friends or neighbors. In this environment, fearful stories move quickly from one household to another. A community clinic manager in San Diego explained:

> In the immigrant community, it is very much driven by what the word of mouth is, what people are saying, what they are saying to their neighbors. People are a little bit more willing to apply for Medi-Cal than they were in the past. But it can change very quickly. In March we were at 60 percent of our patients being fee for service [Medi-Cal], and now we are up to 75 to 80 percent. In just a few months it can change dramatically.

Regaining trust within this close-knit, word of mouth environment is a challenge. The medical social worker must become a trusted part of this word of mouth system. Successful strategies used by social workers to foster trust include: first, understanding and incorporating their patients' personal, ethnic, or migration histories into the medical model; second, attending to the concerns of the patient's family as a whole; and third, following through with consistent, reliable information.

First, when working with immigrants, understanding their ethnic or migration background may be indispensible.[11] A social worker at a Bay Area hospital illustrated this point as follows:

> [A]n immigrant comes in with whatever their symptoms are but, in addition, they also come in with the experience of being an immigrant and that's a complicated experience. We need to start thinking about how the migration affects what's going on with this family right now. For example, we had an immigrant family—an El Salvadoran family—their infant was born with a condition called NEC, which is a problem with your intestines. The intestines kind of got twisted up and so they had to go in there and do a surgical intervention and they had to give this child a device, which meant that he went [to the bathroom] through a bag while his intestines were healing. It was a temporary measure to give his intestines time to heal.
> The family came from a rural area in El Salvador and, you know, going to a hospital was something that you only did when you were going to die, so everything in between was handled [internally] unless it was some emergency. But this family adjusted pretty well to this really

weird way of caring for their child. The interesting thing is that, when the time came for this child to be reconnected—which meant that the surgery was going to be done to put his bowels back so he could go [to the bathroom] normally; the family up until that point was very excited about having the surgery—all of a sudden the mother started having these enormous feelings of anxiety. In working with her, I found out that her story was directly related to their immigration, which had occurred a number of years before.

What happened is that she started having dreams that her brother had started coming to her. Now this is a brother who had died. It turned out that the brother had been a victim of the war in El Salvador and that he had been murdered. The family—because of that danger—had to come to the United States. They applied for political asylum here and once they got here, they didn't want to look back. Even though they had adapted pretty well into our society—they were working, they were following up with all of the medical care—because they had this trauma, this tremendous loss, it started to interfere with the health of this child. The brother visited the mother in her dreams prior to this child's surgery and she thought, "Oh, my God. That means he is going to come and take my child." So she was ready at that point to cancel the surgery.   So, as this story came out, we then realized the complicating factor. I think it's an important story for providers to hear and understand that migration is a big deal and people come for different reasons. Providers need to start seeing what is really going on with them because that's affecting their health care.

In the end, this social worker was able to work with the mother in allaying her fears. After a number of lengthy discussions, the mother trusted her son's health care providers enough to go ahead with the surgery. The son survived the surgery. This trust was in large part gained through the social worker's ability to show the mother that she understood her predicament. As an immigrant from Latin America herself, the social worker was able to provide the kind of bilingual and knowledgeable intervention that is crucial to developing a relationship between the patient and the health care provider.

The second crucial factor when working with immigrant communities is addressing the needs of the family. This is certainly evident in the failed attempts to enroll low-income immigrant children into state-funded child health insurance programs. Covering one child but not the entire family made many immigrants reluctant to enroll.[12]

The health care concerns of low-income immigrant families are intricately connected to a number of other key issues, including finances, employment, housing, transportation, and child care. Social workers point out that all these issues bear directly on one's access to health care. One social worker discussed a recent dilemma as follows:

I had a phone call from a mother that I am working with that has 2 children that are one year apart. The oldest one is about 17 months old but she was born a few months early, so her correct age is really 14 months. She was a single parent, immigrant, isolated. Doesn't have any family. Doesn't have a support system at all. She called and I was so thankful that I happened to be at my desk. She was calling from a phone booth. She had a problem with some people that she was living with and she was living on the street. She spent the weekend on the street. Now it's sad enough to be homeless, but when you're homeless with medically fragile infants, a baby can get into trouble just like that. When I realized what was going on, I talked to her about shelters. So the first shelter number that I called said that they had a bed available and then after we started getting into some details.

I said, "This is a Spanish speaking mom,"

And this is when they commented, "Oh, she's Spanish speaking, we can't take her."

"What do you mean you can't take her in the shelter?"

I said, "You do have a bed available?"

And she said, "Yeah, we do have a bed available but, we don't have any staff that speaks Spanish and in order for them to come into our program, they have to participate in our activities and we have group meetings and unless she's able to bring a translator with her ... does she have somebody who can?"

I said, "Look, if she had somebody that could come and translate for her then she'd probably have a support network and we wouldn't be making this phone call in the first place."

The fact that there is a very skeletal infrastructure set up that is supposed to attend to families that are in crisis . . . unless you have staff that has the capacity to work with a range of people who are really in the communities, what's the point? I think that's a very critical point to be made. There's not enough staff that can really meet the realistic and the cultural needs of the people who are out there.

This passage makes an important point, in that the failing of the shelter is similar to the failings of the broader safety net health care system. Although lack of insurance is a major reason why many people choose not to utilize health services, language is also a consistent barrier to care. In this case, a desperately needed bed goes empty. Likewise, the safety net system is not functioning as it should if it cannot or will not care for those it was created to serve. Given the tremendous need for quality social services for the working poor, its inaccessibility due to something as basic and obvious as language competency seems nonsensical. And yet, the importance of effectively communicating through some form of shared language and cultural knowledge is repeatedly stressed by social workers. This limitation has considerable impact in California where there is a high concentration of immigrants. As a social worker based in San Francisco's Asian immigrant community explained:

Language competency is primary and the most important ingredient in providing good health care to our population. And home visitation, . . . I really believe it is the best and most effective and most cost effective way of serving this population. Because if you ask them to go to such and such place to seek help, 80 percent of them wouldn't go. But if you bring your service to them, then at least they will be there to visit and make a decision in terms of what they need to do. It is a relationship. So the more you see them, the more they trust you, and then you will be able to help them in whatever way they need.

Organizations whose outreach workers engage in constant and consistent advocacy, and are from the very communities that they serve, appear the most effective in maintaining the trust of immigrant communities. An outreach worker in the Bay Area discussed the importance of advocacy programs for Asian immigrants as follows:

Asian immigrant families have a lot of difficulty divulging their own personal information, like how much you have in the bank, and what kind of car you have, and things like that. [That is] very personal stuff, and they usually don't want to put it down. So, what we do is, we will assist them to fill out those forms, encourage them to get check stubs, whatever, if they have those kinds of things, and then [you] have to submit it in a timely manner, because if you don't submit it in a timely manner, you get cut off. And a lot of people don't understand that. Or they receive something they cannot read, then they have to find someone to read it for them. They may not be able to do it right away, they just put it away. I do remember, especially with the Southeast Asian community, they have the hardest time, because many of them do not read, let alone English. They do not even read their own language. So when they receive something in the mail, they throw it away. So, many times, they miss the deadline of rereporting or whatever, and then they panic when their aid is cut off or when their Medi-Cal got cut off. So, that is why this kind of advocacy program is very, very important. Especially with the Southeast Asian group.

This outreach worker highlights an important awareness that she gained from her experiences. The regular disclosure of private financial and personal information mandated by the state adds to an already very uncomfortable and difficult situation. Having to ask for help in reading one's mail or simply trying to decipher the bureaucratic jargon of government notices requires further exposure and a show of weakness in asking for help at all. Unfortunately, the subsequent avoidance often leads to moments of crisis, which is when the outreach worker usually intervenes. The level of trust that exists between the health care clinic and the patient mediates the intensity of the crisis.

With this trust, the social worker can become a reliable and consistent source of information. While the relationship between health care provider and patient is a tenuous one, it is evident that once a strong connection is made, it is invaluable in maintaining access to prenatal care. One outreach worker said,

I always [joke] with my coworkers that somebody at the border must be telling people my name because a lot of them will know my name. They've never met me but they'll say, "You're Maria." And I say, "Yes." And then they say, "Oh, they told me to make sure I talked to you."

Given the number of patients requesting this particular social worker, it is evident that Maria is a rarity. Another social worker experienced an intergenerational connection:

> Just this week again, I got a phone call from a mother that I had worked with in the Orthopedic Clinic. I had worked with her child when she was a kid and now the child is 16. I don't know how she found me. She called me and she said that there are not a lot of other programs out there. She was able to trust me. It's not that I'm so great. Who else is she going to call if she has a problem?

Despite these strong ties between immigrant women and safety net providers, as noted earlier, the confusion regarding public charge greatly jeopardized the latter's role as sources of reliable information. Consequently, social workers focused more intensively on outreach services. A community outreach coordinator commented, "[B]ut still it was very hard because they didn't trust us for a long time. It was hard to convince them that we really were not going to deport them for using our services." Health care providers learned very quickly that rebuilding trust the second time was twice as hard as the first time.

Normalizing Care

In order to "repackage" the utilization of state-funded health insurance as a "normal" phenomenon, social workers contest the treatment of low-income immigrant women and their children as public burdens. Caring for the "whole" person and her family with consistent and reliable information is an important step toward this end. Interestingly enough, social workers sometimes find themselves fighting an uphill battle not only in trying to convince the mainstream community about immigrants' right to access Medicaid, but also within immigrant communities themselves. A community clinic administrator described the change that occurred after 1996 as follows:

> Once Welfare Reform passed, the feeding frenzy around interpreting it in the most punitive way really just set us back. . . . Even if we only had

one or two cases—I think that the ripple effect in the community is say-ing, "I don't care how much that person tells you that you are eligible for this program, stay away from it."

Some social workers view their jobs as an opportunity to empower low-income immigrant women. One social worker at a prenatal clinic dis-cussed how her patients were "amazed" once they realized how the child was developing in their womb. She used these appointments as an oppor-tunity to answer any questions they had and to arm them with informa-tion regarding the process of labor and delivery. The social worker com-mented, "You know, they want to be treated right when they go to deliver and we expose them to all of that." This social worker, like so many others, is helping immigrants understand their rights—that they deserve to be treated with kindness and respect.

The fact that many of the social workers are members of immigrant com-munities also helps to "normalize" access to Medi-Cal. One social worker in a rural part of Fresno replied, "I come from a migrant family. That's one of the reasons I think I've stood with this hospital; because I can do so much with everybody that I serve." The credibility that this community connection confers counts for a lot in the minds of immigrants when they weigh the costs and benefits of enrolling in Medi-Cal and accessing health care.

Social workers play a pivotal role in this dilemma, as they are the link to the low-income immigrant community. In our study of public charge effects, we found that the degree of awareness of state and federal policies rests largely on the availability of resources at the clinic or hospital. For organizations which have the resources, a key staff member is available whose job, in part, is to keep abreast of the policy changes that impact low-income immigrant women. They then filter the information to the front-line social workers, outreach workers, and health practitioners who work directly with the patients and/or the immigrant communities. A pro-gram manager for a relatively well-funded community clinic in San Diego told us, "[Public charge] was an issue that we had been monitoring very closely. . . . We did get notification through various lobby groups and in-formation from the INS." Subsequently, their role in allaying the fears that arose from the information sharing between the DHS and the INS, and the confusing and intimidating bureaucracies associated with Medi-Cal and the use of prenatal care became more important than ever.

However, many of the safety net clinics and hospitals we visited did not have such luxuries. A Perinatal Services Coordinator in San Francisco stated:

> Funding for activities for outreach is a big problem. Letting women know that low cost or free pediatric or perinatal care is available [is one of our goals], and yet there is no funding for outreach to tell them. We do have services available for low-income women and children but they don't know how to access the services and don't know . . . they are free and low cost.

The majority of these organizations stated that if they had the proper funding to provide outreach, more women would be able to access health care without fear. When organizations choose not to invest or do not have the funds to support strong community outreach programs, the effect is dramatic. Such was the case for one community clinic for Korean immigrants in Los Angeles County that experienced a significant drop in their OB (obstetrics) clientele due to fears of deportation and forced repayment for health services. The clinic director said:

> Undocumented women, we used to have a lot, about maybe 80 percent of the clients who came were undocumented pregnant women for Medi-Cal. But these days we do not have any. Yes, I think this happened last summer. You know, the state announced that they cannot issue Medi-Cal to undocumented women for a short period. But it affects a lot.

This drop in patient numbers occurred despite the fact that prenatal care for undocumented women, while threatened, remained intact. She explained:

> Still, one time the state said they cannot provide the Medi-Cal care for the undocumented women. And it was published in the newspaper. So they got scared. And also, we have some complaints from a Medi-Cal beneficiary who had a delivery. The women went to Korea and when they came back to America, they had a problem. They received a letter, saying that she has to pay back the full amount of the hospital fee. We received more than five complaints last December.

More than six months later, the number of OB and prenatal care patients remained low and the clinic had had little luck in regaining the trust and sense of comfort of their clients. This was not the case for a clinic in San Diego that initiated a strong community outreach effort. The director of this clinic discussed how her clinic learned from California's earlier Proposition 187:

> What we have found is that ever since Prop. 187—initially when that was approved—the clinic numbers overall dropped. And we got a lot of calls, a lot of concern about people being afraid to apply for Medi-Cal or even to go into a clinic and use its services for fear that we would report them. That changed pretty quickly. We got the word out fairly quickly that the clinic was not doing that. And then publicity about Prop. 187 going to the courts was pretty widely publicized in the Latino community. People quickly got the idea that we were not going to report them, and so that was not a worry.

This level of outreach was also necessary for some clinics to maintain clients following the 1996 welfare reforms. For these clinics, an immediate outreach campaign following the particular hostile policies or threats of policies worked to maintain a certain level of trust among low-income immigrants, especially those who were undocumented.

Unfortunately, there are significant barriers preventing most safety net health service providers from instituting such programs. Their positions are particularly vulnerable in unstable economic times. Every health care provider I interviewed reported severe financial constraints, inadequate personnel, and the overwhelming health care needs of their patients. Many were operating at capacity and had not had the opportunity to familiarize themselves with particular policy concerns. Such health care providers— witnessing their patients' intense fear and confusion in trying to decide whether or not to apply for Medi-Cal—experienced the impact of public charge as simply one in a long line of anti-immigrant initiatives, albeit a particularly hostile one.

Given the seemingly constant anti-immigrant pressure on low-income communities, safety net social workers perform an important role in "normalizing" low-income immigrant women's access to prenatal care. Effective communication and knowledge regarding their patients' history, understanding the broader circumstances of the whole family, persistence in staying up to date on policy changes, and treating their clients with respect have helped rebuild a certain level of trust. By doing so, social workers have helped to legitimize immigrant mothers among both immigrant communities and the public at large, so that they are seen as deserving of publicly funded health care.

The next chapter pays closer attention to the issue of access to immigrant prenatal care within the political cauldron of the U.S.-Mexico border. Systemic stresses and strains take on an extra level of gravity in San Diego, as immigrant women's reproduction becomes political fodder for larger national ideological anxieties.

CHAPTER 5

Fear and Loathing at the Border

[W]hat this county as a whole is more concerned about is fraud and fraud prevention than they are in provision of services, so everything they do is geared toward making sure the wrong people don't get it and if that means that many people who may be eligible don't get it in the process too, well that's just the way it goes.

—Health care advocate, San Diego

Borders are contradictory. They have the potential to both enable and constrict ideas and actions. For this reason, borders are spaces of power. Whether they demarcate literal, physical place or figurative, abstract space, borders are socially constructed entities with the potential for real, lived consequences. Geographer David Sibley explains that boundaries can provide security and comfort as well as provoke risk and fear, depending upon where you stand and with what resources.[1] Subsequently, the ability to cross boundaries—or, to move from a familiar to an alien space—can be an anxious experience. In some circumstances it can be fatal. At the Mexico-U.S. border, the deaths of hundreds of Latin American women working in maquiladora factories in Juarez[2] are a graphic example.

Borders are also powerful locations for defining who is included or excluded, and how. As liminal spaces, they are messy locations in which the contradictions of boundary maintenance are exposed. Legal scholar Robert Chang observes, "The Border is everywhere" and yet can be rendered invisible. "It is through this invisibility that the border gains much of its power."[3] Chang notes that because national borders are imperfect, supplementary mechanisms for exclusion are deployed. As such, welfare and health care policies function to supplement immigration policies in deciphering who belongs and who does not. In doing this, each mechanism roots out the foreign as a threat thereby necessitating systematic observation, control, and potential deportation. Welfare and health policies, then, inconspicuously extend the power of the border far beyond the literal, physical fence.

At the same time, the international border in San Diego County has undergone very conspicuous changes during the neoliberal 1990s. In his investigation of the Operation Gatekeeper program, Joseph Nevins writes, "Nowhere along the boundary are integration and boundary policing as pronounced as they are in the San Diego-Tijuana region. . . . In addition, it is the location of the most intense economic and demographic growth of the U.S.-Mexico border region—the fastest developing border zone in the Americas, and perhaps the world."[4] With the passage of the North American Free Trade Agreement (NAFTA) in 1994, trade between the United States and Mexico grew from $80 million to $200 billion in 2000.[5] This increase in capital was accompanied by an increase in the flow of people. Nevins documents:

> About 60 million people and 20 million cars per year now enter San Diego from Mexico through the San Ysidro port of entry, making it the busiest land crossing in the world. And an estimated 40,000 people cross the border each day to work, including several thousand who manage and work in maquiladoras (export-oriented assembly plants) in Tijuana, but live in the San Diego area.[6]

The population of those who live on both sides of the border numbers 12 million.[7] This is a relatively new phenomenon. Only since the 1970s has the U.S.-Mexico border region housed large-scale cities. Some urban studies scholars have identified the San Diego-Tijuana region as a new urban ecological space or "transfrontier metropolis."[8] Since its creation in 1848, the two thousand-mile international boundary between the United States and

Mexico has run across a sparsely populated, rural edge of two vast nation-states. Beginning in the 1950s, a dramatic transformation occurred in the borderlands region of both nations, turning what was once a dusty frontier into permanent, economically driven cities. The population of cities along the border increased faster than the national average in both countries.

Propelling this dramatic urbanization and its accompanying tension at the border is the concentration of global capital and growing demand for cheap labor in the region. Nestor Rodriguez argues that the economic reality of the new transfrontier metropolis soon became incompatible with the existing nation-state boundary. He writes, "the 'crisis' of the border is not that 'illegal aliens' are swarming across the U.S.-Mexico border, but that global capitalist growth is overwhelming nation-states as units of social-economic development."[9] But, despite the strong pressures brought to bear by neoliberal economic policies, the nation-state borders held their ground. In fact, the border took on even greater symbolic and cultural importance for national identity during the 1990s.

Certainly, anxiety regarding national security helped to solidify the southern borderlands as a tangible front in the frequently intangible "global war on terror." At the same time, the rapidly growing immigrant population began to move into nontraditional destination states. Work opportunities in the Southeast, Midwest, and Rocky Mountain states attracted immigrants away from the usual coastal cities. The foreign-born population more than doubled in many of these new destinations between 1990 and 2000.[10] The Urban Institute notes, "The dispersal of our newest arrivals to regions that historically have attracted relatively few immigrants means that the integration issues previously confined to only a handful of states—issues such as access to language classes, health care, welfare benefits, and jobs—are now central concerns for most states."[11] In fits and starts, immigration has topped the agenda in many towns across the nation—from Aspen, Colorado to Carpentersville, Illinois to Nashville, Tennessee.[12] As Alex Kotlowitz found in his analysis of Carpentersville, a small town in Illinois with 37,000 residents, immigration politics is experienced in a very personal way and has a strong tendency to turn very nasty.

Carpentersville is described as a town "without a center." Long-time residents report a growing sense of alienation and isolation within a global economy that dramatically changed the racial demographics from 17 percent Latino in 1990 to 40 percent a decade later.[13] And, while scholars such as Kitty Calavita, Ruth Milkman, and others emphasize the historical fact that wage levels fell and income inequality grew as a result of deindustrialization, capital flight, economic restructuring, and the dismantling of labor unions in the 1970s and 1980s, *before* the current influx of immigrants into middle America, immigrants remain easy targets during these unsettling times.[14] The militarization of the Mexico-U.S. border is now seen as necessary in order to regain a sense of national stability, particularly perhaps for those further away from the borderlands who see their communities in the "heartland" changing in ways they do not like, ways that destabilizes their experience as the central and sole identity for their town.[15]

Mike Davis describes the southern California border as "a state-sanctioned system of violence: physical, environmental, economic, and cultural."[16] In 1993, the INS budget for border enforcement was $400 million. Four years later, this number doubled to $800 million. Subsequently, the number of Border Patrol agents increased from 4,200 in 1994 to 9,212 by 2000. Throughout the 1990s, and continuing into the 2000s, boundary enforcement efforts have increased precipitously. In his analysis of Operation Gatekeeper, a border enforcement program launched during the Clinton Administration, Nevins shrewdly assesses that rather than solving the problem of Mexican immigration, the program in fact created it. The Gatekeeper program's very existence helped to create the specter of an invasion by Mexican "illegal aliens." He writes,

> The geographical epicenter of these concerns and efforts was the state of California, whose southern boundary with Mexico, especially in the area of San Diego, was probably the gateway for the majority of unauthorized entries into the United States. The San Diego section of the boundary became a platform for politicians, government officials, and political activists in favor of immigration restriction, who were eager to communicate their messages advocating a crackdown to an increasingly anxious public. [17]

He concludes, "Gatekeeper's greatest significance is that it embodies the pinnacle of a historical geographical process that has made the boundaries of the United States and their accompanying social practices seem increasingly normal and unproblematic, thus placing them largely beyond question."[18] This program, which solidifies the border as an institution and frames the policy of exclusion as a solution to major social problems, paves the road for the re-emergence of public charge through port of entry fraud detection programs.

The underlying role of these border-making enforcement measures is what DeGenova articulates as "deportability." He writes, "The U.S. nation-state's enforcement of immigration law and policing along the U.S.-Mexico border, notably, have long sustained the operation of a revolving-door policy—simultaneously implicated in *im*portation as much as (in fact, far more than) deportation."[19] The border and its programs create their own legitimacy through the production of migrant "illegality" or criminality. At the same time, illegality and the possibility of deportation facilitates importation by sustaining immigrant labor's vulnerable status. And for all the efforts toward militarizing the border, there is little to be proud of.

In his analysis, Douglas Massey and his coauthors write, "In the end, U.S. policies transformed what had been a relatively open and benign labor process with few negative consequences into an exploitative underground system of labor coercion that put downward pressure on the wages and working conditions not only of undocumented migrants but of legal immigrants and citizens alike."[20] While the characterization of border crossing in the 1980s as "benign" may be contested, the failure of border enforcement in the 1990s is clear. Tripling the number of Border Patrol agents and quadrupling the Border Patrol budget did nothing to reduce the influx of undocumented migrants.[21] Instead, it has created a bottleneck effect in which migrants who would regularly cross the national border (sometimes multiple times a year) in keeping with their work schedules are now residing permanently in the United States, along with their families. Massey et al. write, "A perverse consequence of draconian border enhancement is that it does not deter would-be migrants from trying to enter the country so much as it discourages those who are already here from returning home."[22] This process has actually doubled the number of undocumented Mexican immigrants during a time of increased border enforcement.[23]

In addition, there is a greater reliance on coyotes, or professional smugglers, who are increasing the cost for their services to $3,000 per person as the risks increase. And the risks have increased precipitously as migrants cross more remote and hazardous terrain. Wayne Cornelius writes, "Between 1995 and 2006, there were over 3,700 *known* migrant fatalities due to unauthorized border crossings; dehydration and hypothermia were the most common causes of death. The actual death toll undoubtedly was much higher, including bodies yet undiscovered."[24] For women, more of whom are making this arduous journey than before, the militarization of the border has brought with it the risk of rape and sexual harassment—a risk sometimes also faced by men. Independent organizations that monitor the U.S.-Mexico border, including Amnesty International, Human Rights Watch, and the American Friends Service Committee, consistently report rape and sexual abuse of immigrants by Border Patrol agents.[25]

And yet, despite its many failures, as a social and legal force the border remains as strong as ever. In Massey's view, "Immigration and border policies after 1986 were not grounded in any real understanding of Mexico-U.S. migration or its role in North American integration, but in cold war ideology, anti-drug hysteria, and crude ethnic scapegoating."[26] Similarly, Rodriguez concludes, "Solemn treaties formalize international boundaries, but it is the daily reproduction of ideas and myths that socially construct borders."[27] Clearly, modes of exclusion that maintain the border go far beyond the physical fence. And as the ambiguity of inclusion spreads internally, the border becomes increasingly important in upholding certain myths. In studying the impact of public charge fears in welfare and immigration legislation, it is evident that social policies can feed the myths necessary for border maintenance. I would argue that pregnant immigrant women actually *embody* the fears associated with the border, marking them as a social problem to be solved by new modes of exclusion.

Immigrant health care advocates in the border town of San Diego witness this myth making and its impact on a firsthand basis. They experience dual pressures—those emanating from all the localized anti-immigrant anger across the country and those resulting from the hostility of their own local politics. In the following section I discuss in more detail the experiences of health care workers in the borderlands of San Diego who care for low-income pregnant immigrant women and the way their work reflects the social reality of our deeply racialized border politics.

Making "Illegal" Spaces

In researching San Diego County, immigrant health care providers consistently described the local political climate as one in which low-income immigrants were assumed to be fraudulent unless proven otherwise. Of the three regions included in this study, San Diego was repeatedly noted as particularly harsh on immigrant applicants. Interestingly, the same federal and state mandates that are passed down to local county governments are operationalized in very different ways by different counties. Take, for instance, the intimidating signs in the San Diego DSS (Department of Social Services) offices where women apply for Medi-Cal, as discussed in chapter 2. The signs, which stated that personal information would be sent to the INS, deterred immigrants from applying for services for which they were eligible. San Diego's social services offices were the only ones in the region required by the County Board of Supervisors to hang up such signs. A community clinic prenatal care program manager in San Diego assessed the political climate for her immigrant clients as follows:

> [T]he County Board of Supervisors has really endeavored to make its policies quite hostile to the undocumented. And so, for example, there are notices that are posted in the Department of Social Services offices saying that the information that you give to the Medi-Cal offices could be forwarded to the INS. And there was actually a pilot program where they were running border-crossing cardholders' names through the INS files. There was a pilot program [in which] they were comparing people who were applying for Medi-Cal to the INS rolls. There also was a time when those notices saying that your information could be forwarded to the INS were actually mailed to applicants, and included as part of the orientation packet. So these were extremely hostile actions that were taken toward the undocumented in San Diego County.

San Diego County, with its receptive Board of Supervisors, functions as a frontier for border enhancement experiments. Health care workers were witnesses to these efforts. The same program manager added:

> And it is borne out also by the statistics that we have. We know for example that in San Diego County, about 30 percent of Medi-Cal applications are granted and that about 70 percent are put into pending status. Whereas in Los Angeles County, it is the complete opposite. About 70 percent are approved and about 30 percent are put into pending status. And these are two counties that geographically are very close together.

But it is really due to the political environment here, and there is much greater consciousness in this area of people being undocumented, much more concern about people taking advantage of medical services.

While San Diego has exhibited hostile tendencies toward immigrants in the past, the added fear from recent immigration and welfare legislation has exacerbated the local politics of the border. A health care advocate in San Diego's North County explained:

> One of the biggest problems is that we are across the border and we do have situations and circumstances in which people do cross the border simply to access our services, and we know that that does occur, but the percentage of people doing this is probably very small and what this county as a whole is more concerned about is fraud and fraud prevention than they are in provision of services, so everything they do is geared toward making sure the wrong people don't get it and if that means that many people who may be eligible don't get it in the process too, well that's just the way it goes.[28]

Another graphic example of hostility toward immigrant health care use is the growing number and strategic presence of the Border Patrol. An outreach worker at a women's clinic near downtown San Diego reported that the Border Patrol deported a number of her patients in the midst of their prenatal care. She said:

> This lady said she went to the Laundromat and she was washing and suddenly the immigration man came and people were kind of rounded up and asked for papers and the ones that didn't have it were put on the van and taken to the border.

According to this outreach worker, stories of similar deportations are common among the immigrant communities in the region. Most community members know at least one other member who was taken and dropped on the other side of the Mexico-U.S. border. Moreover, Border Patrol vans are familiar to many immigrants and constantly reinvigorate immigrants' fears of how health care use can lead to deportation. One clinic worker explained that pregnant immigrant women have skipped prenatal care visits after sighting these vans in their neighborhoods. Another clinic that cares for a large number of undocumented women has had to deal with Border Patrol vans that park conspicuously in the clinic's parking lot. Understandably, the number of patients drops considerably on such days.

In response, clinics and hospitals have had to advocate for their patients beyond their health care. In one case, a San Diego nurse recalled:

> I remember one case where there was a teenager and she was a U.S. citizen and she has a grandma or someone in Mexico and [Border Patrol] handcuffed her and they called from the border saying they have this patient and they're not going let her come [across]. She was a U.S. citizen, she had her birth certificate and she was living here. They saw her pregnant and they asked her where she was going for her prenatal [care] and that's why they called here.

The nurse was asked to vouch for her patient's legitimate presence in the United States. The birth certificate and evidence of a U.S. address provided by the young Mexican patient were not enough to convince the Border Patrol agent. Her pregnancy raised the level of scrutiny and the agent took the extra precaution of actually calling a health care clinic to verify her legal status. Undoubtedly, the handcuffs raised the stakes as well. They spoke to the agent's level of seriousness and marked the teenager as a criminal.

Another nurse practitioner at a clinic that serves immigrants, including a high proportion of those who are undocumented, described the border as a place of "violence":

> The whole immigration fear that we see has to do with knowing that they are not in this country legally and that at any one time they can just yank me outta here. The Border Patrol does it every day. People are put in vans and taken across. It is a reality that people see. People feel it—there is violence.

An employee from the San Diego Department of Health described her county as having a "siege mentality." The County officials apparently see themselves as battling the forces of Mexico and their immigrants. This mentality works to increase the distance between immigrants and the health care they need. In response, the advocates in these hostile regions have had to increase their efforts to secure a level of trust among immigrants who need the health care for which they are eligible. Over time, community health clinics have found themselves having to follow the ebb and flow of local political whims. The impact of local politics cannot be overstated. A program manager of a hospital north of the city of San Diego, which serves a high number of immigrant workers, explained her circumstances in 2000 as follows:

> The political climate had a huge impact on women accessing prenatal care here in San Diego County. Now the pendulum is swinging. We have more women getting Medi-Cal. At one point, when Governor Wilson was constantly talking about eliminating prenatal care for undocumented women and also when the local Board [of Supervisors] was being very aggressive with fraud prevention, we were seeing about 50 percent of our patients in our prenatal program being on the cash program and 50 percent on Medi-Cal. Now it's probably about 90 percent Medi-Cal and 10 percent cash. So it has really made an impact. The women that were paying cash, unfortunately, we charged them $2,500 for prenatal care and the delivery at the hospital, which is pretty competitive, but by the time they put $2,500 together, they were well into the third trimester. [Now], qualifying for presumptive eligibility Medi-Cal, which is a temporary Medi-Cal that's good for two months while they get their pregnancy-related Medi-Cal together, and then qualifying for Medi-Cal, we're getting these women into prenatal care much, much faster.

When the state eased off on local fraud investigations and threats, the level of Medi-Cal use went up from 50 percent to 90 percent for prenatal care in this one hospital alone. Apparently, policy impacts work both ways— just as anti-immigrant policies have a strong impact, so do pro-immigrant policies. Without overstating the case and calling the change in direction in San Diego County's political climate a complete turnaround, one clinic program manager reported seeing positive trends in prenatal care use as a result of fairly subtle political changes:

> What we've also seen in San Diego County, which isn't necessarily true of other counties in California, is that the political climate has changed and especially the Department of Social Service where they are getting less aggressive about denying people Medi-Cal. They are getting a little

more customer-service-oriented. . . . We are seeing a lot of our pregnant women being granted Medi-Cal upon interviewing with the DSS worker, where in the past they would have been placed in investigatory status and the case would have been continued for sixty days.

However, throughout these fluctuations, the demand for prenatal care was consistent. Even when hostility toward immigrant health care was high, many immigrant women sought prenatal care, paying out of pocket if necessary. Many hospitals also adjusted to the local political environment and found ways to ensure quality care. This is a tricky endeavor in a system in which even sympathetic DSS workers must tread carefully. A community mediator explained,

[I]n fact many of these people [DSS] would really like to make things work well and flow but they also have to make sure that they don't make too big of a deal out of some of these things because it may call too much attention to them and could create some other ramifications that could cause problems at another level, so you have a political philosophy in this county that is basically anti-immigrant.

The community mediator also recounted her own experience of applying for a grant from the county for immigrant prenatal care:

There are some really difficult things to overcome when your whole community is not necessarily prohelp—they would really like to see as much negative immigrant eligibility as possible. As a matter of fact, we were told very bluntly with this grant—because our primary focus is on immigrant pregnant women—that this is a group of people this county chooses not to serve. *Specifically.*

Another community clinic advocate discussed the pressures on county social service workers. She said, "Once a DSS worker told me that they have to treat each case, or each person, as if they are lying to them, and that's what you have to prove to them—that they're not." Another clinic manager observed, "We had DSS workers that, I think, really enjoyed making their clients cry, I swear. I think now it's better, but some of these people have been there for thirty years and it's really hard to change their style."

Across all the regions in this study, there were consistent concerns regarding language and cultural competency, transportation, and childcare, all of which continue to contribute to a general sense of fear and frustration in accessing Medi-Cal and health care. Without childcare and transportation, many women are unable to leave their family responsibilities to keep prenatal care appointments. Lack of accessible transportation created the greatest barrier in the Central Valley, where neighborhoods are more isolated and the public transportation systems are less comprehensive.

And, as discussed in the previous chapter, language and cultural barriers have continued to cause difficulties for advocates and providers in communicating with their target populations. For instance, providing culturally appropriate advocacy for the many different Asian immigrants—who represent a wide range of cultural backgrounds, languages, and histories—is at times very difficult. Linguistic competency, which is so crucial in the health care setting, is further compromised for groups that have high illiteracy rates in their own languages. Moreover, the level of fear and misunderstanding is even greater for communities without culturally sophisticated outreach workers.

At the same time, each region interviewed displayed distinctive traits in its treatment of immigrants and prenatal care, particularly toward the undocumented population. The actions of the Board of Supervisors in each area are but one indication of the regional variation. In comparing the three regions—the San Francisco Bay Area, San Diego County, and the Central Valley—the Bay Area appeared most receptive to immigrants' health care needs while San Diego County was by far the most hostile. People and institutions both in and outside San Diego echoed this sentiment consistently.

Disseminating Myths: The Media and Legal Trade

In general, key informants from the San Francisco Bay Area appear to be the best informed of the three regions about public policies affecting immigrant women's health care coverage—specifically public charge and the Port of Entry Fraud Detection programs. In telephone interviews and focus groups, Fresno and San Diego reported a lower degree of awareness. In these two counties, it was apparent that health care providers were less familiar with the term "public charge." While almost all the informants were quite familiar with the concerns of low-income immigrant women in accessing Medi-Cal and utilizing prenatal care, they were unaware of the term itself. For instance, the director of a prenatal care clinic in San Diego replied, "I'm not sure," when we asked if she was aware of the public charge policy. Once we had defined the term, the director responded, "Yeah. I didn't know what it was called." This exchange occurred more often in Fresno and San Diego where there was less policy outreach, making the jargon of "public charge" more obscure. However, the real-life implications of this policy were clearly understood in all regions.

However, even in San Francisco there remains considerable confusion about the details of public charge determinations and their current implications for future immigration status. One's degree of awareness of state and federal policies evidently depends on the availability of resources at the clinic or hospital. This is true across the three regions. Those organizations that have the resources have a key personnel member whose job, in part, is to keep abreast of the policy changes that impact low-income immigrant women. They then filter the information to the front-line social workers, outreach workers, and health practitioners who work directly with the patients and/or the immigrant communities. Unfortunately, many safety net clinics and hospitals do not have such luxuries.

Some of the hostility or "feeding frenzy" in San Diego County can be attributed to the local media—including the ethnic news media—and immigration attorneys. It appears that while both entities serve a valuable purpose, some have also helped to create greater confusion and frighten immigrant communities. A hospital administrator reported that they experienced a "huge increase" in the number of pregnant women who walked into the emergency room with no prenatal care as a result of alarming but ill-informed rumors about Medi-Cal that they had heard on the Spanish language radio. In her experience, the media played an integral part in unnecessarily increasing the overall level of fear among immigrant communities:

> The media makes it harder, I think. Because they talk about laws being passed and then the general public does not understand that it has been held up in the courts. And so, we end up doing a lot of education of these people, that they can apply for Medi-Cal.

In San Diego, the local mainstream English-language media outlets regularly focus on stories of Mexicans receiving costly health care in the United States. A community clinic coordinator recalled some of these cases:

> There were a number of high profile cases where people who lived in Mexico were using the Medi-Cal system to obtain very costly services, like kidney transplant or heart transplant, and those cases really generated a lot of concern in the media and in the public and among politicians that the undocumented were taking advantage of medical services. So, for those reasons, there is a lot of fear in the community about applying for Medi-Cal. And so what we see is that we have a lot more late care patients. We have patients who are afraid to apply for Medi-Cal and who delay getting prenatal care, specifically for that reason.

She went on to add that when media coverage of Medi-Cal cases died down, so did immigrants' fears, and more immigrant women began applying for Medi-Cal again: "Now, we are seeing more patients being willing to apply for Medi-Cal. And I think that is because the prenatal care for the undocumented issue has not been in the news now for a while." This negative assessment of local media effects is unfortunate, given the potentially useful role that both mainstream and ethnic media can play in disseminating important health policy information. Focus group participants reported hearing some attempts at dissemination through Spanish-language newspapers like *La Opinión* and Spanish-language TV. But participants reported that the coverage was inconsistent and confusing. Though many Latino immigrants receive most of their health information from Spanish-language media,[29] respondents reported that health policy coverage was dismal.

Immigration attorneys and other providers of legal advice received equally negative reviews. One exasperated health care advocate had this to say about lawyers' impact on Medi-Cal access, "I think the immigration lawyers were the worst. They have been the slowest . . . I mean, you still hear lawyers now saying to you, two years later, 'Don't apply.'" A clinic director described the confusion that some immigration attorneys have created among her patients: "[T]hey are being told, in [some] cases incorrectly by their immigration attorneys, that if you apply for Medi-Cal, you will be denied residency. And of course, there is the whole public charge issue, which is very complicated, very difficult to explain." While some attorneys in San Diego— including Friends of Legal Aid—have played a significant role in providing sound legal assistance to immigrant communities, their work is outweighed by the disreputable effects of many others in the border region that profess legal authority. In terms of legal advice, the borderland is the wild frontier. Paralegals, notaries, and even check cashing stores charge exorbitant fees to provide legal advice to those in legal limbo. Completely unregulated, temporary legal storefronts open and close overnight to take advantage of the growing confusion. Community clinics and hospital outreach workers try to stay abreast of these businesses. A hospital program manager told me,

> We try to pass out the information to places where people go for legal advice in the immigrant community, which, as you probably know, is often not attorneys per se but paralegals, filing services, notaries, check cashing places. Those are places where people go often in the immigrant community to get so-called legal advice. It's really important for those centers to be aware of the changes. We've often had people say, "Well, you're an outreach worker. Why should I believe you when my attorney says such-and-such?" It's really difficult, it's been difficult for people to take our word over, for example, whom they're paying for legal advice and saying this is really true. So we're trying, not very successfully, to reach them.

Another outreach worker at a nearby hospital told a similar story:

> [I]n our [western] office, which is in a pretty small community, all of a sudden our case load dropped—what was it, by 11 or 12 percent? Like within a few days, we were like what happened? But we found out, we traced it back to someone who gave a talk in the community. It was a notary public that gave a talk that said that WIC was a public charge, I mean our case load plummeted and we had to regain it and let them know and get word out but that's how fast it happens.

An advocate who works with migrant workers in the county explained the significance of notaries public:

The problem is that in Mexico, and in my culture too, I'm from South America, a public notary is somebody that went at least five or six years to college and they are the level of a lawyer. I mean, they are really important, trusted people in the community for the Latino world. So, if I go and talk to a public notary here, I go in with my mind from South America that this guy is the same as a lawyer, so whatever this guy is going to tell me is going to be the gospel truth.

Clear, consistent, reliable, and low-cost legal representation is in great demand among both documented and undocumented immigrants. What currently passes as legal counseling is wholly inadequate, creating an environment that essentially allows for further exploitation of already vulnerable people. The need is particularly acute at the border, where rules and regulations are regularly bent and stretched according to both local and national political inclinations.

San Diego's Safety Net: The Last Frontier

San Diego County boasts the lowest support for safety net health care (for medically indigent adults who are not eligible for Medi-Cal) of any large urban area in the state.[30] San Diego essentially privatized their safety net public hospital beginning in the late 1960s. The University of California, San Diego (UCSD) negotiated a contract to run the San Diego County General Hospital at that time. By 1981, UCSD bought the hospital outright. While UCSD is a state university, the hospital is run by a separate nonlocal, academically oriented governance. The facility, now called UCSD-Hillcrest, promised to continue providing indigent care and the county agreed to make annual payments toward this care. However, county contributions fell precipitously each year, explicitly citing concerns over caring for undocumented immigrants. In the 1990s, the county cut its support of UCSD-Hillcrest from $10 million to a mere $2.1 million in 1999, again citing its displeasure over assisting undocumented immigrants. As permitted under California law, counties are allowed to limit their County Medical Services funds to their legal residents. However, the hospital argues that the free care it does provide to undocumented immigrants is mandated under federal law as medical emergencies. UCSD-Hillcrest remains the leading provider of uncompensated care in the region and most of its safety net support comes directly from state subsidies.[31]

Consequently, county politics that target undocumented immigrants have ramifications for all uninsured and underinsured persons in the border region. Underfunding of safety net health services can negatively affect broader public health goals, including ensuring prenatal care for pregnant women, immunizations for school age children, and health maintenance for working men and women. And at the most fundamental level, basic safety net health care is a matter of social justice. There are currently 47 million uninsured people in the United States,[32] and two-thirds of them are near or below federal poverty levels. Local public hospitals have historically functioned as the last stop for medical care for disadvantaged families. Public hospitals provide not only emergency care but also urgent care and primary care through outpatient clinics.[33] A recent study found that medical costs are the leading cause of personal bankruptcies and that 78 percent of these cases had some form of health insurance.[34] For the low-income and uninsured, health problems can be even more devastating. The basic health care provided by safety net hospitals and clinics constitute a thin, but absolutely necessary buffer, keeping many people from truly hitting bottom.

During the 1990s, as fiscal pressures on public hospitals intensified, the county increasingly looked toward community clinics as low-cost alternatives for medical care for the indigent and working poor.[35] Community clinics have become an important part of the safety net, particularly in the city of San Diego, which lacks a public hospital. The clinics we visited were telling examples of the state of San Diego's safety net health care and its providers. The following sections focus on two such clinics.

Operation Samahan

Operation Samahan is a community clinic located in National City, a few minutes from the U.S.-Mexico border. "Samahan," a Tagalog word meaning "working together," began in 1973 in a small barbershop in downtown San Diego. It was started by a group of Filipino health professionals as a way to assist their elderly. San Diego is home to the largest community of Filipinos in the nation. What began as informal health education gatherings expanded into a nonprofit, private community clinic that serves low-income families from diverse ethnic backgrounds. One of two locations, the clinic site we visited was located in a small one-storied building within a neighborhood of strip malls and fast food chains. I noted these observations in my field notes:

> The place feels a bit barren: no trees, lawns, or shrubs. The small, narrow waiting room was quiet with one family patiently waiting to be called. We've come during the lunch hour (with food), when it's quiet. There is a television that's turned off adjacent to a roll of generic stackable chairs leaning against a wall. There is a worn-looking glass panel that separates the "front" waiting room from the "back."
>
> A friendly receptionist takes us to the back, through locked doors. It was a maze of small rooms, with equipment and people overflowing into the halls. The corridors are so narrow that you must turn to the side to pass another person. Our interview takes place in the break room that also doubles as an office for the nurse practitioners, staff lunch room, and conference room. The room was filled to capacity with people, two desks, a copy machine, a large conference/lunch table, microwave, refrigerator, and a kitchen sink.
>
> During the interview, people moved in and out of the room continuously—something easily done since the room has no door. There are 16 people squeezed into the room. We are sitting and standing everywhere—I'm plugged into a corner next to the copy machine and a desk and I'm trying not to disturb all the paperwork on the desk. It's obvious that many have come for the free lunch. All the health care providers are people of color—mostly Latino/a and Filipino/a. They are very warm.
>
> It is evident, in the course of the focus group interview, that the term "public charge" is not used often at the clinic although fear and frustration are everyday occurrences. They, as exemplified by the space, are functioning at capacity and have been for some time. Concerns regarding public charge are viewed as all part of the usual struggle experienced by immigrants for many years. It is nothing new and they do not have the luxury of alarm at every "new" invention that the state comes up with – many of these providers have been working at the clinic for years and they've pretty much seen it all.

The clinic workers collectively agreed that there is still a great deal of fear about accessing health care for women and children, much less any other kind of public benefits. Their patients, 90 percent of whom are foreign-born, are suspicious of any government program, including the U.S. census. As a clinic of last resort, patients who need specialized care beyond preventive screenings, immunizations, and preliminary diagnosis, are at a loss. A doctor explained,

> One woman fell and needed an MRI—she had some serious injuries—but she didn't have insurance and we could only give her a diagnosis. We have to refer her elsewhere for treatment but she doesn't have the money. She had come to us because she was referred here. I don't know what happened to her. She just left and we never saw her again.

I asked if there was somewhere else she could go. The doctor replied, "No. There is no county hospital. There's no place else." Many uninsured low-income immigrants are left to manage their own health care. Some diagnose themselves or go to alternative community healers. Others medicate themselves through unlicensed backdoor pharmacies. And still others go across the border to Mexico for affordable medical care and pharmaceuticals.

St. Vincent de Paul Family Health Center

St. Vincent's is part of a larger "village" of social services for people who are uninsured and/or homeless. Along with prenatal, medical, psychiatric, and dental care in the Family Health Center, St. Vincent also runs short-term and long-term homeless shelters where it provides chemical dependency classes, counseling groups, parenting classes, and children's services, including a Head Start program. It also has an on-site school for homeless children and distributes over two thousand free meals a day. Off-site, it has a low-income apartment building funded by HUD, a ranch in the mountains for runaway teens, three different houses for people with HIV, and a teen center that houses up to thirty youth at any given time. In the health center, I spoke with five women who work in the prenatal program where they care for between a hundred and a hundred and forty patients at a time. While the actual delivery takes place at UCSD-Hillcrest Hospital, twenty-three volunteer doctors from three area hospitals provide care at

St. Vincent's free of charge. The clinic gets its funding from a combination of federal and state government grants, private foundation support, and donations from thrift stores and local charities. The clinic, in downtown San Diego, was first established by the Catholic diocese and became independently licensed as a nonprofit in 1987. St. Vincent is today's version of a charity hospital for the poor.

The prenatal coordinator described her patient population as mostly Latina, approximately 80 to 85 percent. The remaining 15 percent were homeless white and black women. She said,

> Basically, we see anyone who doesn't have access to health care. We see a lot of patients that are getting prenatal care in another clinic but they couldn't get Medi-Cal and they were referred to us. We have a lot who get presumptive Medi-Cal and then they didn't pursue getting the [regular] Medi-Cal because they are afraid to, or they heard from friends or investigators from the DHS that they were not eligible for that because they are not legal residents here.

When pregnant women are denied public health insurance coverage and they do not have enough money to pay out of pocket, they come to St. Vincent's. Many of the patients at St. Vincent's have complex health issues and the staff must deal with challenging cases each day. A health care advocate recounted three cases that occurred earlier that day—a traumatized twelve-year-old girl who was pregnant after a rape, a homeless mother who went into labor with her fourth child while begging on the street, and a man who was badly burned at his job and was dropped off at the clinic instead of a hospital to avoid paying for his medical treatment. "We really see here in our agency, just some of the most horrible things that happen to people. It's almost a daily occurrence. We have an emergency that comes through our door every day."

For their immigrant patients, fear of the INS and Border Patrol is a constant worry in addition to their health problems. The program manager explained, "Quite a few women have serious illnesses but won't do anything about it because they're afraid that they'll be deported or that their family will be deported or somehow somebody in their family is going to get in trouble for this. No matter what we say or do, it has not changed their opinion." A recent case exemplified her frustrations:

There was one woman who really needed a hysterectomy. She has uterine cancer. She wouldn't go any further with the treatment. A big problem is word of mouth. I don't think it's from the medical profession. It's the people that they relate to on a day-to-day basis telling them, "Oh no, you can't do that, you'll be deported." They believe those people instead of the people who actually can say, "No, no one's going to be notified. You're not going to be deported." There's still the fear of doing it.

I asked what her response was in these situations. She said,

I try to be as strong and firm as I can when I talk to them and try to get them to understand that I don't care where they're from. All I know is they have a medical need that needs treatment. Without it there are going to be serious consequences. I try to take that approach and say, "I'm not going to notify the police or the INS or anybody." Sometimes it's very hard. They keep coming back and they want us to do something, but we tell them what we need to do and they don't want to do it. But they still expect that the medications will cure everything, even though we've already told them repeatedly, "No, you have cancer and this needs to happen in order for you to feel better." They don't go through with it, and we can't force them to go through with it. Yet they keep coming back and saying things are getting worse, "I don't feel good." We go over the whole thing all over again. It can be very frustrating. It's like a revolving circle.

Low-income immigrants with a serious medical condition are in an impossible situation. How much do you risk for medical care? Deportation would devastate your family but so would your illness and death. Many of the patients go to St. Vincent's precisely to avoid governmental surveillance but find that their care requires yet another referral back to a hospital with the appropriate equipment and professional expertise. Going to a hospital will require more forms and more questions. Those lucky enough not to have to worry about deportations but ineligible for Medi-Cal or other health insurance coverage also find themselves in a very difficult situation, in which the high costs can lead to personal bankruptcies and other significant stressors on their family. St. Vincent's program manager discussed the staff's limitations in caring for their patients:

We don't have any cancer drugs here. It's a very basic clinic. If she had the hysterectomy or whatever was needed, that in many cases could stop the cancer from spreading. We don't have chemotherapy here. We have no access to it. Most patients don't have the insurance or the resources for that. They would have to apply for Medi-Cal for the emergency treatment, but then Medi-Cal would report it to the INS.

As the program manager at St. Vincent's stated, "We're the safety net, we're the last resort." And where do these patients go in the end? What do they decide? Health care providers at both Operation Samahan and St. Vincent's say they don't know and do not hear from them again. They disappear.

Women on the Verge

One of the most detrimental aspects of national immigration policy is its fixation on border control. Saskia Sassen notes that this is a pivotal flaw in many countries. She writes, "Yet with all these differences immigration policy and the attendant operational apparatus in all these countries reveal a fundamental convergence regarding immigration. The sovereignty of the state and border control, whether land borders or airports, lie at the heart of the regulatory effort."[36] This popular preoccupation with the literal U.S.-Mexico border is the easy way out. It provides a big bang for the political buck that in reality does little to actually achieve national "security." Instead, we whittle away the most basic civil rights and social safety net for the most vulnerable—both citizens and noncitizens. In considering the state of prenatal care in San Diego County, it is clear that border control cannot guide our national immigration policy. For many women enduring the fear of deportation, it is the thought of their children's placement in foster care in addition to their own displacement south of the border that frightens them.[37] Deportation and its accompanying fears raise questions that are intergenerational, transnational, and constitutional.

The militarization of the southern border also has significant ramifications for health care for low-income uninsured immigrants and Americans who must cobble together a transnational strategy to cover their medical needs. Across the border regions, Mexican health care functioned as the safety net for a number of immigrants and Americans.[38] In southern Texas, one study found that over a six-month period 14 percent of their survey respondents had crossed the border to Mexico for medical treatment, 28 percent for dental care, and almost 30 percent for pharmaceuticals.[39] In the border town of Nogales, Arizona, 14 percent of women and their children sought doctors in Mexico for their regular medical care. [40] And in southern New Mexico, 65 percent of respondents in one survey went to Juarez, Mexico for medical treatment, while another study found that 87 percent of the clients at a rural clinic in New Mexico purchased pharmaceuticals in Juarez during a two-month period. [41] The tightening of the border has restricted all types of movement across the border. In terms of health care, the United States was benefiting from Mexico's relatively affordable medical care. Now these strategies are no longer viable for many of the uninsured.[42]

The assumption of fraud by Medi-Cal applicants worked to discourage all applicants; furthermore, the mistrust of health care providers and the unreliability of legal advice creates a chaotic environment with implications for people beyond the borderlands. The history of public charge designations has profound implications for the extent and reach of the state as well as the volatility of national belonging and the instability of social citizenship. Through passage of the 1996 immigration and welfare reforms, the federal government in effect made the legal illegal for particular members of our society. This uncertainty in the application of the law has implications for everyone.

These policies have a profound reach beyond a person's actual documentation status. Those who "look" or are perceived to be "foreign" are easily caught within the dragnet of a broad range of legislation that applies a reverse logic of law and order —racialized foreigners are assumed to be guilty until they can prove otherwise. And the burden of "proof" continues to rise, particularly after 9/11. Likewise, border control has detrimental gendered impacts that affect women and men, in conjunction with their racialization. Low-income immigrant pregnant women are assumed to be guilty of fraud and criminal dependency. From the point of view of border control, when these women have babies they are engaging in morally suspicious behavior that warrants greater surveillance. Eithne Luibheid writes, "The policing of immigrant women on the basis of sexuality also enabled the discursive production of exclusionary forms of nationalism that took concrete shape in immigration laws and procedures, but extended well beyond the border to produce particular visions of the U.S. nation and citizenry."[43] As reproduction becomes increasingly central to "border control," anxieties about national boundaries become embedded within immigrant women's bodies. Giving birth becomes an act of illegal crossing and the resulting child is politically and socially marginalized as the next generation of public charge, regardless of his or her status as a legal citizen. The growing encroachment of state control upon women's bodies, the explanation of immigrant poverty in terms of an intractable underclass, the disregard for children's rights, and the dilution of the meaning of citizenship and its accompanying rights are all serious concerns that affect all members of society. The decision to link the core of our national identity and political consciousness to the laws and procedures that form the U.S.-Mexico border has been shortsighted and disastrous for everyone.

Consequently, a person's immigration and citizenship status are *not* the point of these federal and state policies. Though these laws designate a complicated matrix of eligibility for particular services and protections, (legal or illegal, qualified or unqualified, and so on), the fact is that the state can and has altered the meaning of and rights associated with these statuses. Eligibility, then, has nothing to do with de jure citizenship. But citizenship remains significant as a state mechanism that allows for the possibility of inclusion.

This then leads to the question of inclusion as a goal for social justice. Not only does inclusion appear to be impossible, but the more you want it, the more elusive it becomes. Like illusions of consumptive satisfaction via capitalist accumulation, efforts toward inclusion within a capitalist system may simply function as a tool for behavioral discipline. Immigrants are already included; in fact, immigrants are fundamental to the current functioning of neoliberal capitalism. And the way in which immigrants are included actually produces injustice for many in order to benefit the few. The central focus for immigrant social justice cannot rest simply on inclusion within the state. As noted, immigrants are already included, just differentially so (i.e., as cheap labor). In this way, true immigrant rights lie beyond what is dictated by neoliberal capital doctrine. Instead, it is a central site for resistance against inequality and the pursuit of greater social justice for all working people.

CHAPTER 6

Bearing the Burden of Welfare Reform

> If I'm not who you say I am, then
> you're not who you think you are.
> —James Baldwin[1]

On September 9, 2009, Representative Joe Wilson interrupted President Barack Obama's speech to a joint session of Congress by loudly shrieking, "You lie!" This unprecedented outburst occurred when the president was specifically addressing the issue of undocumented immigrants' access within his new health care reform plan. As a *New York Times* editorial later stated, "Illegal immigration is an all-purpose policy explosive."[2] Why is this? What makes this issue so volatile? Undocumented immigrants are and will remain ineligible for Medicaid under the president's new plan.[3] And yet, the ensuing debate over whether Rep. Wilson should have formally apologized on the senate floor spurred a flood of campaign donations for and against this little known representative from South Carolina. It is evident that "the immigrant" triggers a fundamental national anxiety regarding access to essential public goods such as health care. The politics of deservingness and social belonging have clearly entered a stridently hostile era and concerns about immigrant dependency and personal responsibility have reached a level of moral panic.

In this book, I document the formal return of the immigrant as a "public charge," setting the precedent for this later moment of outrageous rancor. Using the vantage point of health care workers at the front line of this heated exchange, I investigate how the politics of immigration, health care, and welfare are intertwined. After interviewing almost two hundred key health care social workers, medical personnel, and policy advocates who work closely with low-income pregnant immigrant women, I found that the major welfare and immigration reforms passed in the 1990s had devastating effects on health care access for low-income immigrants, which in turn have larger reverberating implications for the nation. The legal consequences of these policy enactments alone have historic significance. However, the broader social significance is even greater.

In chronicling these policy effects, access to prenatal care for low-income Latina and Asian immigrant women is an important site because these women embody a political subjectivity that make them a walking target for the expression of a number of national anxieties about race, class, gender/sexuality, and nation. This in turn makes services geared toward them deeply contentious. The mere accusation of public charge functions as a powerful state mechanism to promote a neoliberal understanding of personal responsibility and criminal dependency.

Beginning with the Port of Entry Fraud Detection programs at the Mexico-U.S. border and at the Los Angeles and San Francisco airports, the State of California specifically targeted immigrant women with children as an innovative approach to addressing health care fraud. Rather than viewing these practices as isolated events, I see them as part of a concerted effort by various government and private entities to control the quantity and quality of our citizenry. Debates regarding who should have access to public services such as health care are important avenues for understanding the shifting boundaries of society and its relationship with its various members.

Social Citizenship in the Neoliberal Age

Federal welfare and immigration reforms and state health care policy changes are clearly targeted at low-income immigrants, despite the continued need for their labor. Embedded within this dilemma is the implicit question of national *belonging*—of social citizenship—particularly for immigrants with limited means. Social citizenship is understood as the final stage of modern citizenship that goes beyond civil and political rights to social belonging. T. H. Marshall, in his seminal work "Citizenship and Social Class" (1964), defines this final stage of citizenship as the ability to "share in the full social heritage and to live the life of a civilized being according to the standards prevailing in the society."[4]

Nancy Fraser and Linda Gordon extend Marshall's ideas in their examination of why the United States never developed this ideal stage of citizenship, which embody a distinct set of rights as "full members of society entitled to equal respect." Analyzing contemporary welfare politics, they highlight a two-tiered "contract-versus-charity" dichotomy, which differentially privileges waged labor (as contract) at the same time that it derogates women's unpaid care work (as charity). Historian Barbara Nelson calls this the "two-channel" welfare state model, which ideologically separates public support for wage earners from that of childbearers.[5] This ideology was administratively enforced in the Progressive Era when benefits devised for mostly male, white industrial workers were strongly linked to welfare capitalism and scientific management, while those devised for a select group of mothers (impoverished white widows with young children) were linked to the poor law tradition and the administrative practices of the Charity Organization Society movement.[6] Consequently, the Workman's Compensation program was judicial, public, and routinized in its administration while the "Mother's Aid" program was characterized by "moralistic, diffuse decision criteria, high levels of bureaucratic discretion, and many levels of managerial cross-checking. While it was designed to be efficient and accountable, it was also cumbersome and repeatedly intrusive."

By the 1990s, the growing presence of immigrants of color further complicated the concept of social citizenship. And while Marshall's frame of citizenship as membership of a community, not merely the nation-state, opened our discourse on multiple levels, the role of race in relation to class and gender/sexuality in constructing social citizenship remains a central and unfinished priority.[7] Far more complex than a simple dichotomous classification between the legal and the illegal, the documented or the undocumented, Kathleen Canning and Sonya O. Rose explain that citizenship is

one of the most porous concepts in contemporary academic parlance
[that] can be understood as a political status assigned to individuals
by states, as a relation of belonging to specific communities, or as a set
of social practices that defines the relationships between peoples and
states and among people with communities.[8]

Citizenship, then, is a normative ideology that dictates how particular
members of a given nation-state are included or excluded at particular
historical moments. As porous as this concept is, specific social markers
that denote one's race, class, and gender have been consistently relevant
in determining one's social citizenship status throughout U.S. history. For
example, Richard Delgado outlines the current implications of restricting
citizenship to white men of property during the birth of the U.S. constitution.[9] For those who do not possess the "proper," largely ascribed characteristics of race (being white), class (propertied), and gender (heterosexual
male), making a claim upon the state is an everyday struggle. What is a
taken-for-granted *entitlement* for one person becomes a morally questionable *handout* for another—usually based upon the person's race, class, and
gender.

The moralistic language constructed during the Progressive Era is ever-
present in the current public obsession over the dependency and responsibility of immigrants—so much so that even scholars critical of welfare
reform do not venture far from the confining discourse of individual behavior. In his work on welfare-to-work programs, Sanford Schram observes
that this approach neglects the social context created by this legislation
and instead "imputes to the poor the identity of self-interested, utility-max-
imizing individuals who need to be given the right incentives so that they
will change their behavior."[10] Interestingly, these character traits are viewed
as quintessentially "rational" in neoliberal terms for those of privilege, and
yet when ascribed to the disadvantaged, it becomes a way to portray them
as morally deficient for unfairly taking "advantage" of services or programs
for which they do not deserve. These "incentives" are disciplinary measures that look more like punishments. A prime example is welfare reform,
which was designed to instill a work ethic in mothers who are assumed to
be too lazy to raise their children. Jane Collins argues that welfare reform,
which construes poverty as the result of individual dysfunctional choices,
has forced low-income mothers to work longer hours outside the home.[11]

Given that poverty is actually a "politically constructed, institutionally mediated, legally regulated process,"[12] greater numbers of working mothers has not led to poverty alleviation. Rather, it has led to smaller numbers of women being eligible for welfare benefits while poverty rates have increased. Unfortunately, mainstream understandings of poverty remain mired in the realm of individual dependency and responsibility.

Apparently, we are still looking for the "welfare queen" driving a Cadillac instead of focusing on the social, structural context of poverty. The crown is now shared with low-income immigrants, particularly those from Latin America. This is why public charge provisions will continue to remain a part of the nation-state's repertoire of exclusionary mechanisms. Historically, the argument of public burden has been particularly useful against immigrant women. In assessing the impact of immigration and welfare policies on immigrant women workers, apparently it is irrelevant whether someone is "dependent" or "irresponsible." What makes one person responsible renders the next person irresponsible. There is no consistency in its application. Instead, the underlying point of these laws is to maintain a vulnerable and necessary reserve pool of labor through capitalist discipline, as articulated by Aihwa Ong.[13] Consequently, it is possible for immigrant women workers to be both responsibly and irresponsibly *independent* as well as *dependent* upon the state. Either way, low-income immigrant women are always excessive or deficient in relation to the state. What is consistent within this logical knot is that one's designation as "good" or "bad" for the state is based on whether an individual is acting in a way that benefits capital accumulation. For instance, despite the political rhetoric promoting independence from the state, some level of dependency is seen as responsible, particularly for low-income people, since poverty is largely understood as resulting from bad decision making by the individual. This paternalism and its ability to instill a sense of shame and social vulnerability is one of the most powerful mechanisms for discipline. In fact, some amount of connection, documentation, and surveillance is enforced not just on immigrants, but on all "good" citizens—enough to benefit capital markets as cheap labor but not so much that it incurs additional, irresponsible costs. The threshold of irresponsibility apparently fluctuates depending upon one's social status, based on race, class, gender/sexuality, and nation. Irresponsible costs for low-income immigrants of color include social service use, health care access, pregnancies, and livable wages—all of which are taken for granted by those deemed "deserving."

Low-income Latina and Asian immigrants further complicate this shortsighted understanding, given their paradoxical construction both as public burdens and as (too) hardworking. In other words, their social citizenship is denied on the basis that they are lazy but also because they take other people's jobs. Low-income immigrant women fall between the increasingly large cracks in the two-channel welfare state. Historian Alice Kessler-Harris writes, "[W]hen the federal government began, in the 1930s, to legislate an array of social benefits and tax incentives designed to ensure economic security for the American family, it attached its most valuable benefits not to families but to wage work."[14] By linking old age pensions and unemployment insurance to jobs, beneficiaries were treated as independent and upstanding citizens. Kessler-Harris adds, "Work, wage work, had long marked a distinction among kinds of citizens: intimately tied to identity, it anchored nineteenth-century claims to political participation. But when the federal government linked wage work to tangible, publicly provided rewards, employment emerged as a boundary line demarcating different kinds of citizenship."[15]

Wage labor, then, forms the basis of social citizenship. Yet, low-income immigrant women are denied national inclusion regardless of their employment. And if they become pregnant, they are also excluded as public burdens for using health care—again, regardless of whether or not they are employed. Wage labor apparently does not function in the same way for everyone. The logic of public charge is not predicated on immigrants' actual lived experience. Immigrants are assumed burdens unless proven otherwise—and in the policies of the neoliberal 1990s, the accusation of public charge reached a level of criminality and the burden of proof to show otherwise was nearly impossible.

The Irresponsibility of State and Capital

In the 1990s, the responsibility of the state and capital dwindled while the public became increasingly incensed about the perceived irresponsibility of low-income individuals. The neoliberal language of personal responsibility allowed for greater privatization to replace social protections that were once an obligation of employers and the state.[16] Lisa Duggan writes that welfare reform promotes the privatization of the costs of social reproduction, along with the care of human dependency needs, through personal responsibility exercised in the family and in civil society—thus shifting costs from state agencies to individuals and households. This process accompanies the call for tax cuts that deplete public coffers, but leave more money in the "private" hands of the wealthy.[17]

In his now classic article from 1976, sociologist Michael Burawoy wrote that the economic value of migrant labor was predicated on the transnational separation of work and family: "One consequence of a system of migrant labor is the externalization, to an alternate economy and/or state, of certain costs of labor-force renewal—costs normally borne by the employer and/or state of employment.[18] More recently, Tamar Diana Wilson has argued that the anti-immigrant legislations that increasingly militarized the border, sharpened threats of deportations, and denied social citizenship, were an effort to "re-separate" the process of reproduction (family) and production (wage-work).[19] This reseparation comes as the presence of Latina and Asian immigrants increases and assumes greater permanence.

Social programs such as the Port of Entry Fraud Detection program in California shift the responsibility of reproduction back to "other" nation-states.[20] And as these social programs make clear, this reseparation requires intense state regulation—or statecraft. Such heavy-handed regulations, which force families to repay the state for benefits appropriately received, are needed because there is in fact nothing "natural" about the rationale driving this separation. Those who are not citizens or native-born are no more dependent, lazy, or criminal than anyone else—to believe otherwise requires structural reinforcement. Neoliberalism works to mask this strenuous effort. Kanishka Jayasuriya writes, "Though neo liberalism is often identified in terms of the retreat and withdrawal of the state from the allocation of social and material goods, I propose that its more profound impact lies in the way it entrenches new forms of social and economic regulation of the market."[21] He argues that welfare is statecraft and that this form of social regulation will yield even greater influence in facilitating a new relationship between citizen and the state—that of market citizenship. The "social" becomes wholly absorbed into the "economic," so that concerns about social citizenship are replaced by economic

citizenship, wherein the pursuit of inclusion and participation is economically defined. In this way, Jayasuriya views neoliberalism as being much
more than an economic program. Rather, it is "a set of often diverse political or statecraft projects intended to reshape the boundaries of the state
and also the nature of the relationship between state and civil society."[22]

In framing welfare as statecraft, a key understanding derived from neoliberalism is that this is a *process* in development. It is a project in the
making. And while "unmaking" something (policy, in particular) may not
be as easy, it is not impossible. At every level in California, a number of immigrants, their advocates, and safety net providers worked to devise ways
to alleviate (if not overturn) the effects of federal and state legislation.
While the true impact of their efforts may be debatable, individuals and
organizations provided some measure of social belonging to their patients
by working hard to encourage immigrants to use health care, for which
they are eligible. The following section outlines some of the coordinated
efforts by various organizations to mitigate the public charge fears of pregnant immigrant women.

Ensuring Belonging: Programmatic Strategies

At the federal level, advocates applied persistent and organized pressure
on the INS to provide clearer guidelines to exempt the use of Medicaid
benefits from determinations of "public charge" when applicants applied
for a change in immigration status. Organizations also addressed the need
for a systematic and continuous flow of timely information at the state,
county, and community levels to ensure appropriate decision making
based on accurate and up-to-date information. Below are some examples
of the measures taken by the advocates and providers we interviewed.

State and local advocacy organizations for immigrants worked to
provide clear, linguistically appropriate information through organized
channels, which respond to the specific concerns articulated by both immigrants and their caregivers. Through their own organizations and in
collaborative efforts with other agencies, advocates tried to clarify the
specificities of welfare and immigration legislation as it relates to the use
of Medi-Cal. Because of the vague and confusing implementation of the
new laws, advocates tried to clarify the issues and respond to the new regulations and practices with a steady flow of information designed to raise

community awareness and to enable providers to make sound decisions regarding their immigrant patients' care.

Legal advocates and immigrant health organizations also collaborated in order to better disseminate accurate and up-to-date information to health providers and other immigrant organizations. One of the organizations we interviewed[23] was a collaborative initiative called the Health Consumer Alliance. The Alliance consists of the National Health Law Program, the Western Center for Law and Poverty, and six consumer education programs. The Alliance was established through the National Health Law Program, to provide ombudsman-type advocacy for health consumers in six managed care regions: Fresno, Los Angeles, Orange, San Diego, San Mateo, and San Francisco counties. The plan also includes a hotline and a source for streamlined education and advocacy within each county. An immigration attorney described the center in San Diego, as follows: "It will be the first of its kind in the country because it will actually not just take phone calls to try to help people through managed care, but will also advocate both systematically, policy-wise and individually on behalf of consumers, and we're going to concentrate on poor consumers to begin with."

The California Immigrant Welfare Collaborative is another example of a partnership among legal, immigrant, and health advocates. Its purpose is to enhance the effectiveness of advocacy at the state level, and to inform immigrants of the impact of legislation on their communities and their access to health care. The Collaborative consists of four organizations: one is in the Bay Area (the Northern California Coalition for Immigrant Rights) and three are in the Los Angeles area (the National Immigration Law Center, the Coalition for Humane Immigrant Rights of Los Angeles, and the Asian Pacific American Legal Center of Southern California). Formed in August 1996 in reaction to Proposition 187, the Collaborative is an organization devoted to federal, state, and local advocacy to preserve immigrant rights to public benefits. Its work to date has focused on legislative advocacy, as well as provider and public outreach, and education about welfare and immigration reforms through regular distribution of informational updates on such issues as public charge, prenatal care, and Healthy Families.[24]

Other effective advocacy organizations are the Legal Aid Society in San Diego, El Concilio in Fresno, and Maternal and Child Health Access in Los

Angeles. Though not created in response to the welfare or immigration legislation, they have made significant strides in mitigating the stigma of health care use in the communities they serve and helping women access pregnancy-only Medi-Cal. They offer legal counsel to immigrants about their immigration status and welfare applications. The Legal Aid Society is a traditional organization of lawyers offering pro bono services. El Concilio is a local, grassroots organization serving communities in the Central Valley. The organization consists of two staff members who provide legal advice to immigrants with regard to health care and immigration law cases. Maternal and Child Health Access was formed as a community-based organization to provide direct services to immigrant women and their families in the community, as well as training and education to other community-based organizations in the Los Angeles area.

In addition, legal advocates help to create a more positive view of the use of Medi-Cal in the minds of immigrants. To encourage them to view Medi-Cal as an opportunity rather than an obstacle, advocates developed state legislation that simplified the Medi-Cal application (SB 780 and AB 1015). The legislation addressed such important issues as language access and eligibility standards and procedures in order to make the process more user-friendly and less intrusive for applicants. As one state advocate noted, although the initiatives developed on the Medi-Cal front are not specific to immigrants, they will have a significant impact on immigrants by making the application process less intimidating. Other proposed state legislation included efforts to funnel state funds directly to community-based organizations in California for education and community outreach in order to increase public awareness of the rights open to low-income communities and to build trust.

To address people's fears about the application process for Medi-Cal, providers are trying to do as much as possible to prepare women at the health care site. Some community clinics and hospitals across the state with significant numbers of low-income patients have a DSS "outstation" on the premises. Some clinics also have legal advocates on staff to help patients within the trusted clinic environment to address legal questions about the Medi-Cal application and public charge issues. Clinics and hospitals have also utilized outreach workers to approach immigrant families in their own communities to build a sense of trust among those seeking health care. One clinic administrator said:

> We recently hired an outreach worker . . . and I think that there is a sig-
> nificant plus for us, in that she, of course, is Hispanic, and she has been
> able to go out into the areas where [Hispanics] are and talk to them
> about the importance of prenatal care, and assist them with some of
> their questions and help them to get in, to navigate the system and re-
> assure them that they will not be reported to Immigration ... and that
> sort of thing. So, I think outreach is really critical.

Some clinics we interviewed have also played a key part in advocacy at
the state and county levels. A few clinic representatives, like those from
Asian Health Services in Oakland, had their own policy analysts to help
them assume advocacy roles. Asian Health Services developed a program
called the Language Cooperative, which serves as a countywide resource,
supplying language interpreters to their own providers and contracting
to local hospitals, private doctors, and health maintenance organizations.
Along with La Clínica de la Raza, Asian Health Services is part of an initiative called Community Voices, which was developed to respond to immigrant health care legislation and to develop an affordable insurance product that would be marketable to immigrant communities.

Finally, clinic and hospital providers in several counties developed alternative payment mechanisms for immigrants who may be reluctant to go
through the Medi-Cal eligibility process. Health care providers described
their fears of not being fully compensated for services if women were unwilling or unable to establish their eligibility. They feared losing staff members if they lost additional revenue through uncompensated care and were
uncertain about what to do while decisions regarding Medi-Cal coverage
were pending. In response, many clinics developed and promoted cash
payment programs for women without insurance. One clinic in San Diego
initiated a nationally recognized "Fund for Moms," a microloan program
in coordination with a local bank. The clinic also provides loans through
its own resources to women who do not qualify for bank loans. Providers'
payment programs usually involve financial packages that can be paid in
installments. Fee-for-service arrangements, which would enable women to
pay per visit, were generally avoided since they ran the risk of immigrants
making fewer visits to reduce total out-of-pocket costs. The providers emphasized the importance of flexibility and patience with regard to payment. They noted that most women who are financially able are willing to

pay for their services but that they need considerable time to accumulate the required resources.

As a program, Presumptive Eligibility (PE) for Medi-Cal during pregnancy represents both an opportunity and a risk from the provider's perspective. By giving pregnant women sixty days of prenatal coverage while the Medi-Cal application is being reviewed, it enables staff to encourage women to come in early for care.[25] Clinic administrators have sometimes combined Presumptive Eligibility with a self-pay plan to ensure both the provision and compensation for the care. Unlike prenatal care, the hospital costs of delivery were more difficult to adequately address through payment packages because the hospital costs were generally much higher. Some clinics provided a prenatal-only package so that the cost was not insurmountable. This arrangement allowed the women to deal with hospital delivery charges in some other manner. Some clinics and hospitals also offered a total financial package including prenatal and delivery services. However, in the end, providers acknowledged that there were some women for whom all of these alternatives were out of their reach.

The Question of Burden

Increasingly, health care is privatized into the home and out of the hospital. As with other industries, the structure of health care services has also transformed under neoliberalism. Production became more "flexible" as services were fragmented into "parts" through greater specialization and dispersed to alternative, cheaper locations. In order to save costs, hospitals have increasingly "externalized" health services to nonmedical sites, including nursing facilities and private homes. At the same time, women are increasingly entering the paid labor market as more households experience a decline in income.[26] Carolyn Cartier writes,

> Economic restructuring in health care services combined with the widespread entry of women into the workforce and demographic shifts in the US population have resulted in new health care needs and reorganization of health services provision. As the baby boomer generation looks ahead to retirement and end of life, more people will need long-term

care, and the traditional care providers within families—women—will not be readily available to step into care-giving roles.[27]

The combination of these social factors—neoliberal economic restructuring, women care providers leaving the home, and elderly baby boomers—has produced intense demand for affordable (i.e., cheap) home health care workers. And given the very difficult working conditions, it is immigrant women workers with limited employment choices who fill this labor market.[28]

The "externalization" of hospital costs simply shifts the burden of care to the patient, his or her family, and the home health care provider. Likewise, neoliberalism simply restructures the burden or cost of (re)production elsewhere—into the private sphere or to other nations. As the United States increasingly relegates its role as provider of public safety net services to others, individual families struggle to find affordable care and migrant workers continue to fulfill the growing gap. Immigrants caught in the midst of this outsourcing are in a very vulnerable position as many American families experience the stress of increasing demands on their diminished time and income. Defying logic, low-income immigrants in this scenario are constructed as a public charge—burdensome, inadequate bodies always marginal to the state.

Market logic has always belittled the range of human capabilities. However, the market was viewed as one of a number of powerful rationales of human interaction and organization. In the 1990s, as articulated by the welfare, immigration, and health care legislations discussed in this book, the neoliberal twist of this logic has taken a grave, formidable turn in its depth and breadth. Aihwa Ong argues that "individual internalization of neoliberal traits" is now the new norm.[29] Ong views neoliberalism as a political philosophy that has been internalized to such as a degree as to make it "normal" or taken for granted. Similarly, political theorist Wendy Brown identifies contemporary neoliberalism as

> more than a set of free market economic policies that dismantle welfare states and privatize public services in the North, make wreckage of efforts at democratic sovereignty or economic self-direction in the South, and intensify income disparities everywhere. Certainly neoliberalism comprises these effects, but as a political rationality, it also involves a specific and consequential organization of the social, the subject, and the state.[30]

Here, Brown argues that neoliberalism has become a normative political rationality that has restructured the meaning of citizenship. By limiting social membership to individual entrepreneurs and consumers, citizenship is reduced to "self-care" and is "divested of any orientation toward the common, thereby undermining an already weak investment in an active citizenry and an already thin concept of a public good from a liberal democratic table of values."[31] Brown warns that the implications for the state and the practice of democracy are serious. It could be reduced to an individual consumer good with no attention to issues of equality, difference, and public accountability.

The future of many federal and state benefits for the working class and poor is in dire straits. Certainly, California's Medicaid programs face grave cuts, if not outright elimination. And in the midst of all this uncertainty, what remains is our fixation on rooting out those deemed criminally dependent upon the state and irresponsible in their behavior. In reviewing the amount of effort and time devoted to criminalizing immigrants, one has to wonder why. Sunaina Maira argues that citizenship within neoliberalism is based on "the legal and economic regulation of citizens and workers,"[32] and that this regulation is constructed in the context of the need for a low-wage, undocumented, or noncitizen labor pool. In effect, immigrant labor not only fuels globalization but is also used to mask the realities of social inequality and the imperial nature of neoliberal notions of citizenship that presumably promote liberal-democratic ideals of individual freedom.[33]

And in the age of "terrorism," immigrants are more important than ever as politically potent symbols that justify greater militarized sovereignty and nativist nationalism. While a flexible, underground reserve pool of labor may be the ultimate neoliberal dream, immigrants are also useful as social problems (morally deviant, criminally inclined, terrorists/enemies of the state) to be solved. Consequently, immigrants are central in a very complex political and economic struggle. And those who work as advocates with these communities must strike a very delicate balance between multiple interests while at the same arguing for justice, particularly for pregnant immigrant women. Dorothy Roberts notes the significance of immigrant women as a powerful symbol of our nation's boundaries and the conditions of citizenship within it. She writes,

An important strand of political theory regarding immigration holds that exclusion at the border is necessary for political citizenship to flourish within. But the regulation of membership in the national community does not only involve patrolling our borders to prevent disfavored groups from entering. The present nativism also includes efforts to restrict who may give birth to citizens within the nation's boundaries.[34]

The struggle against welfare reform identifies the practice of neoliberalism and its logic. The fight for immigrant rights—in which the value of a human being is beyond market costs and benefits—is a crucial site for global social justice. The struggle against public charge legislation illuminates the need to wrestle the state from capital so that its main function is no longer to secure private property rights on behalf of markets. Most important, we need to challenge the normative assumptions of market-based citizenship and the notion that individual freedom is guaranteed by freedom of the market. Rather, the struggle for immigrant health care makes it is clear that free enterprise is anything but free or normal.

Since 1987, when Gloria Anzaldúa wrote her seminal text, *Borderlands/ La Frontera*, borders have taken on increasingly fearful tones, with triple layers of technological surveillance and a vast arsenal of deportation tools, and those who cross them have had to take ever greater risks. The oppositional, revolutionary possibilities in the flexibility and mobility of the borderlands exalted by Chicana feminists have been wrestled away and appropriated by global capitalists. It is time to take them back for all our sakes.

Research Methods

From September 1998 to December 2001, 196 participants were inter-viewed in two different stages for this study. Using qualitative methods, key respondents were interviewed to document the impact of recent im-migration and welfare reforms on health care access for low-income preg-nant immigrant women in California. Initially, we focused on four areas of the state that together comprise more than 75 percent of California's foreign-born population: San Diego, Los Angeles, the San Francisco Bay Area, and the Central Valley. These four areas were selected because they include the majority of the state's urban and nonurban immigrant popula-tion. This sampling strategy provided "information-rich"[1] interviews that il-luminated the variation of experiences among the many immigrant groups that reside in California.

In this first stage, we selected a purposive sample of 101 key individuals from 76 different organizations knowledgeable about pregnant immigrant women's health care in California since 1994. These respondents came from three different types of organizations to reveal the multiple dimen-sions of immigrant women's experiences with health services. These orga-nizations include:

Safety net providers: County and community hospitals and clinics.
Immigrant organizations: National, state, and local legal and health policy
    advocates.
G*overnment agencies*: State and county public health, Medi-Cal, and social
    service agencies.

We spoke with 41 safety net providers, 35 immigrant health care advocates, and 25 government personnel across the state of California.

To select particular organizations and individuals, we relied on a combination of sampling measures. The first was a "snowball" method, which identified cases of interest from knowledgeable individuals. For this project, we began the snowball process by contacting government agencies, safety net clinics and hospitals, and immigrant advocacy organizations known to the research team. A careful literature and Internet web search, and strategic calls to other researchers and policy advocates were an important part of this process. We then asked these initial contacts to identify other key individuals in the field. This process continued until no new relevant cases were identified, thereby signaling an exhaustive search.

The list compiled by snowball sampling was then narrowed or stratified by particular government agencies, safety net providers, and immigrant advocacy organizations. This step helped facilitate comparisons across the different categories. Finally, a third sampling method, "criterion," was incorporated to narrow the cases even further. Individuals within the stratified sample were selected according to particular criteria (i.e., position, title, and so on). Criterion is a useful tool for quality assurance among the interviewees. The selection for community clinics and hospitals included in the sample required that they be among the three largest providers to foreign-born or ethnic patients in the county area.[2]

In choosing interviewees, our goal was to identify "individuals who possess special knowledge, status, or communication skills, who are willing to share their knowledge and skills with the researcher and who have access to perspectives."[3] The screening process to identify respondents began with several telephone conversations. The respondents fell into seven general categories: legal advocate, immigrant advocate, clinical practitioner, coordinator, director, outreach/social worker, and eligibility worker. We experienced little resistance to our requests for interviews. On the whole, the individuals we approached showed interest in the issue and readily agreed to the interview. However, there were difficulties in the scheduling of interviews.

Understandably, safety net providers and advocates for this vulnerable population were extremely busy, and finding the time for interviews proved to be a significant constraint. As a result, telephone interviews were preferred over face-to-face interviews. However, some face-to-face group interviews were conducted in the Bay Area, at the respondents' request.[4]

We preceded each interview by providing a short description of the research project (verbal and written) and an introductory letter with our contact information. We also provided individual confidentiality, unless explicitly refused. We conducted both formal and informal interviews. The formal interviews were semistructured with specific core interview questions for all respondents, identified through criterion sampling. Questions, probes, and prompts were asked in an open-ended format. Interviews lasted thirty minutes to an hour. We used an audio recorder, with the written permission of the interviewees, to supplement our notes and for data coding and analysis purposes. The face-to-face group interviews were also audiotaped.[5]

All audio recordings of the interviews were transcribed. Also, all additional notes from both formal and informal interviews by all the interviewers were compiled to begin the coding process. To do this, a template or analysis guide was applied to the text. Rather than a statistical process, this method of analysis discerns themes, patterns, and interrelationships in an interpretive manner. Built into this method is the ability to undertake revisions after reading and analyzing the text. The template was derived from a summary reading of the text and follows the issues outlined in the core interview questions. The responses to each core interview question by all interviewees were analyzed separately. The data analysis process involved multiple coders. We began by first reviewing the transcripts and initiating an open coding process.[6]

We identified and investigated five main issues affecting low-income pregnant immigrant women: first, access to Medi-Cal; second, access to pregnancy-related services; third, utilization of community clinics; fourth, utilization of hospitals; and fifth, strategies immigrant women and their health care providers use to reduce the barriers to health care. My central objective was to assess the impact of the welfare reform law that had passed just two years prior. We came away from these interviews with a clear sense of fear on behalf of immigrant women's access to the health care for which they are eligible. Informants identified this fear as a "chilling effect," the result of recent policy implementations that marked low-income immigrants as potential public charges.

A little over a year later, I returned to the respondents and interviewed them once again to document any changes that might have taken place in their access to health care. This time, I limited my sample size to three geographical areas to provide greater depth: the San Francisco Bay Area, Fresno County, and San Diego County. The San Francisco Bay Area remained the northern California sample, Fresno the rural, Central Valley sample, and San Diego the southern California sample. However, we found a high turnover rate in these positions, making it difficult to locate the same individuals we had interviewed earlier. Consequently, we spoke with the people who had been newly hired in the same positions whenever possible. In some instances, the positions had been eliminated altogether. My objective in this second phase of data collection was to document whether the women and their health care providers experienced less confusion in the aftermath of a number of key attempts by different government agencies to clarify federal and state health care policies for immigrants. I paid particular attention to federal policy clarifications regarding public charge.

We interviewed a total of 95 key informants in this second stage. Telephone interviews were conducted between August 2000 and November 2000 and lasted thirty minutes to an hour. We also conducted two focus groups in the Fresno region, two in the San Francisco Bay Area, and four in the San Diego region. Overall, 63 participants from these regions participated in focus groups. Each of these meetings ran for one to two hours. All interviews were audiotaped and transcribed. The transcript and field notes and discussion from the debriefing were used for this analysis. As in the first stage, I reviewed the transcripts and initiated an open coding process. I then read through all the transcripts repeatedly, theoretically working through the main issues that were most prominent in the data. In the end, the arguments and narratives presented here reflect the concerns and hopes articulated by the informants.

APPENDIX B

Summary of Provisions of Federal Welfare and Immigration Reform Affecting Health Care Access

The 1996 Personal Responsibility and Work Opportunities Act (PRWORA) created two categories of immigrant eligibility for means-tested programs: "qualified" and "not qualified." Those considered qualified include:

Lawful permanent residents (LPRs)

Refugees, persons granted asylum or withholding of deportation/removal, and conditional entrants

Persons granted parole by the Department of Homeland Security for a period of at least one year

Cuban and Haitian entrants

Certain abused immigrants, their children, and/or their parents.

In addition, these qualified immigrants must have arrived prior to August 22, 1996 (when PRWORA was enacted) in order to be eligible. All other immigrants, both documented and undocumented, are considered "not qualified." Those arriving after August 22, 1996 are ineligible for nonemergency Medicaid for the first five years in the United States. In years six through ten, the sponsor's resources are counted, or "deemed," in the eligibility review. Also, those states choosing to provide state or local public benefits to "not qualified" immigrants must enact new laws to do so.

The 1996 Illegal Immigration Reform and Immigrant Responsibility Act (IIRIRA) required sponsors to demonstrate their ability to maintain the sponsored immigrant at a minimum annual income of 125 percent of the federal poverty level. This policy also made the affidavits of support legally enforceable for the costs of certain means-tested programs. In addition, it required states requesting reimbursement for emergency Medicaid services to unqualified immigrants to verify the immigration status

TABLE APPENDIX B
Immigrant Eligibility for Federal Medicaid Benefits

Program	Qualified Immigrants (before 8/22/1996)	Qualified Immigrants (after 8/22/1996)	Not Qualified Immigrants
Emergency Medicaid (includes labor and delivery)	Eligible	Eligible	Eligible
Medicaid(full scope)	Eligible	Restricted*	Restricted**

*Eligible only if: 1) Were granted asylum or refugee status or withholding of deportation/removal, Cuban/ Haitian entrant, Amerasian, or Iraqi or Afghan special immigrant status; 2) Veteran, active duty military, including spouse, unmarried surviving spouse, or child; 3) Receiving federal Foster Care; 4) Have been in "qualified" immigrant status for 5 years or more; 5) Children under 21 (state option); and 6) Pregnant women (state option).
**Eligible only if: 1) Were receiving SSI on 8/22/96 (in states that link Medicaid to SSI eligibility); 2) Certain American Indians born abroad; 3) Victims of trafficking and their derivative beneficiaries; 4) Lawfully residing children under 21 (state option); and 5) Lawfully residing pregnant women (state option).
Source: National Immigration Law Center, April 2010.

of patients for whom the payment was made. However, it also amended PRWORA to extend nonemergency public benefits to a group of battered or abused spouses and required the Attorney General and the Secretary of the Department of Health and Human Services to establish procedures to provide proof of citizenship in a "nondiscriminatory manner."

Despite all these changes, labor and delivery remains available for all immigrants, regardless of documentation status and time of arrival, as a form of emergency health care.

NOTES

CHAPTER 1

1. All names of interviewees are pseudonyms unless otherwise stated. Also, some personal details were altered or omitted to ensure confidentiality.

2. California State Auditor, *Department of Health Services*, 9.

3. PRWORA dismantled the sixty-year-old federal cash assistance program, Aid to Families with Dependent Children (AFDC), and replaced it with Temporary Assistance to Needy Families (TANF)—block grants to states governed under a new set of time limits and restrictions (Marchevsky and Theoharis, *Not Working*, 5).

4. U.S. Citizenship and Immigration Services. http://www.uscis.gov. Website last accessed on July 12, 2010.

5. U.S. Citizenship and Immigration Services, *Fact Sheet: Public Charge*. Last accessed July 12, 2010.

6. See Luibheid, *Entry Denied*, 9.

7. See Fairchild, *Science at the Borders*, 14. By 1903 the PHS began to formally classify diseases in accordance with this law.

8. Gardner, *The Qualities of a Citizen*, 89.

9. Ibid., 88.

10. Ibid., 91.

11. See L. Park, "Perpetuation of Poverty through Public Charge."

12. Scheer, "The Governor's Brave Stand on Birth Control."

13. Ibid.

14. See Goldman and Sood, "Rising Medicare Costs: Are We in Crisis?"

15. Ibid. Forty-five percent of Los Angeles County residents are foreign-born. The researchers found that nonelderly, adult immigrants (documented and undocumented) made fewer visits to doctors and hospitals than native-born nonelderly adults.

16. See Lu et al., "Elimination of Public Funding of Prenatal Care for Undocumented Immigrants in California: A Cost/Benefit Analysis."

17. Murray and Bernfield, "The Differential Effect of Prenatal Care on the Incidence of Low Birth Weight among Blacks and Whites in a Prepaid Health Care Plan."

18. See Henderson, "The Cost Effectiveness of Prenatal Care: Health Care Needs of Vulnerable Populations."

19. Misra and Guyer, "Benefits and Limitations of Prenatal Care," 1662.

20. Ibid.

21. For example, cases of domestic violence are brought to the attention of health care providers, who then contact local immigrant advocates against domestic violence.

22. The prison system (i.e., "immigration detention centers") is also increasingly used for these purposes.

23. D. Roberts, "Who May Give Birth to Citizens?" 208.

24. See Smith, *Entitlement Politics.* Medicare and Social Security are also major national entitlement programs.

25. Rosen, *Caring for Our Future, the Content of Prenatal Care.*

26. Kotelchuck, "The Adequacy of Prenatal Care Utilization Index."

27. The program is administered by the California Department of Health Services (DHS) and at the county level, a Department of Social Services (DSS) member functions as the Medi-Cal eligibility worker. At the federal level, the Health Care Financing Administration (HCFA) of the U.S. Department of Health and Human Services (DHHS) oversees the federal Medicaid program. See Medi-Cal Policy Institute, *Understanding Medi-Cal: The Basics.*

28. Alexander and Kotelchuck, "Quantifying the Adequacy in Prenatal Care"; Braverman et al., "Validity of Insurance Information on California Birth Certificates"; Kogan et al., "The Changing Pattern of Prenatal Care Utilization in the United States, 1981–1995."

29. See Ventura and Taffel, "Childbearing Characteristics of U.S.- and Foreign-Born Hispanic Mothers"; and California Department of Health Services, "Adequacy of Prenatal Care Utilization: California 1989–1994."

30. Similar effects were also documented in Texas by Hagan et al., "The Effects of Recent Welfare and Immigration Reforms on Immigrants' Access to Health Care." For more details on the new eligibility rules, see Appendix B.

31. See Ellwood and Ku, "Welfare and Immigration Reforms: Unintended Side Effects for Medicaid"; Zimmerman and Fix, *Declining Immigrant Applications for Medi-Cal and Welfare Benefits in Los Angeles County*; and Fix and Passel, *Trends in Noncitizens' and Citizens' Use of Public Benefits following Welfare Reform, 1994–97.*

32. David Harvey defines neoliberalism as "a theory of political economic practices that proposes that human well-being can best be advanced by liberating individual entrepreneurial freedoms and skills within an institutional framework characterized by strong private property rights, free markets, and free trade." See Harvey, *A Brief History of Neoliberalism.* See also Duggan, *The Twilight of Equality?* and Sparke, "A Neoliberal Nexus."

33. See Massey et al., *Beyond Smoke and Mirrors,* 14; Sassen, *Globalization and Its Discontents.*

34. Massey et al., *Beyond Smoke and Mirrors*, 14.

35. Schram, *Words of Welfare*, 61.

36. Ibid.

37. See Marchevsky and Theoharis, *Not Working*, 10.

38. Ibid., vii.

39. Ibid., 2. Similar investigations are conducted for those applying for public health insurance, as described in chapter 2.

40. Fraser and Gordon, "A Genealogy of Dependency," 315.

41. Solinger, "Dependency and Choice," 62.

42. Ibid., 65.

43. Lisa Duggan (*Twilight of Equality*, xix) argues that "Neoliberals in the ranks of U.S. conservative party politics began to slowly and unevenly shed the 'culture wars' alliances with religious moralists, white supremacists, ultra nationalists, and other antiliberal forces that had helped guarantee their political successes during the 1980s. Neoliberal new Democrats, led by Bill Clinton, included civil right/ equality politics within a framework that minimized any downwardly redistributing impulses and effects."

44. Roberts, "The Future of Reproductive Choice for Poor Women and Women of Color," 284.

45. Ibid.

46. Solinger, *Beggars and Choosers*, 200.

47. Petchesky ("The Body as Property," 387) notes, "[R]eproductive politics is in large part about language and the contestation of meanings."

48. Ruhl, "Dilemmas of the Will," 643.

49. De Beauvoir, *The Second Sex* (cited in Ruhl, "Dilemmas of the Will," 650).

50. Ruhl, "Dilemmas of the Will," 645.

51. Valverde, "'Despotism' and Ethical Liberal Governance."

52. Ruhl, "Dilemmas of the Will," 656.

53. Ibid., 660.

54. Petchesky, "The Body as Property."

55. Ibid., 388.

56. Ibid., 389.

57. Williams, *The Alchemy of Race and Rights*, 219.

58. Ibid., 220.

59. Burton, "Childhood Adultification in Economically Disadvantaged Families"; P. Collins, *Black Feminist Thought*; Stack, *All Our Kin*.

60. Sunaina Maira (*Missing*, 69) states that "the War on Terror is an extension of the 'war on immigrants,' revived by the Right and stoked by nativists since the late 1980s." See also Deepa Fernandes, *Targeted*; and Tram Nguyen, *We Are All Suspects Now*.

61. Here, I borrow from Jonathan Xavier Inda (*Targeting Immigrants*, 6): "The technological is that domain of practical mechanisms, devices, calculations, procedures, apparatuses, and documents through which authorities seek to shape and instrumentalize human conduct."

62. De Genova, *Working the Boundaries*, 8.

63. See Schram, *After Welfare*.

64. Sparke, "A Neoliberal Nexus: Citizenship, Security and the Future of the Border."

65. Marchevsky and Theoharis (*Not Working*, 5) note: "Welfare was no longer a social safety net but a temporary program designed to encourage marriage and other 'family values' among the nation's poor and to move welfare recipients as quickly as possible into the work force."

66. Young, "Autonomy, Welfare Reform, and Meaningful Work," 43–44.

67. Ibid., 59 (footnote #14). Young advocates for a language of "autonomy" as the primary means for achieving greater freedom and respect, apart from the demands of the state or corporations.

68. Marchevsky and Theoharis, *Not Working*, 18.

69. Fraser and Gordon, "A Geneology of Dependency," 325.

70. Ibid.

71. See P. Collins, *Black Feminist Thought*.

72. Ibid., 75.

73. Ibid., 73.

74. See Fraser and Gordon, "Contract versus Charity," 123.

75. Harvey, *A Brief History of Neoliberalism*, 203.

76. This was made very clear once again during the immigration policy debates in 2006. The Sensenbrenner bill (H.R. 4437) is just one such example.

77. See Solinger, *Beggars and Choosers*, 206.

78. Popular anxiety over "anchor babies" attests to this later concern. See Huang, "Anchor Babies, Over-Breeders, and the Population Bomb," 385.

79. See Zucchino, *Myth of the Welfare Queen*; and P. Collins, *Black Feminist Thought*.

80. Solinger (*Beggars and Choosers*, 219) cites a personal letter written by a single mother to the House Ways and Means Committee during the 1996 welfare reform debates: "Why is it that a woman who, because she is of a privileged economic class, chooses to stay home and raise her children is performing the most important job in the world, but a poor woman is a lazy, no good cheat?"

81. Johnson, *The "Huddled Masses" Myth*, 281.

82. Ibid., 386.

83. See also Fujiwara, "The Impact of Welfare Reform on Asian Immigrant Communities."

84. Chavez, "A Glass Half Empty," 69.

85. Fujiwara, "The Impact of Welfare Reform on Asian Immigrant Communities."

86. Stern, *Eugenic Nation*, 60. It is also noteworthy that the treatment of Chinese immigrants during the Gold Rush revealed major anxieties around the boundaries of whiteness and the position of the white male worker and his masculinity. As in the 1990s, the vast majority of people in California during the Gold Rush were immigrants, but they were Europeans defined as white, while the "Foreign Miner's Tax" was applied exclusively to Chinese immigrants. Then the Working Man's Party and other groups emerged to define "working class" in California as white and male. The similarities to the 1990s and the early twenty-first century are quite strong.

87. *San Diego Union-Tribune*, Feb. 6, 1993.

88. See Berk et al., "Health Care Use among Undocumented Latino Immigrants"; Eisenstadt and Thorup, *Caring Capacity vs. Carrying Capacity*; Fix, Passel, and Zimmerman, *Facts about Immigrants' Use of Welfare*.

89. The Economic Policy Institute (Chapman and Bernstein, *Immigration and Poverty*, 8) reports that immigrants, especially those recently arrived, experience a poverty rate that is over twice that of U.S. native-born. In California, the poverty rate for the native born was 10.4 percent while for immigrants it was 20.5 percent in 1999.

90. See Hughes and Runyan, "Prenatal Care and Public Policy"; Tannenbaum, "Medicaid Eligibility Policy in the 1980s"; and Sardell, "Child Health Policy in the U.S."

91. This is evident in eugenic and sterilization programs, which rationalize their targeting of particular racial ethnic groups. See Briggs, *Reproducing Empire*; Gutierrez, *Fertile Matters*; Kline, *Building a Better Race*; Ordover, *American Eugenics*; Schoen, *Choice and Coercion*; Smith, *Conquest*; and Stern, *Eugenic Nation*.

92. Hing, *Defining America through Immigration Policy*, 28.

93. Ono and Sloop, *Shifting Borders*, 3.

94. Ibid., 3–4.

95. Moss et al., "Perspectives of Latina Immigrant Women on Proposition 187."

96. Zimmerman and Fix, *Declining Immigrant Applications for Medi-Cal and Welfare Benefits in Los Angeles County*.

97. Pre-enactment immigrants are those who entered the United States before August 22, 1996, when the Welfare Reform bill was signed into law and post-enactment immigrants are those who entered on or after August 22, 1996. Both these categories of immigrants are documented and therefore "legally" reside in the United States. See Appendix B for a more detailed explanation of immigrant eligibility for Medicaid.

98. See Marchevsky and Theoharis, *Not Working*, 5.

99. MaCurdy and O'Brien-Strain, *Reform Reversed?* Also, the Center for Law and Social Policy (Greenberg et al., *Welfare Reauthorization*) found that decline of the immigrant caseload accounted for over half of the welfare savings that year, surpassing earlier predictions.

100. Espenshade et al., "Implications of the 1996 Welfare and Immigration Reform Acts for US Immigration."

101. After the terrorist attacks on U.S. soil on September 11, 2001, then President George W. Bush created the Department of Homeland Security in 2003, bringing together twenty-two federal agencies, including the Immigration and Naturalization Service (INS). Subsequently, the activities of the INS were distributed across different agencies within the department: Immigration and Customs Enforcement, Citizenship and Immigration Services, and U.S. Customs and Border Protection.

102. Morse et al., *America's Newcomers.*

103. To make things even more difficult, the federal welfare reform legislation now explicitly prohibits states from offering nonemergency services to nonqualified aliens, including the undocumented, unless the state passes new legislation providing state funding for such coverage.

104. California Legislature Senate Office of Research, *Federal Welfare Changes Affecting California's Immigrants.*

105. See Moss et al., "Perspectives of Latina Immigrant Women on Proposition 187"; Scholsberg and Wiley, *The Impact of INS Public Charge Determinations on Immigrant Access to Health Care;* Rodriguez and Hagan, "Fractured Families and Communities"; Ku and Matani, "Left Out"; Fujiwara, *Mothers without Citizenship.*

CHAPTER 2

1. Ong, *Buddha Is Hiding,* 9.

2. Ibid.

3. See Sassen, *The Mobility of Labor and Capital;* and Sassen, *Globalization and Its Discontents.*

4. Sassen, *Guests and Aliens,* 136–137.

5. Mae Ngai and others have critiqued the common reading of this legislation as an "open door" for immigrants. Ngai writes, "[I]t continued and, indeed, extended the reach of numerical restriction, a policy that would reproduce the problem of illegal immigration, especially from Mexico, to the present day" (*Impossible Subjects,* 227). "Indeed, the persistence of numerical restriction in the postwar period, with its emphasis on territoriality, border control, and deportation of illegal aliens, suggest[s] that in some respects immigration reform only hardened the distinction between citizen and alien" (p. 229).

6. Mink, *Welfare's End,* 22.

7. See Amott, "Black Women and AFDC," 287.

8. Ibid., 289.

9. Mink, *The Wages of Motherhood*.

10. Ibid., 177.

11. Gordon, *Pitied but Not Entitled*, 1.

12. Mink, *Welfare's End*, 6.

13. Gordon, *Pitied but Not Entitled*, 2.

14. Mink, *Welfare's End*, 22.

15. See Pear, "Immigrants Face Medicaid Hurdle for Infant Care," A1.

16. See Abramovitz, *Regulating the Lives of Women*.

17. See Burchell et al., *The Foucault Effect*; and Foucault, *Society Must Be Defended*; and Foucault, *Discipline and Punish*.

18. See Soss et al., "The Third Level of U.S. Welfare Reform: Governmentality under Neoliberal Paternalism."

19. Ong, *Spirits of Resistance and Capitalist Discipline*, 4–5.

20. At the federal level, the Health Care Financing Administration (HCFA) of the U.S. Department of Health and Human Services (DHHS) oversees the federal Medicaid program (Medi-Cal Policy Institute, *Understanding Medi-Cal: The Basics*).

21. Schlosberg and Wiley, *The Impact of INS Public Charge Determinations on Immigrant Access to Health Care*.

22. In its most general interpretation, an "informal economy" is defined as income-generating activities unregulated by the state in places where similar activities are generally regulated. See B. Roberts, "Informal Economy and Family Strategies," 6; Castells and Portes, "World Underneath"; Feige, "Defining and Estimating Underground and Informal Economies."

23. Pregnancy-Only Medi-Cal is a temporary form of Medi-Cal that covers the mother's health care during her pregnancy.

24. National Immigration Law Center, *Public Charge*.

25. After September 11, 2001, the INS was reorganized into the Immigration and Customs Enforcement (ICE) agency, operating under the new Department of Homeland Security.

26. Morse et al., *America's Newcomers*.

27. California Legislature Senate Office of Research, *Federal Welfare Changes Affecting California's Immigrants*.

28. Of course, immigrants are not the only group who are uninsured. The 2005 census data show that a record 46.6 million Americans are uninsured, or 15.9 percent of the total U.S. population. (Center on Budget and Policy Priorities Report, *The Number of Uninsured Americans Is at an All-Time High*.)

29. Ladd-Taylor and Umansky, *"Bad" Mothers*, 6.

30. Ibid., 7.

31. Ibid., 3.

32. Ibid., 9.

33. See also Zelizer, *Pricing the Priceless Child*.

34. Glenn, "Social Constructions of Mothering," 14.

35. Ibid., 5.

36. D. Roberts, "Who May Give Birth to Citizens?" 206.

37. Ladd-Taylor and Umansky, *"Bad" Mothers*, 2.

38. Cooey, "'Ordinary Mother' as Oxymoron."

39. Hays, *The Cultural Contradictions of Motherhood*, 125.

40. See Hancock, *The Politics of Disgust*; Kozol, *Rachel and Her Children*; Sidel, *Keeping Women and Children Last*; Zucchino, *Myth of the Welfare Queen*.

41. D. Roberts, "Poverty, Race, and New Directions in Child Welfare Policy," 47.

42. See Saito, "The Politics of Adaptation and the "Good Immigrant."

43. See L. Park, *Consuming Citizenship*.

44. See Hochschild, *The Commercialization of Intimate Life*, 37.

45. Hondagneu-Sotelo and Avila, "I'm Here, but I'm There," 552.

46. Ibid., 563.

47. See D. Roberts, "Who May Give Birth to Citizens?"

48. Ibid., 215.

CHAPTER 3

1. California State Auditor, *Department of Health Services*, 9.

2. Duster (*Backdoor to Eugenics*, 13) writes, "The last reforms and regulations of the Progressive Era, the immigration laws of the 1920s, and two powerful movements (labor and temperance) were all substantially influenced by this immigration."

3. Ibid., 4.

4. See ibid., 4.

5. See Kline, *Building a Better Race*, 13.

6. Ibid., 14.

7. Ibid., 19 and 29.

8. Duster, *Backdoor to Eugenics*, 4.

9. Ibid.

10. Gutierrez, "Policing 'Pregnant Pilgrims.'"

11. Gutierrez, *Fertile Matters*.

12. See Luibheid's (*Entry Denied*, 67) discussion of the central role of immigrant childbirths in the Japanese exclusion movement in the 1920s.

13. McClintock, "'No Longer in a Future Heaven,'" 91.

14. Ibid.

15. See Rollins, *Between Women;* Romero, *Maid in the U.S.A.;* Hondagneu-Sotelo, *Domestica.*

16. See Calavita, *U.S. Immigration Law and the Control of Labor,* 68–91; and Calavita, *Inside the State,* 6.

17. Unofficially, the DHS had initiated an earlier version of this program in the mid-1980s after the INS notified the DHS that foreigners were entering the country with Medi-Cal benefit documents.

18. Department of Health Services, All County Letter #94-75, September 20, 1994.

19. Department of Health Services, All County Letter #95-18, March 16, 1995. Forbidding reentry at the border is far less bureaucratically taxing than formal deportation.

20. A letter from the Department of Health Services to all county welfare program directors, administrative officers, and Medi-Cal program specialists, states, "The primary purpose of this program is to prevent Medi-Cal fraud from occurring by investigating potential ineligibility before Medi-Cal approval." Department of Health Services, All County Letter #94-75, September 20, 1994.

21. The "success" of these investigations was determined solely by its ability to deter access to Medi-Cal, resulting in "substantial cost savings" for the state. Whether or not these applications were actually fraudulent did not appear to be a primary concern.

22. Department of Health Services, All County Letter #94-75, September 20, 1994.

23. Willes et al., "Abuse by Officials at the Border."

24. Nonimmigrants are those with some form of documentation, including a temporary border pass, U.S. tourist visa, student visa, or a temporary visa. There is continuous debate about the Medi-Cal eligibility measures of nonimmigrants (those holding valid border crossing cards or temporary visas). See All County Welfare Directors Letters 96-47, 96-27, 97-06, 98-48. Of note is the punitive or narrow reading of eligibility until August 11, 1998, when the California Court of Appeal sided with the plaintiffs in Latino Coalition for a Healthy California vs. Belshé et al. (California Court of Appeal No. A081229) and forced the DHS to rescind its latest efforts to restrict residency.

25. This is the case even after the punitive effects of federal welfare reform, which eliminated federally subsidized pregnancy-related health care for immigrants. Following a 1988 legislation that authorized Medi-Cal to use state-only funds to provide nonemergency pregnancy-related services to alien women, California is supposed to cover prenatal care and delivery for low-income immigrants. See All County Welfare Directors Letter 97-22.

26. Telephone interview, January 25, 1999.

27. Ibid.

28. Ibid.

29. It was not stated whether she spoke to the DHS and the INS together or separately.

30. Rocio vs. Belshé, US District Court of Southern District of California, 3/19/1997, p.1.

31. Ibid, p. 3.

32. They are cited as coplaintiffs in the case. Sofia argued that the DHS program negatively impacted them as a nonprofit legal advocate for immigrants, since they were spending all their resources in dealing with PED and its accompanying public charge concerns.

33. Rocio vs. Belshé, p. 5: "Since or before November 1994, defendant had been operating a project known as the 'Border Project.' Although a general description of the project was published in a DHS 'All County Letter,' this letter is not a formal regulation" [ACL 95-18].

34. National Immigration Law Center, "Immigrants and Public Charge: Resource Book 1998–99," 1998.

35. See 42 U.S.C. § 1396, 1396a (a) (8) (19); 42 C.F.R. § 435.402, et seq. and Personal Responsibility and Work Opportunity Reconciliation Act of 1996 ("Welfare Reform" Act), Sec. 401(a), 410(b), 431.

36. According to the lawsuit (pp. 6, 7), "State Medicaid programs must provide safeguards to restrict use or disclosure of information concerning applicants and recipients to purposes directly connected with the administration of the state's Medicaid plan. 42 U.S.C. § 1396a(a)(7)." In addition, the plaintiff notes that "Aliens who apply for 'full scope' Medicaid benefits and claim to have a qualifying legal immigration status, sign a release to have their status verified by the INS. Aliens who apply for emergency benefits only do not give permission to have their immigration status verified by the INS and, under federal confidentiality provisions, cannot be reported to the INS by the state."

37. "42 U.S.C. § 1396p(b)(1) provides that no adjustment or recovery of any medical assistance correctly paid on behalf of an individual under a state's Medicaid plan may be made, except in certain limited cases involving recovery from the estates of certain deceased recipients who received nursing home care or care after age fifty-five. The exceptions set forth in Section 1396p do no apply to class members in this case" (p. 8).

38. The fifth and fourteenth amendments of the U.S. Constitution require that notice and a hearing be provided prior to recovery of a Medicaid overpayment. See also 42 U.S.C § 1396a(a)(3)(4); 42 C.F.R. § 431.200, et seq.; Calif. Gov't Code § 11340, et seq. Federal and state laws require states to make readily available to the public all Medicaid rules, and also to provide an opportunity for a fair hearing or comment prior to policy implementation.

39. ACWDL No. 00-12, March 14, 2000.

40. Ibid., 1.

41. ACWDL No. 00-12 on March 14, 2000 and ACWDL No. 03-03 on January 9, 2003.

42. The District Court granted the proposed modification to the settlement agreement on October 9, 2002.

43. California State Auditor, *Department of Health Services.*

44. Ibid., 17.

45. Ibid.

46. Ibid., 9.

47. Ibid. There were other instances that illustrate the DHS's overstepping its authority, including PED program investigators at the San Ysidro port of entry allowing the destruction of a person's immigration documents by a county eligibility technician during an interview (ibid., 15).

48. Ibid., 13.

49. Ibid.

50. Ibid.

51. Ibid., 11.

52. Ibid., 1. However, the audit also notes that they caught DHS investigators at CARR continuing to send requests for repayments until at least November 1998—six months after they had signed a legal agreement to stop such requests. The audit concluded that oversight is a continued problem (ibid., 21).

53. Programmatic abuses by DHS included: (1) improperly changing eligibility procedures to discontinue or deny Medi-Cal benefits to eligible resident aliens; (2) soliciting and receiving repayment of Medi-Cal benefits without complying with state regulations; (3) inappropriately soliciting repayments in exchange for implied improvements in immigration status; and (4) influencing INS decisions about whether to admit immigrants and visitors into the United States (ibid., 13).

54. Ibid., 20.

55. USCIS, *Fact Sheet.*

56. A derogatory term for the INS.

57. Perhaps the only unwavering aspect of public charge policy is that it is not applicable to refugees or aliens seeking asylum.

58. This new requirement is found in Sections 212 and 213A of both legislations.

59. Employment-based immigrants who will work for a close relative or for a firm in which a U.S. citizen or lawful permanent resident relative holds a 5 percent or greater ownership interest are also required to have a qualifying sponsor submit an affidavit of support on their behalf.

60. In 1999, 125 percent of the poverty level for a family of four was $20,875.

61. Park and Park (*Probationary Americans*, 30) note that an earlier form of public charge existed in the eighteenth century before federal immigration rules existed. The concept dates back to colonial governments in U.S. history.

62. See Evans, "Likely to Become a Public Charge," vi.

63. Ibid., 11.

64. *New York Times*, "Hispanic and Asian Populations Expand."

65. Schevitz, "California Minorities Become Majority," A1.

66. This law redefined deportable offenses and retroactively reclassified minor offenses as felonies. This worked in tandem with the immigration reform of that same year, which removed the right to judicial review in many deportation cases and authorized "expedited removal" of people who arrived at U.S. airports and other borders without proper documents. More recently, after 9/11, with the creation of Homeland Security and the passage of the USA PATRIOT Act, which allows for broad sweeps and raids, the repertoire of deportation possibilities increased exponentially. See Hing, *Deporting Our Souls*.

67. Foreshadowing events, Patricia Evans wrote, "As long as immigration remains an administrative law, requiring interventionist judiciary and broad interaction between regulator, regulatee, and the general citizenry; and there are no powerful domestic advocates for the alien, it will remain an administrative anomaly" ("Likely to Become a Public Charge," 257).

68. See Fairchild, *Science at the Borders*, 14.

69. U.S. Department of Justice, *1998 Statistical Yearbook of INS*, 200.

70. Ibid., 204.

71. In fact, Thomas J. Espenshade and his colleagues ("Implications of the 1996 Welfare and Immigration Reform Acts for US Immigration") argue that there were a number of unintended consequences as a result of the 1996 policies: (1) limited legal migration, and (2) increase in undocumented migration.

72. Sassen, *Globalization and Its Discontents*, 49.

73. Fix and Passel, "Immigration and Immigrants: Setting the Record Straight." Also, DeFreitas (*Immigration, Inequality, and Policy Alternatives*) notes that immigration at current levels does not harm domestic wages or employment. In fact he reports that immigrants contribute more in federal, state, and local taxes than they use in public assistance and services.

74. Fraser and Gordon, "A Genealogy of Dependency."

75. Fix and Zimmerman, "Immigrant Families and Public Policy: A Deepening Divide."

76. Amott and Matthaei, *Race, Gender, and Work.*

77. Fraser and Gordon, "A Genealogy of Dependency."

CHAPTER 4

1. California Association of Public Hospitals and Health Systems, *On the Brink*, 2. By 2003, public hospitals and clinics in California comprised only 6 percent of hospitals statewide but provided 55 percent of the cost of health care to the uninsured. They serve a patient population that is 76 percent people of color, including more than 50 percent Latino.

2. Madigan, "Los Angeles Emergency Care Crisis Deepens," A8.

3. Schlosberg and Wiley, *The Impact of INS Public Charge Determinations on Immigrant Access to Health Care*.

4. Ibid.

5. Singer, "Immigrants, their Families and their Communities in the Aftermath of Welfare Reform," 6–7.

6. Park et al., "Impact of Recent Welfare and Immigration Reforms on Use of Medicaid for Prenatal Care by Immigrants in California."

7. Deeming refers to the attribution of the income and resources of an immigrant's sponsor(s) to the immigrant to determine eligibility for public funds.

8. The issue of deeming remains unclear even after the clarification of public charge determinations.

9. Fee-for-service Medi-Cal is the traditional method of paying for care in which health care providers are reimbursed for particular services such as office visits, medical procedures, and prescriptions rather than a flat fee for the entire prenatal care service. Roughly 60 percent of Medi-Cal beneficiaries in California participate in this program (Medi-Cal Policy Institute, *Understanding Medi-Cal*).

10. CPSP refers to the Comprehensive Perinatal Services Program. This program provides prenatal and postnatal services—including psychosocial, nutrition, and health education services—for Medicaid-eligible pregnant women.

11. Ku and Matani ("Left Out") stress this point in their research. They argue that immigration status helps to explain the racial and ethnic inequality in insurance coverage and access to care.

12. Fix and Zimmerman, *All under One Roof*.

CHAPTER 5

1. Sibley, *Geographies of Exclusion*.

2. See Camacho, *Migrant Imaginaries*.

3. Chang, "A Meditation on Borders," 246.

4. Nevins, *Operation Gatekeeper*, 6.

5. Ibid., 5.

6. Ibid., 6.

7. Ibid., 5.

8. See Herzog, *Where North Meets South*; and Herzog, "The Transfrontier Organization of Space along the United States-Mexico Border."

9. Rodriguez, "The Social Construction of the U.S.-Mexico Border," 226.

10. Capps et al., The Dispersal of Immigrants in the 1990s.

11. Ibid. (p.1): "In 2000, over two-thirds of the nation's total foreign-born population lived in six 'major destination' states: California (28) percent, New York (12 percent), Texas (9 percent), Florida (9 percent), New Jersey (5 percent), and Illinois (5 percent). However, the overall share of the immigrant population living in these six states declined significantly, from 75 percent in 1990 to 68 percent in 2000."

12. For discussion of Aspen, Colorado, see Park and Pellow, *The Slums of Aspen*. For Carpentersville, Illinois, see Kotlowitz, "All Immigration Politics Is Local (and Complicated, Nasty and Personal)." For Nashville, Tennessee, see Harris, "City of Nashville Rejects English-Only Law."

13. Kotlowitz, "All Immigration Politics Is Local (and Complicated, Nasty and Personal)," 33.

14. See Calavita, "Deflecting the Immigration Debate." See also Milkman, *L.A. Story*, 9.

15. See Rodriguez, "The Social Construction of the U.S.-Mexico Border," 226. And Kotlowitz "All Immigration Politics Is Local (and Complicated, Nasty and Personal)."

16. Forward for Nevins, *Operation Gatekeeper*, x.

17. Nevins, *Operation Gatekeeper*, 2–3.

18. Ibid., 10.

19. DeGenova, *Working the Boundaries*, 8.

20. Massey et al., *Beyond Smoke and Mirrors*, 5.

21. See ibid.; and Cornelius, "Introduction: Does Border Enforcement Deter Unauthorized Immigration?"

22. Massey et al., *Beyond Smoke and Mirrors*.

23. Passel, Size and Characteristics of the Unauthorized Migrant Population in the United States: Estimates Based on the March 2005 Current Population Survey.

24. Cornelius, "Introduction: Does Border Enforcement Deter Unauthorized Immigration?" 4–5.

25. See Luibheid, *Entry Denied*, 121. It is also the case that women are at risk of rape by coyotes, police on both sides of the border, and other fellow-immigrants during their passage.

26. Massey et al., *Beyond Smoke and Mirrors*, 4–5.

27. Rodriguez, "The Social Construction of the U.S.-Mexico Border," 223.

28. One study reviewed 184 cases of Mexican women who gave birth in California between 1982 and 1987 and found that 10.4 percent crossed the border to give birth in the United States. Contrary to fears of an invasion of "anchor babies," these are fairly small numbers during a time of relatively lax border control. They also found that most of these deliveries were in the private sector and paid for out of pocket, representing a very low public burden. See Guendelman and Jasis, "Giving Birth across the Border."

29. Brodie et al., "Perceptions of Latinos, African Americans, and Whites on Media as a Health Information Source."

30. Wulsin et al., *Clinics, Counties and the Uninsured.*

31. Bovbjerg et al., Health Care for the Poor and Uninsured after a Public Hospital's Closure or Conversion, 23.

32. Seven million nonelderly Californians are uninsured. (Schauffler and Brown, *The State of Health Insurance in California.*)

33. Ibid., 1.

34. Arnst, "Study Links Medical Costs and Personal Bankruptcy."

35. Bovbjerg et al., *Health Care for the Poor and Uninsured after a Public Hospital's Closure or Conversion,* 33.

36. Sassen, *Guests and Aliens,* 150.

37. Kalofonos and Palinkas ("Barriers to Prenatal Care for Mexican and Mexican American Women," 149) documents these fears, fueled by anecdotes of INS raids at health clinics.

38. Macias and Morales, "Crossing the Border for Health Care."

39. Thompson, "Cross-Border Health Care Utilization and Practices of Mexican-Americans in the Lower Rio Grande Valley."

40. Homedes and LaBrec, *Health Services Utilization across the Arizona-Sonora Border.*

41. Geography and Urban Planning Programs, "Sunland Park Community Survey"; Tabet and Wiese, "Medications Obtained in Mexico by Patients in Southern New Mexico."

42. It is also noteworthy that migrants who regularly cross the border use the U.S. health care system the least. A study by Chavez et al. ("Mexican Immigrants and the Utilization of U.S. Health Services," 100–101) found that male migrants who temporarily stay in the United States as laborers are typically young and healthy. They write, "If they develop a serious but non-acute health problem, they usually return to Mexico where their dependents—if any—remain in the place of origin. The heaviest users of health services among the Mexican immigrant population are whole family units which settle permanently or on a long-term basis in the United States, especially those who do so as legal resident aliens."

43. Luibheid, *Entry Denied,* xi.

CHAPTER 6

1. Quoted in Addis, "'Hell Man, They Did Invent Us,'" as cited in Chang, "A Meditation on Borders," 247.

2. *New York Times*, editorial, September 11, 2009.

3. Under the reform passed in March 2010, documented immigrants are given limited federal health care coverage while undocumented immigrants are not eligible for Medicare, nonemergency Medicaid, or the Children's Health Insurance Program. Undocumented immigrants are also restricted from purchasing private health insurance at full cost and are not eligible for health care-related tax credits or cost-sharing reductions. However, they remain eligible for emergency care and can seek nonemergency health services at community health centers or safety net hospitals. See National Immigration Law Center, *How Are Immigrants Included in Health Care Reform?*

4. Marshall, "Citizenship and Social Class."

5. Nelson, "The Origins of the Two-Channel Welfare State," 145.

6. Ibid., 124.

7. See Yuval-Davis, "The Citizenship Debate: Women, Ethnic Processes and the State," 61. See also Lister, *Citizenship*; and Hobson and Lister, "Keyword: Citizenship."

8. Canning and Rose, "Gender, Citizenship and Subjectivity," 427.

9. Delgado, "Citizenship."

10. Schram, *Words of Welfare*, 4.

11. J. Collins, "The Specter of Slavery," 131.

12. Ibid.

13. Ong, *Spirits of Resistance and Capitalist Discipline*, 4–5.

14. Kessler-Harris, *In Pursuit of Equity*, 4.

15. Ibid.

16. See Harvey, *A Brief History of Neoliberalism*, 53.

17. Duggan, *The Twilight of Equality?* 14.

18. Burawoy, "The Functions and Reproduction of Migrant Labor." In this article he also notes the limitations of understanding migration as an individual decision making process (i.e., push/pull): "[W]hat is of interest is not how migrants adapt to their new environment but how structural, particular political and legal, constraints make permanent "integration" impossible. The issues are not ones of assimilation and acculturation but of enforced segregation through such "total" institutions as the compound and labor camp and the corresponding persistence of race and ethnic differentiation" (p.1051).

19. Wilson, "Anti-Immigrant Sentiment and the Problem of Reproduction/Maintenance in Mexican Immigration to the United States," 191.

20. Much of the time, this responsibility is absorbed by individuals rather than other nation-states.

21. Jayasuriya, *Statecraft, Welfare, and the Politics of Inclusion*, 3.

22. Ibid.

23. This is by no means a complete list of advocacy groups and actions in California. This is only meant to serve as an example of the types of advocacy responses deployed during our research.

24. Healthy Families is California's State Children's Health Insurance Program (SCHIP), which provides low-cost health insurance for children and teens.

25. The risk is that the patient's application may be denied at the end of the sixty-day review period and the cost of her care uncovered.

26. See Cartier ("From Home to Hospital and Back Again," 2293): "During the period 1977–1999, 80 percent of US households, as a group, experienced a decline in their share of national income from 56 percent to under 50 percent." Cartier adds, "Both social inequality and income polarization (i.e., the highest income households increased income the fastest while lower income households experienced income decline) have increased in the US in the final quarter of the 20th century."

27. Ibid., 2289.

28. On home health care working conditions, see Burbridge, "The Labor Market for Home Care Workers"; Feldman, "Labor Market Issues in Home Care, Nursing Homes and Home Care"; and Yamada, "Profile of Home Care Aides, Nursing Home Aides, and Hospital Aides."

29. Ong, *Neoliberalism as Exception*, 11.

30. Brown, "American Nightmare," 693.

31. Ibid., 694–695.

32. Maira, *Missing*, 138.

33. Ibid., 137.

34. D. Roberts, "Who May Give Birth to Citizens?" 205.

APPENDIX A

1. Patton, Qualitative Research and Evaluation Methods.

2. For community clinics and hospitals to be included in the sample, they had to be one of the three largest providers of pregnancy-related services in their county in 1994 for both foreign-born ethnic groups (Latino or Asian American) and Medicaid and uninsured patients. For clinics, this determination was made with the *1996 Community Clinic Fact Book* (Campos 1998). In each region, our selections were based on: (1) clinic size; (2) provision of prenatal care; (3) number of patients on Medi-Cal; (4) number of patients uninsured; (5) ethnic breakdown; (6)

number of patients for whom English is not the first language. For hospitals, the inclusion determination was made with 1994 electronic birth records for California. Using the 1994 electronic birth records, we selected for: (1) type of hospital; (2) number of births to foreign-born mothers; (3) percentage of births to foreign-born mothers; (4) percentage of births to foreign-born Asian mothers; (5) percentage of births to foreign-born Hispanic mothers; and (6) number of Medi-Cal and uninsured patients.

3. Gilchrist and Williams, "Key Informant Interviews."

4. The group interviews were one or more hours in length and conducted by two or three interviewers. Only three such group interviews were conducted and all were located in the Bay Area. The number of respondents in each interview session were two, six, and twelve, respectively. While the interview with the two respondents functioned largely like an individual formal interview, the other two larger groups were interviewed using a focus group format. In this format, core issues were raised by the interviewers who functioned largely as facilitators of the respondents' discussions.

5. The formal, individual telephone interviews were conducted by two members (out of four) of the research team. One interviewer led the discussion, while the other acted as a participant observer documenting critical anecdotes and points, and asking probing questions when needed. A short debriefing meeting was scheduled after each interview for the interviewers to discuss central points made by the informant and key insights gained. These debriefing sessions were also useful for identifying points that were still unclear and that needed further attention when the tapes and transcripts were reviewed. The informal interviews, on the other hand, were relatively brief and generally not audio recorded. They followed a more open format that did not necessarily address all the interview questions. These interviews generally focused on one particular interest or concern, as indicated by the respondent.

6. Strauss, *Qualitative Analysis for Social Scientists.*

BIBLIOGRAPHY

Abramovitz, Mimi. *Regulating the Lives of Women: Social Welfare Policy from Colonial Times to the Present.* Boston: South End Press, 1996.

Addis, Adeno. "'Hell Man, They Did Invent Us': The Mass Media, Law, and African Americans." *University of Buffalo Law Review* 41 (1993): 523–626.

Alexander, Greg R., and Milton Kotelchuck. "Quantifying the Adequacy of Prenatal Care: A Comparison of Indices." *Public Health Reports* 111, no. 5 (1996): 408–419.

Amott, Teresa L. "Black Women and AFDC: Making Entitlement Out of Necessity." *Women, the State, and Welfare.* Edited by Linda Gordon. Madison: University of Wisconsin Press, 1990: 280–298.

Amott, Teresa, and Julie Matthaei. *Race, Gender, and Work: A Multi-Cultural Economic History of Women in the United States.* Boston: South End Press, 1996.

Anzaldúa, Gloria. *Borderlands/La Frontera: The New Meztiza.* San Francisco: Aunt Lute Books, 1987.

Arnst, Catherine. "Study Links Medical Costs and Personal Bankruptcy." *BusinessWeek,* June 4, 2009.

Beauvoir, Simone de. *The Second Sex.* New York: Alfred A. Knopf, 1952.

Berk, Marc L., Claudia L. Schur, Leo R. Chavez, and Martin Frankel. "Health Care Use among Undocumented Latino Immigrants." *Health Affairs* 19, no. 4 (July/August 2000): 51–64.

Bovbjerg, Randall R., Jill A. Marstellar, and Frank C. Ullman. *Health Care for the Poor and Uninsured after a Public Hospital's Closure or Conversion,* Occasional Paper No. 39. Washington, D.C.: The Urban Institute, 2000.

Braverman, Paula, M. Pearl, S. Egerter, K. Marchi, and R. Williams. "Validity of Insurance Information on California Birth Certificates." *American Journal of Public Health* 88 (1998): 813–816.

Briggs, Laura. *Reproducing Empire: Race, Sex, Science, and U.S. Imperialism in Puerto Rico.* Berkeley: University of California Press, 2002.

Brodie, Mollyann, Nina Kjellson, Tina Hoff, and Molly Parker. "Perceptions of Latinos, African Americans, and Whites on Media as a Health Information Source." *Howard Journal of Communications* 10, no. 3 (August 1999): 147–167.

Brown, Wendy. "American Nightmare: Neoliberalism, Neoconservatism, and De-Democratization." *Political Theory* 34, no.6 (2006): 690–714.

Burawoy, Michael. "The Functions and Reproduction of Migrant Labor: Comparative Material from Southern Africa and the United States." *American Journal of Sociology* 81, no. 5 (March 1976): 1050–1087.

Burbridge, L. C. "The Labor Market for Home Care Workers: Demand, Supply, and Institutional Barriers." *Gerontologist* 33 (1993): 41–46.

Burchell, Graham, Colin Gordon, and Peter Miller, eds. *The Foucault Effect: Studies in Governmentality.* Chicago: University of Chicago Press, 1991.

Burton, Linda M. "*Childhood Adultification in Economically Disadvantaged Families: An Ethnographic Perspective.*" *Family Relations* 56 (2007): 329–345.

Calavita, Kitty. "Deflecting the Immigration Debate: Globalization, Immigrant Agency, 'Strange Bedfellows', and Beyond." *Contemporary Sociology* 37, no. 4 (2008): 302–305.

——. *Inside the State: The Bracero Program, Immigration, and the I.N.S.* New York: Routledge, 1992.

——. *U.S. Immigration Law and the Control of Labor, 1820–1924.* London: Academic Press, 1984.

California Association of Public Hospitals and Health Systems. *On the Brink: How the Crisis in California's Public Hospitals Threatens Access to Care for Millions.* 2003.

California Department of Health Services. "Adequacy of Prenatal Care Utilization: California 1989–1994." *Morbidity and Mortality Weekly Review.* Centers for Disease Control 45 (1996): 655.

California Legislature Senate Office of Research. *Federal Welfare Changes Affecting California's Immigrants.* Sacramento, Calif.: Senate Office of Research, 1996.

California State Auditor. *Department of Health Services: Use of Its Ports of Entry Fraud Detection Programs Is No Longer Justified.* Sacramento, Calif.: Bureau of State Audits, 1999.

Camacho, Alicia Schmidt. *Migrant Imaginaries: Latino Cultural Politics in the Mexico-U.S. Borderlands.* New York: NYU Press, 2008.

Canning, Kathleen, and Sonya O. Rose. "Gender, Citizenship and Subjectivity: Some Historical and Theoretical Considerations." *Gender and History* 13, no. 3 (2001): 427–443.

Capps, Randolph, Michael E. Fix, and Jeffrey S. Passel. *The Dispersal of Immigrants in the 1990s.* Washington, D.C.: The Urban Institute, 2002.

Cartier, Carolyn. "From Home to Hospital and Back Again: Economic Restructuring, End of Life, and the Gendered Problems of Place-Switching Health Services." *Social Science and Medicine* 56 (2003): 2289–2301.

Castells, Manuel, and Alejandro Portes. "World Underneath: The Origins, Dynamics, and Effects of the Informal Economy." *The Informal Economy: Studies in Advanced and Less Developed Countries.* Baltimore: Johns Hopkins University Press, 1989.

Center on Budget and Policy Priorities Report. *The Number of Uninsured Americans Is at an All-Time High.* August 29, 2006.

Chang, Grace. *Disposable Domestics: Immigrant Women Workers in the Global Economy.* Boston: South End Press, 2000.

Chang, Robert S. "A Meditation on Borders." *Immigrants Out! The New Nativism and the Anti-Immigrant Impulse in the United States.* Edited by Juan Perea. New York: NYU Press, 1997.

Chapman, Jeff, and Jared Bernstein. *Immigration and Poverty: Disappointing Income Growth in the 1990s Not Solely the Result of Growing Immigrant Population.* Briefing Paper. Washington, D.C.: Economic Policy Institute, 2002.

Chavez, Leo R. "A Glass Half Empty: Latina Reproduction and Public Discourse." *Women and Migration in the U.S.-Mexico Borderlands: A Reader.* Edited by Denise A. Segura and Patricia Zavella. Durham: Duke University Press, 2007.

Chavez, Leo R., Wayne A. Cornelius, and Oliver Williams Jones. "Mexican Immigrants and the Utilization of U.S. Health Services: The Case of San Diego." *Social Science & Medicine* 21, no. 1 (1985): 93–102.

Collins, Jane. "The Specter of Slavery: Workfare and the Economic Citizenship of Poor Women." *New Landscapes of Inequality.* Edited by Jane Collins, Micaela di Leonardo, and Brett Williams. Santa Fe: School for Advanced Research Press, 2008: 131–153.

Collins, Patricia Hill. *Black Feminist Thought: Knowledge, Consciousness, and the Politics of Empowerment.* London: Routledge, 1991.

Cooey, Paula M. "'Ordinary Mother' as Oxymoron: The Collusion of Theology, Theory, and Politics in the Undermining of Mothers." *No Easy Task: Dilemmas Confronting Contemporary Mothers.* Boston: Beacon Press, 1999.

Cornelius, Wayne. "Introduction: Does Border Enforcement Deter Unauthorized Immigration?" *Impacts of Border Enforcement on Mexican Migration: A View from Sending Communities.* Edited by Wayne Cornelius and Jessa M. Lewis. La Jolla: Center for Comparative Immigration Studies, University of California, San Diego, 2007.

DeFreitas, Gregory. *Immigration, Inequality, and Policy Alternatives.* New York: Russell Sage Foundation, 1995.

De Genova, Nicholas. *Working the Boundaries: Race, Space, and "Illegality" in Mexican Chicago.* Durham: Duke University Press, 2005.

Delgado, Richard. "Citizenship." *Immigrants Out! The New Nativism and the Anti-Immigrant Impulse in the United States.* Edited by Juan Perea. New York: NYU Press, 1997: 318–323.

Duggan, Lisa. *The Twilight of Equality? Neoliberalism, Cultural Politics, and the Attack on Democracy.* Boston: Beacon Press, 2003.

Duster, Troy. *Backdoor to Eugenics.* New York: Routledge, 2003.

Eisenstadt, Todd A., and Cathryn L. Thorup. *Caring Capacity vs. Carrying Capacity: Community Responses to Mexican Immigration in San Diego's North County*. La Jolla: Center for U.S.-Mexico Studies, University of California, San Diego, 1994.

Ellwood, Marilyn R., and Leighton Ku. "Welfare and Immigration Reforms: Unintended Side Effects for Medicaid." *Health Affairs* 17, no. 3 (May–June 1998): 137–151.

Espenshade, Thomas J., Jessica L. Baraka, and Gregory A. Huber. "Implications of the 1996 Welfare and Immigration Reform Acts for US Immigration." *Population and Development Review* 23, no. 4 (December 1997): 769–801.

Evans, Patricia R. "'Likely to Become a Public Charge': Immigration in the Backwaters of Administrative Law, 1882–1933." Ph.D. dissertation, George Washington University, 1987.

Fairchild, Amy L. *Science at the Borders: Immigrant Medical Inspection and the Shaping of the Modern Industrial Labor Force*. Baltimore: Johns Hopkins University Press, 2003.

Feige, Edgar L. "Defining and Estimating Underground and Informal Economies: The New Institutional Economics Approach." *World Development* 18, no. 7 (July 1990).

Feldman, P. H. "Labor Market Issues in Home Care, Nursing Homes and Home Care." *Home-Based Care for a New Century*. Edited by D. M. Fox and J. Raphael. Malden, Mass.: Blackwell, 1997: 155–183.

Fernandes, Deepa. *Targeted: Homeland Security and the Business of Immigration*. New York: Seven Stories Press, 2007.

Fix, Michael E., and Jeffrey S. Passel. Immigration and Immigrants: Setting the Record Straight. Washington, D.C.: The Urban Institute, 1994.

———. Trends in Noncitizens' and Citizens' Use of Public Benefits Following Welfare Reform, 1994–97. Washington, D.C.: The Urban Institute, 1999.

Fix, Michael E., Jeffrey S. Passel, and Wendy Zimmermann. *Facts about Immigrants' Use of Welfare*. Washington, D.C.: The Urban Institute, 1996.

Fix, Michael E., and Wendy Zimmerman. *All under One Roof: Mixed-Status Families in an Era of Reform*. Washington, D.C.: The Urban Institute, 1999.

———. *Immigrant Families and Public Policy: A Deepening Divide*. Washington, D.C.: The Urban Institute, 1995.

Foucault, Michel. *Discipline and Punish: The Birth of the Prison*. New York: Vintage Books, 1995.

———. *Society Must Be Defended: Lectures at the College de France, 1975–76*. New York: Picador, 2003.

Fraser, Nancy, and Linda Gordon. "Contract versus Charity: Why Is There No Social Citizenship in the United States?" *The Citizenship Debates*. Edited by Gershon Shafir. Minneapolis: University of Minnesota Press, 1998: 113–127.

———. "A Genealogy of Dependency: Tracing a Keyword of the U.S. Welfare State." *Signs* 19, no. 2 (Winter 1994): 309–36.

Fujiwara, Lynn H. "The Impact of Welfare Reform on Asian Immigrant Communities." *Social Justice* 25, no. 1 (1998): 82–104.

———. *Mothers without Citizenship: Asian Immigrant Families and the Consequences of Welfare Reform.* Minneapolis: University of Minnesota Press, 2008.

Gardner, Martha. *The Qualities of a Citizen: Women, Immigration, and Citizenship, 1870–1965.* Princeton: Princeton University Press, 2009.

Geography and Urban Planning Programs. *Sunland Park Community Survey: Summary.* Las Cruces: Earth Sciences Department, New Mexico State University, January 1991.

Gilchrist, Valeria J., and Robert L. Williams. "Key Informant Interviews." *Doing Qualitative Research.* London: Sage Publications, 1992.

Glenn, Evelyn Nakano. "Social Constructions of Mothering: A Thematic Overview." *Mothering: Ideology, Experience, and Agency.* Edited by Evelyn Nakano Glenn, Grace Chang, and Linda Rennie Forcey. New York: Routledge, 1994.

Goldman, Dana P., and Neeraj Sood. "Rising Medicare Costs: Are We in Crisis?" *Health Affairs* 25, no. 5 (November 2006): 389–390.

Gordon, Linda. *Pitied but Not Entitled: Single Mothers and the History of Welfare.* New York: Free Press, 1994.

Grant, Madison. *The Passing of the Great Race: or, The Racial Basis of European History.* New York: Scribner's, 1916.

Greenberg, M., et al. *Welfare Reauthorization: An Early Guide to Issues.* Washington, D.C.: Center for Law and Social Policy, July 2000.

Guendelman, Sylvia, and Monica Jasis. "Giving Birth across the Border: The San Diego-Tijuana Connection." *Social Science & Medicine* 34, no. 4 (February 1992): 419–426.

Gutierrez, Elena R. *Fertile Matters: The Politics of Mexican-Origin Women's Reproduction.* Austin: University of Texas Press, 2008.

———. "Policing 'Pregnant Pilgrims': Situating the Sterilization Abuse of Mexican-Origin Women in Los County." *Women, Health and Nation: Canada and the United States since 1945.* Montreal: McGill-Queen's University Press, 2003.

Hagan, Jacqueline, Nestor Rodriguez, Randy Capps, and Nika Kabiri. "The Effects of Recent Welfare and Immigration Reforms on Immigrants' Access to Health Care." *International Migration Review* 37, no. 2 (2003): 444–463.

Hancock, Ange-Marie. *The Politics of Disgust: The Public Identity of the Welfare Queen.* New York: NYU Press, 2004.

Harris, Pat. "City of Nashville Rejects English-Only Law." *Reuters,* January 22, 2009.

Harvey, David. *A Brief History of Neoliberalism.* New York: Oxford University Press, 2005.

Hays, Sharon. *The Cultural Contradictions of Motherhood.* New Haven: Yale University Press, 1996.

———. *Flat Broke with Children: Women in the Age of Welfare Reform.* New York: Oxford University Press, 2003.

Henderson, James W. "The Cost Effectiveness of Prenatal Care: Health Care Needs of Vulnerable Populations." *Health Care Financing Review* (June 22, 1994): 21–32.

Herzog, Lawrence A. "The Transfrontier Organization of Space along the United States-Mexico Border." *Geoforum* 22, no. 3 (1991): 255–269.

———. *Where North Meets South: Cities, Space and Politics on the U.S.-Mexico Border.* Austin: CMAS/ILAS/University of Texas Press, 1990.

Hing, Bill Ong. *Defining America through Immigration Policy.* Philadelphia: Temple University Press, 2004.

———. *Deporting Our Souls: Values, Morality, and Immigration Policy.* New York: Cambridge University Press, 2006.

Hobson, Barbara, and Ruth Lister. "Keyword: Citizenship." *Contested Concepts in Gender and Social Politics.* Edited by Barbara Hobson, Jane Lewis, and Birte Siim. Northampton, Mass.: Edward Elgar Publishing, 2004.

Hochschild, Arlie Russell. *The Commercialization of Intimate Life: Notes from Home and Work.* Berkeley: University of California Press, 2003.

Homedes, Nuria, and P. A. LaBrec. *Health Services Utilization across the Arizona-Sonora Border: A Bi-National Maternal and Child Health Project,* Monographs no. 28. Tucson: Southwest Border Rural Health Research Center, College of Medicine, University of Arizona, 1991.

Hondagneu-Sotelo, Pierrette. *Domestica: Immigrant Workers Cleaning and Caring in the Shadows of Affluence.* Berkeley: University of California Press, 2001.

Hondagneu-Sotelo, Pierrette, and Ernestine Avila. "I'm Here, but I'm There: The Meaning of Latina Transnational Motherhood." *Gender and Society* 11, no. 5 (1997): 548<N<571.

Huang, Priscilla. "Anchor Babies, Over-Breeders, and the Population Bomb: The Reemergence of Nativism and Population Control in Anti-Immigration Policies." *Harvard Law & Policy Review* 2 (2008): 385.

Hughes, D. C., and S. J. Runyan. "Prenatal Care and Public Policy: Lessons for Promoting Women's Health." *Journal of the American Medical Women's Association* 50 (1997): 156–163.

Illegal Immigration Reform and Immigrant Responsibility Act of 1996 ("IIRIRA"), Public Law 104-208, 110 Stat. 3008, September 30, 1996.

Inda, Jonathan Xavier. *Targeting Immigrants: Government, Technology, and Ethics.* Malden, Mass.: Blackwell, 2006.

Jayasuriya, Kanishka. *Statecraft, Welfare, and the Politics of Inclusion.* New York: Palgrave Macmillan, 2006.

Johnson, Kevin. *The "Huddled Masses" Myth: Immigration and Civil Rights*. Philadelphia: Temple University Press, 2004.

Kalofonos, Ippolytos, and Lawrence A. Palinkas. "Barriers to Prenatal Care for Mexican and Mexican American Women." *Journal of Gender, Culture, and Health* 4, no. 2 (June 1999): 135–152.

Kessler-Harris, Alice. *In Pursuit of Equity: Women, Men, and the Quest for Economic Citizenship in 20th Century America*. New York: Oxford University Press, 2001.

Kline, Wendy. *Building a Better Race: Gender, Sexuality, and Eugenics from the Turn of the Century to the Baby Boom*. Berkeley: University of California Press, 2001.

Kogan, Michael D., Joyce A. Martin, Greg R. Alexander, Milton Kotelchuck, Stephanie J. Ventura, and Fredric D. Frigoletto. "The Changing Pattern of Prenatal Care Utilization in the United States, 1981–1995, Using Different Prenatal Care Indices." *Journal of the American Medical Association* 279, no. 20 (May 27, 1998): 1623–1628.

Kotelchuck, Milton. "The Adequacy of Prenatal Care Utilization Index: Its U.S. Distribution and Association with Low Birthweight." *American Journal of Public Health* 84 (1994): 1486–1489.

Kotlowitz, Alex. "All Immigration Politics Is Local (and Complicated, Nasty, and Personal)." *New York Times Magazine* (August 5, 2007): section 6.

Kozol, Jonathan. *Rachel and Her Children: Homeless Families in America*. New York: Ballantine Books, 1988.

Ku, Leighon, and Sheetal Matani. "Left Out: Immigrants' Access to Health Care and Insurance." *Health Affairs* 20, no. 1 (January–February 2001): 247–256.

Ladd-Taylor, Molly, and Lauri Umansky. *"Bad" Mothers: The Politics of Blame in Twentieth-Century America*. New York: NYU Press, 1998.

Lister, Ruth. *Citizenship: Feminist Perspectives*, 2d ed. New York: NYU Press, 2003.

Lu, M. C., Y. G. Lin, N. M. Prietto, and T. J. Garite. "Elimination of Public Funding of Prenatal Care for Undocumented Immigrants in California: A Cost/Benefit Analysis."*American Journal of Obstetrics & Gynecology* 182, no. 1 (2000): 233–239.

Luibheid, Eithne. *Entry Denied: Controlling Sexuality at the Border*. Minneapolis: University of Minnesota Press, 2002.

Macias, Eduardo P., and Leo S. Morales. "Crossing the Border for Health Care." *Journal of Health Care for the Poor and Underserved* 12, no. 1 (2001): 77–87.

MaCurdy, Thomas, and Margaret O'Brien-Strain. *Reform Reversed? The Restoration of Welfare Benefits to Immigrants in California*. Public Policy Institute of California, 1998.

Madigan, Nick. "Los Angeles Emergency Care Crisis Deepens." *New York Times*, August 21, 2004, A8.

Maira, Sunaina. *Missing: Youth, Citizenship, and Empire after 9/11*. Durham: Duke University Press, 2009.

Marchevsky, Alejandra, and Jeanne Theoharis. *Not Working: Latina Immigrants, Low-Wage Jobs, and the Failure of Welfare Reform*. New York: NYU Press, 2006.

Marshall, Thomas H. "Citizenship and Social Class." *The Citizenship Debates*. Edited by Gershon Shafir. Minneapolis: University of Minnesota Press, 1998 (1964 original).

Massey, Douglas S., Jorge Durand, and Nolan J. Malone. *Beyond Smoke and Mirrors: Mexican Immigration in an Era of Economic Integration*. New York: Russell Sage Foundation, 2002.

McClintock, Anne. *Imperial Leather: Race, Gender and Sexuality in the Colonial Context*. New York: Routledge, 1995.

——. "'No Longer in a Future Heaven': Gender, Race, and Nationalism." *Dangerous Liaisons: Gender, Nation, and Postcolonial Perspectives*. Minneapolis: University of Minnesota Press, 1997.

Medi-Cal Policy Institute. *Understanding Medi-Cal: The Basics*. 1998.

Milkman, Ruth. *L.A. Story: Immigrant Workers and the Future of the U.S. Labor Movement*. New York: Russell Sage Foundation, 2006.

Mink, Gwendolyn. *The Wages of Motherhood: Inequality in the Welfare State, 1917–1942*. Ithaca: Cornell University Press, 1995.

——. *Welfare's End*, rev. ed. Ithaca: Cornell University Press, 2002.

Misra, Dawn P., and Bernard Guyer. "Benefits and Limitations of Prenatal Care: From Counting Visits to Measuring Content." *Journal of the American Medical Association* 279, no. 20 (May 27, 1998): 1661–1662.

Morse, A., J. Meadows, K. Rasmussen, S. Steisel. *America's Newcomers: Mending the Welfare Safety Net for Immigrants*. San Francisco: Public Policy Institute of California, 1998.

Moss, N., L. Baumeister, and J. Biewener. "Perspectives of Latina Immigrant Women on Proposition 187." *Journal of the American Medical Women's Association* 51, no. 4 (August–October 1996): 161–165.

Murray, J. L., and M. Bernfield. "The Differential Effect of Prenatal Care on the Incidence of Low Birth Weight among Blacks and Whites in a Prepaid Health Care Plan." *New England Journal of Medicine* 219, no. 21 (November 24, 1988): 1385–1390.

National Immigration Law Center (NILC). *How Are Immigrants Included in Health Care Reform?* Los Angeles: National Immigration Law Center, April 2010.

——. Immigrants and Public Charge: Resource Book 1998–99.Los Angeles: National Immigration Law Center, 1998.

——. *Public Charge*. Los Angeles: National Immigration Law Center, 1997.

Nelson, Barbara. "The Origins of the Two-Channel Welfare State: Workmen's Compensation and Mothers' Aid." *Women, the State, and Welfare*. Edited by Linda Gordon. Madison: University of Wisconsin Press, 1990: 123–152.

Nevins, Joseph. *Operation Gatekeeper: The Rise of the Illegal Alien and the Making of the US-Mexico Border.* New York: Routledge, 2002.

New York Times. "Hispanic and Asian Populations Expand." August 30, 2000, A16.

Ngai, Mae M. *Impossible Subjects: Illegal Aliens and the Making of Modern America.* Princeton: Princeton University Press, 2004.

Nguyen, Tram. *We Are All Suspects Now: Untold Stories from Immigrant Communities after 9/11.* Boston: Beacon Press, 2005.

The Number of Uninsured Americans Is at an All-Time High. Washington, D.C.: Center on Budget and Policy Priorities, August 29, 2006.

Ong, Aihwa. *Buddha Is Hiding: Refugees, Citizenship, and the New America.* Berkeley: University of California Press, 2003.

———. *Neoliberalism as Exception: Mutations in Citizenship and Sovereignty.* Durham: Duke University Press, 2006.

———. *Spirits of Resistance and Capitalist Discipline: Factory Women in Malaysia.* Albany: State University of New York Press, 1987.

Ono, Kent A., and John M. Sloop. *Shifting Borders: Rhetoric, Immigration, and California's Proposition 187.* Philadelphia: Temple University Press, 2002.

Ordover, Nancy. *American Eugenics: Race, Queer Anatomy, and the Science of Nationalism.* Minneapolis: University of Minnesota Press, 2003.

Park, Edward J. W., and John S. W. Park. *Probationary Americans: Contemporary Immigration Policies and the Shaping of Asian American Communities.* New York: Routledge, 2005.

Park, Lisa Sun-Hee. *Consuming Citizenship: Children of Asian Immigrant Entrepreneurs.* Stanford: Stanford University Press, 2005.

———. "Perpetuation of Poverty through 'Public Charge.'" *Denver University Law Review* 78 (2001): 1161–1177.

Park, Lisa Sun-Hee, and David N. Pellow. *The Slums of Aspen: Immigrants vs. the Environment in America's Eden.* New York: NYU Press, 2011.

Park, Lisa Sun-Hee, Rhonda Sarnoff, Catherine Bender, and Carol Korenbrot. "Impact of Recent Welfare and Immigration Reforms on Use of Medicaid for Prenatal Care by Immigrants in California." *Journal of Immigrant Health* 2, no. 1 (2000): 5–22.

Passel, Jeffrey. *Size and Characteristics of the Unauthorized Migrant Population in the United States: Estimates Based on the March 2005 Current Population Survey.* Washington, D.C.: Pew Hispanic Center, March 2006.

Patton, Michael Quinn. *Qualitative Research and Evaluation Methods.* Thousand Oaks, Calif.: Sage Publications, 1990.

Pear, Robert. "Immigrants Face Medicaid Hurdle for Infant Care." *New York Times,* November 3, 2006, A1.

Personal Responsibility and Work Opportunity Reconciliation Act of 1996 ("Welfare Reform" Act), Public Law 104-193, 110 Stat. 2105, August 22, 1996.

Petchesky, Rosalind Pollack. "The Body as Property: A Feminist Revision." *Conceiving the New World Order.* Berkeley: University of California Press, 1995.

———. "From Population Control to Reproductive Rights: Feminist Fault Lines." *Reproductive Health Matters* 3, no. 6 (November 1995): 152–161.

Peters, Michael. "Neoliberalism." *Encyclopedia of Philosophy of Education.* London: Routledge, 1999.

Roberts, Bryan. "Informal Economy and Family Strategies." *International Journal of Urban and Regional Research* 18, no. 1 (1994): 6–23.

Roberts, Dorothy. "The Future of Reproductive Choice for Poor Women and Women of Color." *The Politics of Women's Bodies.* Edited by Rose Weitz. New York: Oxford University Press, 2003: 282–289.

———. *Killing the Black Body: Race, Reproduction, and the Meaning of Liberty.* New York: Pantheon, 1997.

———. "Mothers Who Fail to Protect Their Children: Accounting for Private and Public Responsibility." *Mother Troubles: Rethinking Contemporary Maternal Dilemmas.* Edited by Julia E. Hanigsberg and Sara Ruddick. Boston: Beacon Press, 1999: 31–49.

———. "Poverty, Race, and New Directions in Child Welfare Policy." *Journal of Law and Policy* no. 1 (1999): 63–77.

———. "Who May Give Birth to Citizens? Reproduction, Eugenics, and Immigration." *Immigrants Out! The New Nativism and the Anti-Immigrant Impulse in the United States.* Edited by Juan Perea. New York: NYU Press, 1997: 205–219.

Rodriguez, Nestor P. "The Social Construction of the U.S.-Mexico Border." *Immigrants Out! The New Nativism and the Anti-Immigrant Impulse in the United States.* Edited by Juan Perea. New York: NYU Press, 1997: 223–243.

Rodriguez, Nestor, and Jacqueline M. Hagan. "Fractured Families and Communities: Effects of Immigration Reform in Texas, Mexico, and El Salvador." *Latino Studies* 2 (2004): 328–351.

Rollins, Judith. *Between Women: Domestics and Their Employers.* Philadelphia: Temple University Press, 1985.

Romero, Mary. *Maid in the U.S.A.* New York: Routledge, 1992.

Rosen, M. G. *Caring for Our Future, the Content of Prenatal Care.* A Report of the Public Health Service Expert Panel on the Content of Prenatal Care. Washington D.C.: Public Health Service, 1989.

Ruhl, Lealle. "Dilemmas of the Will: Uncertainty, Reproduction, and the Rhetoric of Control." *Signs* 27, no.3 (March 2002): 641–663.

Saito, Leland T. "The Politics of Adaptation and the 'Good Immigrant.'" *Asian and Latino Immigrants in a Restructuring Economy.* Edited by Marta Lopez-Garza and David R. Diaz. Stanford: Stanford University Press, 2001.

Sardell, Alice. "Child Health Policy in the U.S.: The Paradox of Consensus." *Journal of Health Politics Policy and Law* 15, no. 2 (Summer 1990): 271–304.

Sassen, Saskia. *The Global City: New York, London, Tokyo.* Princeton: Princeton University Press, 1991.

———. *Globalization and Its Discontents: Essays on the New Mobility of People and Money.* New York: The New Press, 1998.

———. *Guests and Aliens.* New York: The New Press, 1999.

———. *The Mobility of Labor and Capital: A Study in International Investment and Labor Flow.* Cambridge: Cambridge University Press, 1990.

Schauffler, Helen Halpin, and E. R. Brown. *The State of Health Insurance in California, 1999.* Berkeley: Regents of the University of California, January 2000.

Scheer, Robert. "The Governor's Brave Stand on Birth Control." *Los Angeles Times,* November 5, 1996.

Schevitz, Tanya. "California Minorities Become Majority." *San Francisco Chronicle,* August 30, 2000, A1.

Schlosberg, C., and D. Wiley. *The Impact of INS Public Charge Determinations on Immigrant Access to Health Care.* Washington, D.C.: National Health Law Program and National Immigration Law Center, 1998.

Schoen, Johanna. *Choice and Coercion: Birth Control, Sterilization, and Abortion in Public Health and Welfare.* Chapel Hill: University of North Carolina Press, 2005.

Schram, Sanford F. *After Welfare: The Culture of Postindustrialized Social Policy.* New York: NYU Press, 2000.

———. *Words of Welfare: The Poverty of Social Science and the Social Science of Poverty.* Minneapolis: University of Minnesota Press, 1995.

Schram, Sanford F., Joe Soss, Richard C. Fording, and Linda Houser. "The Third Level of U.S. Welfare Reform: Governmentality under Neoliberal Paternalism." *Citizenship Studies* 14, no. 6 (2010).

Sibley, David. *Geographies of Exclusion: Society and Difference in the West.* New York: Routledge, 1995.

Sidel, Ruth. *Keeping Women and Children Last.* New York: Penguin, 1998.

Singer, Audrey. "Immigrants, their Families and their Communities in the Aftermath of Welfare Reform." *Research Perspectives on Migration* 3, no. 1 (2001): 1–9.

Smith, Andrea. *Conquest: Sexual Violence and American Indian Genocide.* Cambridge, Mass.: South End Press, 2005.

Smith, David. *Entitlement Politics: Medicare and Medicaid, 1995–2001.* New York: Aldine de Gruyter, 2002.

Solinger, Rickie. *Beggars and Choosers: How the Politics of Choice Shapes Adoption, Abortion, and Welfare in the U.S.* New York: Hill and Wang, 2001.

———. "Dependency and Choice: The Two Faces of Eve." *The Subject of Care: Feminist Perspectives on Dependency.* Edited by Eva Feder Kittay and Ellen K. Feder. Lanham, Md.: Rowman & Littlefield, 2002.

Sparke, Matthew. "A Neoliberal Nexus: Citizenship, Security and the Future of the Border." *Political Geography* 25, no. 2 (2006): 151–180.

Stack, Carol. *All Our Kin: Strategies for Survival in a Black Community.* New York: Harper & Row, 1975.

Stern, Alexandra M. *Eugenic Nation: Faults and Frontiers of Better Breeding in Modern America.* Berkeley: University of California Press, 2005.

Strauss, Anselm L. *Qualitative Analysis for Social Scientists.* Cambridge: University of Cambridge Press, 1987.

Tabet, Stephen R., and William H. Wiese. "Medications Obtained in Mexico by Patients in Southern New Mexico." *Southern Medical Journal* 83, no. 3 (March 1990): 271–273.

Tannenbaum, S. J. "Medicaid Eligibility Policy in the 1980s: Medical Utilitarianism and the "Deserving" Poor." *Journal of Health Politics, Policy and Law* 20 (1995): 933–954.

Thompson, William W. "Cross-Border Health Care Utilization and Practices of Mexican-Americans in the Lower Rio Grande Valley." *Border Health Journal* 9, no. 2 (1993): 1–9.

U.S. Citizenship and Immigration Services (USCIS). *Fact Sheet: Public Charge.* May 25, 1999. http://www.dhs.gov.

U.S. Citizenship and Immigration Services. http://www.uscis.gov.

U.S. Department of Justice, Immigration and Naturalization Service. *1998 Statistical Yearbook of the Immigration and Naturalization Service.* Washington, D.C.: U.S. Government Printing Office, 2000.

Valverde, Mariana. "'Despotism' and Ethical Liberal Governance." Economy and Society 25, no.3 (August 1996): 357–372.

Ventura, Stephanie J., and Selma M. Taffel. "Childbearing Characteristics of U.S.- and Foreign-Born Hispanic Mothers." *Public Health Reports* 100, no. 6 (November–December 1985): 647–652.

Willes, M. H., D. F. Wright, M. Parks, and J. Clayton. "Abuse by Officials at the Border." Editorial, *Los Angeles Times*, December 23, 1997, B6.

Williams, Patricia. *The Alchemy of Race and Rights: Diary of a Law Professor.* Cambridge: Harvard University Press, 1991.

Wilson, Tamar Diana. "Anti-Immigrant Sentiment and the Problem of Reproduction/Maintenance in Mexican Immigration to the United States." *Critique of Anthropology* 20, no. 2 (2000): 191–213.

Wulsin, Lucien, Jr., Sepil Djavaheri, Jan Frates, and Ari Shofet. *Clinics, Counties and the Uninsured: A Study of Six California Urban Counties.* Santa Monica: Alliance Healthcare Foundation and the California Wellness Foundation, February 1999.

Yamada, Y. "Profile of Home Care Aides, Nursing Home Aides, and Hospital Aides: Historical Changes and Data Recommendations." *Gerontologist* 42 (2002): 199–206.

Young, Iris Marion. "Autonomy, Welfare Reform, and Meaningful Work." *The Subject of Care: Feminist Perspectives on Dependency.* Edited by Eva Feder Kittay and Ellen K. Feder. Lanham, Md.: Rowman & Littlefield, 2002.

Yuval-Davis, Nira. "The Citizenship Debate: Women, Ethnic Processes and the State," *Feminist Review* 39 (1991): 58–68.

Zelizer, Viviana A. *Pricing the Priceless Child: The Changing Social Value of Children.* Princeton: Princeton University Press, 1994.

Zimmermann, Wendy, and Michael E. Fix. *Declining Immigrant Applications for Medi-Cal and Welfare Benefits in Los Angeles County.* Washington, D.C.: The Urban Institute, 1998.

Zucchino, David. *Myth of the Welfare Queen.* New York: Scribner's, 1997.

INDEX

Abramovitz, Mimi, 34–35
Advocates, 90; collaborations of, 146–50; for Medi-Cal eligibility process, 38. *See also* Legal advocates; Policy advocates
AFDC. *See* Aid to Families with Dependent Children
Aid to Families with Dependent Children (AFDC), 32, 161n3
American College of Obstetricians and Gynecologists, 7
Amott, Teresa, 32
"Anchor babies," 164n78, 175n28
Anti-Terrorism and Effective Death Penalty Act of 1996, 3, 84, 172n66
Anzaldúa, Gloria, 153
Asian Americans, 32, 168n12; Filipino Americans, 131–33
Asian Health Services (Oakland), 149
Asian Pacific American Legal Center of Southern California, 147
Avila, Ernestine, 51

Baby boomers, health care for, 150–51
Backdoor to Eugenics (Duster), 52, 55–56, 168n2
Bad mothers: good mothers compared to, 47–49; immigrant mothers compared to, 48; income and, 49–50
Baldwin, James, 139
Beauvoir, Simone de, 12
Belshé, Kimberly, 63–65. See also *Rocio v. Belshé*

Black mothers, welfare and, 32–33
Black women: motherhood and, 48; stereotypes of, 16–17
Border immigrants: dangers to, 115, 119–20; rape risk of, 120, 174n25
Borderlands/La Frontera (Anzaldúa), 153
Border Patrol, 122–23
Borders, 115; enforcement of, 118–20, 122–23, 136–37; Operation Gatekeeper, 84, 116, 118–19. *See also* San Diego-Tijuana region
Brown, Wendy, 151–52
Burawoy, Michael, 145, 176n18
Burton, Linda, 14
Bush, George W., 166n101

Calavita, Kitty, 57
California: Gold Rush in, 21, 165n86; health care fraud detection programs in, 5; immigrants in, 19–20; majority minority in, 84; SCHIP for, 177–24. *See also* Medi-Cal
California Airport Residency Review (CARR), 60; PED audit and, 69–72, 72; procedure for, 61–63, 170n29; public charge and, 61–62
California Immigrant Welfare Collaborative, 147
Canning, Kathleen, 141–42
CARR. *See* California Airport Residency Review

Port of Entry Fraud Detection Program
(PED), 19, 22, 29, 140; assumptions
of, 59; example in, 1–2; illegality of,
63; immigrant status in, 60, 169n24;
INS and, 59–60; intentions of, 59,
169n17, 169nn19–20; policy advocates against, 74; procedure in, 60–
61; Proposition 187 and, 59; public
charge and, 58, 63, 73; reproductive
health care target in, 1, 60, 169n25;
responsibility shift from, 145, 177n20;
Rocio v. Belshé, 63–68, 81, 170nn32–33,
170nn36–38, 171n42; State Administrative Procedure Act for, 65, 170n33;
"success" for, 59, 169n21; termination
of, 68. *See also* PED audit
Poverty: of immigrants, 21, 165n89;
morality compared to, 4, 9–12; social context of, 142–44
Power: family and, 56–57; immigrant
women's empowerment, 111; of INS,
27; in neoliberalism, 17
Pregnancy: deservingness compared
to, 9–11; Medi-Cal for, 21–22, 44–45,
87, 124–25; PE Medi-Cal during, 38,
101, 150, 167n23, 177n25; public
charge and, 4–5, 6, 161n7
Pregnancy-Only Medi-Cal, 38, 101,
167n23
Pregnant immigrants: central issues
about, 140; fears of, 89, 92–93; outreach to, 111–13; policy shifts and,
100–103; study methods on, 27–28
Prenatal care: cost effectiveness of,
5; delays in, 128; as immigration
incentive, 5; Medi-Cal eligibility
process and, 44–45, 124–25; social
services related to, 4–5, 162n21; at
St. Vincent de Paul Family Health
Center, 133–34; transportation for,

126; U.S. Public Health Service for, 7;
"welfare mothers" and, 34
Presumptive Eligibility Medi-Cal (PE
Medi-Cal), for pregnancy, 38, 101,
150, 167n23, 177n25
Prison system, 162n22
Privatization: family structures and, 14;
of public assistance, 9; from responsibility shift, 177n20; welfare reform
and, 144–45
Progressive Era, 142
Property: bodies as, 13–14; self propriety as, 13
Proposition 187, 5, 20, 22, 169n17; federal welfare reform related to, 27;
Latinas on, 24; PED and, 59; political rhetoric about, 23
PRWORA. *See* Personal Responsibility
and Work Opportunity Reconciliation Act
Public assistance: privatization of, 9.
See also Welfare
Public charge, 28–30, 132, 144; awareness of term, 126–27; CARR and, 61–
62; CIS definition of, 3–4; clarification
of, 74–77, 80–81; continuing consequences of, 78–83, *82*, 171nn57–59,
172n60; continuous existence of,
83–84; costs and benefits related to,
84; Davis, G., and, 81–82; deportability related to, 15, 27, 164n61; Depression and, 83–84; eugenics and, 54–57;
grassroots mobilization and, 75–77;
green cards and, 78, 171n57; health
care and, 26–27; in history, 83, 172n61;
immigrant desirability and disavowal
in, 57–58; immigrants excluded from
U.S. (1892-1990) via, *82*; independent
poor immigrant women compared
to, 52; labor pool related to, 143; legal

Welfare reform, 24–27, 139; privatization and, 144–45; social citizenship and, 140–50; unintended consequences of, 86, 164n80, 172n71. *See also* Proposition 187
Williams, Patricia, 13–14
Wilson, Joe, 139

Wilson, Pete, 5, 23, 59, 82, 124
Wilson, Tamar Diana, 145
Women: alien removals of, 86; citizensons' education from, 47; public charge and, 85–86

Young, Iris Marion, 16, 164n67

ABOUT THE AUTHOR

LISA SUN-HEE PARK is Associate Professor of Sociology and Asian American Studies at the University of Minnesota, author of *Consuming Citizenship: Children of Asian Immigrant Entrepreneurs*, and coauthor of *The Slums of Aspen: Immigrants vs. the Environment in America's Eden* and *Silicon Valley of Dreams: Immigrant Labor, Environmental Injustice, and the High Tech Global Economy*.